# Building Reading Skills

### Revised Edition

LEVEL 1

Level 2

Level 3

Level 4

# Building Reading Skills

## Revised Edition
### LEVEL 1

Gerald G. Duffy
Professor of Education, Michigan State University

Laura R. Roehler
Associate Professor of Education, Michigan State University

**McDougal, Littell & Company**
**Evanston, Illinois**
**New York   Sacramento**

## About the Authors

**Dr. Gerald G. Duffy,** a professor in the Department of Elementary and Special Education, Michigan State University at Lansing, spent ten years as an elementary and middle school teacher and regularly returns to the classroom during his sabbaticals. He received his doctorate in June of 1966 from Northern Illinois University. His pre-service and in-service workshops, field work, and research all center on his continuing interest in teaching reading in the classroom.

**Dr. Laura R. Roehler,** an associate professor and co-ordinator of the Language Arts Project of the Institute for Research on Teaching at Michigan State University, has wide experience in training teachers of reading and in developing materials for their use, both within the university program and in a public school setting. She taught middle grades and junior high school for five years before receiving her Ph.D. in 1972 from Michigan State University.

## Acknowledgments

"About Space," adapted from *The Question and Answer Book of Space* by Ruth A. Sonneborn; copyright © 1965, 1970 by Random House, Inc.; adapted with permission. "Agave," adapted from "Viva Agave!" by Bet Hennefrund as published in *Ranger Rick's Nature Magazine,* November 1979; copyright © 1979 by National Wildlife Federation; adapted with permission. An adaptation of "Ah Kum's Sea House" by Dorothea C. Hill from *Instructor* Magazine, April 1978; copyright © 1978 by The Instructor Publications, Inc.; adapted with permission. An adaptation of "All Shaded Up" by Peggy Simson Curry from *Boys' Life* Magazine, May 1977; copyright © 1977 by The Boy Scouts of America, Irving, Texas; adapted by permission of Lenniger Literary Agency, Inc., New York. "The Artist" from *Tales from Old China* by Isabelle C. Chang; copyright © 1969 by Isabelle C. Chang; reprinted by permission of Random House, Inc., New York. (continued on page 481)

ISBN: 0-88343-806-2

# Contents

## Section 2  Comprehension Skills

## Unit 8   Work and Play   204

### Learn About the Skills

Comprehension Skills   Interpretive Reading
Relating to previous experience   **205**

Study and Research Skills   Reading Techniques
Setting purposes and rate   **207**

### Apply the Comprehension Skills You Have Learned

## Section 3   Study and Research Skills

## Unit 9   Patterns   234

### Learn About the Skills

Study and Research Skills   Study Techniques
Making a study plan   **235**

Comprehension Skills   Implied Meaning
Relevant and irrelevant details   **237**

## Unit 10   Facts and Figures   266

### Learn About the Skills

## Unit 11   Current Events   292

### Learn About the Skills

# About This Book

This is a book about reading. It will help you to read with ease, understanding, and pleasure. You will learn how to apply your skills to the reading you do for your other school subjects. You will also learn how to apply your skills to your reading outside of school.

## The Organization of This Book

This book is divided into four Sections. Each Section emphasizes a major reading skill:

**Vocabulary Development Skills:** pages 2–115. These pages have blue tabs in the bottom outside corners.

**Comprehension Skills:** pages 117–231. These pages have red tabs.

**Study and Research Skills:** pages 233–347. These pages have green tabs.

**Literary Appreciation Skills:** pages 349–463. These pages have yellow tabs.

Each Section is made up of four units. Each unit contains:

### • Four Skills Teaching Pages

**Overview and Purposes for Reading.** This page introduces the theme of the unit and defines your purpose for reading the unit. For example, see page 2.
**Learn About the Skills.** The next two pages teach the major skill covered in the section. The fourth page discusses another type of reading skill. See pages 3–5, for example.

### • Five Reading Selections

These center around the theme of the unit. Each selection is preceded by a Use the Skills page and followed by questions that Check the Skills.

### • Apply What You Learned in the Unit

These pages summarize the theme of the unit and offer further questions to help you check your understanding of the skills.

At the end of each Section, there are several pages that help you to Apply the Skills You Have Learned. These pages provide questions and further discussion about the skills and show how these skills relate to your schoolwork and to your life.

## Additional Help for the Student

**Context Clues.** Some words in the selections may be unfamiliar to you. Many of these have hints to their meanings in other words and sentences around them. These hints are called *context clues*. A word for which there are context clues is followed by a small letter c, like this.c

**Glossary.** Some words in the selections are included in the glossary at the back of the book. A small *g* after a word means the word is in the glossary.

A list of the context clue words and glossary words begins on page 475.

# Section 1  Vocabulary Development Skills

# Real and Make-Believe

## Overview and Purposes for Reading

### The Theme

#### Real and Make-Believe

1.  All the selections in this unit are make-believe. That is, the events never *really* happened as written. But some of the stories *could have* happened. How do you know when a story is only make-believe?

### The Skills

#### Vocabulary Development Skills Word Structure

2.  How can understanding prefixes help you determine the meanings of words?

#### Literary Appreciation Skills Figurative Language

3.  What is figurative language? Why do you need to know?

# Learn About the Skills

## Vocabulary Development Skills Word Structure

It's fun to see how words can be expanded. Take the word *pack*, as in this sentence: *Sam will pack his suitcase.* You might expand the base word *pack* by adding *re-* before it. *Sam will repack his suitcase.* Do you know what *repack* means? There are not enough hints in the sentence, or context clues, to help. You need to know what the prefix *re-* means. If you don't know, perhaps context clues in this sentence will help. *Sam will have to repack his suitcase in order to squeeze everything in.* Were you able to figure out that *repack* means "pack again"?

Context clues helped you decide what *repack* means. But you will not always have context clues to determine the meaning of a word containing a prefix. Sometimes you will have to know the meaning of the prefix. You can find prefixes and their meanings in most dictionaries. When you come across a word in your reading that you are uncertain of, you sometimes will be able to figure it out by "breaking down" that word. First determine what the base word is by removing any prefixes and endings. Then determine the meaning of the prefix. Think about how the prefix affects the meaning of the base word. Then decide on the meaning of the word that has been made by combining the base word and the prefix.

Here is a list of some common prefixes, their meanings, and an example of each.

| Prefix | Meaning | Example |
|---|---|---|
| dis- | not, the opposite of | dislike, disconnect |
| im-, in-, il-, ir- | not | impossible |
| pre- | before | preview |
| re- | again, back | reread, rebound |
| un- | not, the opposite of | uncover |

Understanding prefixes can help you figure out the meanings of many words, but it will not always work. For example, *re-* in the word *react* is a prefix added to the base word *act*. But *re* in *ready* is not a prefix at all. Subtracting the letters *re* does not leave a base word you recognize. When using your skill with prefixes, be certain that, after you remove what you think is a prefix, you are left with a base word. If you don't have a base word, you will have to use some other method to figure out a word you don't know.

**Try the Skill.** You be the detective. Can your knowledge of prefixes help you figure out each word below? Why or why not? Watch for base words!

| | | | |
|---|---|---|---|
| uncle | prefix | real | important |
| regain | preach | unpaid | disprove |

As you read this unit, you will find some words with prefixes. You'll see how to use them to understand the words.

# Literary Appreciation Skills Figurative Language

**Figurative language** uses words and phrases in unusual or imaginative ways. **Literal language** stays with the usual or more common meanings. You can sometimes be confused by what you read if you don't know whether language is being used literally or figuratively.

Here are some examples of figurative language. Ask yourself if what is said could really be true.

1. The train sped through the night like a bullet.
2. The stars were jewels in the sky.
3. The stair groaned under the weight of the heavy man.
4. He was so tall he could see into tomorrow.

In the first sentence the figurative language is a *simile*. In a simile the word *like* or *as* is used to compare two things. The second sentence compares stars and jewels, but the word *like* or *as* is not used. In this type of figurative language one item is said to *be* another. This is called a *metaphor*. The figurative language in the third sentence is *personification*. A human being can groan. A stair cannot. In personification, a lifeless thing is given human qualities. The last sentence is an example of exaggeration. Of course, no one can "see into tomorrow" regardless of how tall that person is. But figurative language lets you know that the person is very tall.

In this unit, you will learn more about figurative language and how to tell the difference between figurative and literal language.

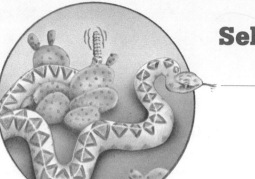

# Use the Skills

### Understanding the Selection

Pecos Bill is the hero of many tall tales. The next selection is one of them.

1. Decide whether any of the events in the story could have happened or if the story is strictly make-believe.

### Vocabulary Development Skills Word Structure

2. Use what you know about prefixes and their meanings to help you figure out the meanings of several words you may not know. Notes in the margin will help you.

### Literary Appreciation Skills Figurative Language

3. Watch for personification and exaggeration.

# THE GREATEST COWBOY

Tom Macpherson

A$^c$ after a word means there are context clues to its meaning. A$^g$ means the word is in the glossary.

Do you think TV cowboys are pretty good? Well, then, you've never heard of Pecos Bill.

Bill was raised by a pack of coyotes. Fact is, he thought *he* was a coyote until somebody pointed out that he didn't have a tail.

When Bill joined up with the humans he became a cowboy—and what a cowboy! On the trail one time, he met a 10-foot rattlesnake. The rattler buzzed at Bill and said he wanted to fight. Bill gave the snake three free bites before he even started to scrap. Then Bill just knocked the poison out of that old rattler.

Farther down the trail, a mountain lion bigger than two steers and a bull calf jumped on Bill. The fur flew for about two minutes. Then the lion gave up and moaned, "Can't you take a joke, Bill?" So Bill slapped his saddle on that lion and rode him down the trail. Bill used the rattlesnake as a whip.

■ The description of the size of the lion is exaggeration. A lion talking like a person is an example of personification.

Bill always claimed he could ride anything with fur on—and some things without. One day he made a bet that he could ride a cyclone$^g$ bareback. So he went up to the Kansas line and caught a cyclone. Bill pulled it down where he could reach it and jumped on its back.

■ Here a storm takes on the qualities of a living horse. This is figurative language, not literal.

Well, this was a real mean cyclone. It went bucking and pitching down through Oklahoma and Texas. It knocked down mountains, blew the water right out of rivers, and cut down all the trees.

Cool as you please, Bill stayed aboard. Every once in a while, he would spur the cyclone in the withers.$^g$ When the cyclone got tired, he whopped it across the ears with a rattlesnake whip.

By the time it reached Arizona, that cyclone was mad! When it saw that it couldn't throw Bill, it just rained out from under him. Bill came down in a rainstorm over California.

Everybody knows that Pecos Bill invented[9] the tarantula[9] to pester his pals. But did you know that he dug the whole Rio Grande River to bring water to his stock from the Gulf of Mexico?

Bill died some time ago. The story is that one day he came upon a fellow from the East all dressed up in a dude[9] cowboy outfit. Bill was so tickled by the sight that he lay down and laughed himself to death.

There are lots more stories about this <u>uncommon</u> man. Look for them in your head some day when your imagination is running as wild as the old West.

■ *Un-* means "not." The base word is *common*. So you know *un- common* means "not ordinary" or "not usual."

# Check the Skills

### Understanding the Selection

1. Do you think any of the events in this story could have really happened? Why or why not? Is this story realistic or only make-believe?

### Vocabulary Development Skills Word Structure

2. Look at the marginal note above. What is the prefix in *uncommon*? What does *un-* mean? *uncommon*?

### Literary Appreciation Skills Figurative Language

3. The description of the lion's size and of its talking are examples of figurative language. How could you figure this out?

# Use the Skills

### Understanding the Selection

Lonesome Star is the main character in the next selection, which is a part of a book based on fact. Lonesome Star was a Crow Indian. She struggled for recognition among her people as a hunter, warrior, and leader. These were qualities usually accepted only in male members of the tribe. This selection begins shortly after Lonesome Star successfully led her first raiding party.

1.   As you read, think about whether or not the events in the story could have really happened in this way.

### Vocabulary Development Skills Word Structure

2.   Try your skill with prefixes to figure out some words you don't know. But be sure the word contains a prefix. Otherwise the skill won't help you. Look back to page 3 if you need to. Notes in the margin will help, too.

### Literary Appreciation Skills Figurative Language

3.   Ask yourself if the author of this selection is less concerned with figurative language than with literal language.

# WOMAN CHIEF

Rose Sobol

Lonesome Star's daring leadership was sung in the camp for many days. Soon it was known to the whole Crow nation.

Within the year, she led seven young men in another raid against the Blackfeet. Fortune continued to smile on her.

■ You know this is personification. Non-living things don't smile. People do.

Her war party stole upon the enemy camp at night and ran off seventy horses. The Blackfeet followed and caught up. After a sharp fight, the Crows got away with most of the horses.

Such horse raids were a means of survival. Without mounts,$^c$ it was impossible for the Crows to live as hunters. The yearly trading with the Flatheads and Nez Percés$^g$ could supply only enough animals to replace losses from disease, old age, and death. Far larger numbers disappeared through theft. Raiders ran off as many as a hundred horses at a sweep. The Sioux$^g$ stole horses from the Assiniboins,$^g$ who stole from the Blackfeet. In turn the Blackfeet stole from the Crows, and the Crows from the Blackfeet. Hence a poor beast might come back to its first owner several times. Among the tribes of the upper Missouri River, the Crows were the richest in horses and the cleverest of horse thieves.

■ The prefix im- means "not." Possible means "able to happen." So impossible means "not able to happen."

■ The base word appear means something like "to come into view." So disappear must mean "not to be in view."

What nation began this circle of warfare no one remembered or cared. Each raid called for an answering raid, either to recover horses or avenge$^g$ a death. This was especially true between Blackfoot and Crow. Seldom did seven days go by without small herds being run off from a Crow or Blackfoot camp.

During the years of her thirties, Lonesome Star led many raids against the Blackfeet, the Sioux, and her former tribe, the Gros Ventres$^g$ of the Prairie. In each she was successful. Although daring, she was never reckless.$^{cg}$ Her first concern was always with the safety of her men.

Her regard for their lives lifted her into the company of the best Crow captains. These were leaders who "never signal a loss." They ranked above leaders who "regularly bring in horses" and leaders who "regularly kill."

Songs in her praise were composed after each of her brave deeds. Young men asked to serve under her. Old men believed she bore a charmed[9] life.

■ If re- means "again," what does *retell* mean?

On state occasions it was the tribal custom to strike a post with a stick and retell heroic deeds. Lonesome Star took her turn ahead of many fine warriors. In every battle she added to her fame.

The time finally came when she could no longer be called Lonesome Star. She deserved a more fitting name, a more respected name.

She received it the day after returning from a raid against the Sioux. She had performed the most daring feat[9] possible. She had cut loose and stolen a Sioux horse picketed[cg] near its owner's tepee.

With this accomplishment, she had performed the fourth of the highest coups,[cg] or tests of courage. Already she had been the first to strike in battle. She had been the leader of a successful raid. She had snatched a gun in a hand-to-hand fight. Now she had stolen a horse within an enemy camp.

Each coup meant a step toward chieftainship. A "chief" was simply a warrior who had succeeded in the four coups at least once. Lonesome Star had earned the title.

A crier[cg] came to her. He bid[cg] her come to the council lodge.

She was expecting him. She had on her best elkskin dress. Little Feather had trimmed it with locks of hair. Each lock represented a coup. Wolf tails were fixed to the heels of her moccasins.

At the council lodge all the advisors and warriors were gathered. Lonesome Star sat down in the place of honor.

War Horse, who was leader of her military club, rose to his feet. He motioned Lonesome Star to do the same.

"From this day forward you shall sit among the chiefs in council," he said. "From this day forward you shall be called Woman Chief."

His voice was not loud. But it seemed to go all over the universe and fill it.

The men left the council lodge. Outside the women greeted them. A crier called everyone to Red Bull's lodge to eat wild-cherry pudding.

Woman Chief lifted her gaze to the skies. She remembered Sharp Knife's words of long ago.

> *Someday when you have performed great deeds, you shall have a new name, and it shall be honored among our people forever.*

Around her she felt the mountains looking down, silently smiling on her.

■ Here is another example of personification.

# Check the Skills

## Understanding the Selection

1.  Do you think Lonesome Star could have really done all the things described in the story? Why or why not? Is this story more realistic than "Pecos Bill"? Or is it strictly make-believe? Why do you think as you do?

## Vocabulary Development Skills Word Structure

2.  a. Look back at the third marginal note on page 11. How could you figure out that *disappear* means "not in view"?

    b. What is the meaning of *retell* on page 12?

## Literary Appreciation Skills Figurative Language

3.  Do you think the author uses more literal language than figurative? Why do you think as you do?

    You may want to read *Woman Chief* by Rose Sobol. This selection was taken from that book. The book is fiction, but it is based on the writings of the real Lonesome Star.

# Use the Skills

### Understanding the Selection

1.  Perhaps you, like Ah Kum in this selection, have at some time been reluctant to invite your friends to your house. As you read, decide if this story is real or make-believe.

### Vocabulary Development Skills Word Structure

2.  Context will help you decide the meanings of words with prefixes. If you need help, refer back to page 3.

### Literary Appreciation Skills Figurative Language

3.  There are some examples of figurative language in this selection. Don't take them literally!

# AH KUM'S SEA HOUSE

Dorothea C. Hill

"Hi, Ah Kum!" called Sing Lee, the Chinese boy standing on the Singapore pier.[9]

"Hi," answered Ah Kum, keeping his Malayan[9] black eyes lowered as he busied himself tying up his boat. Almost two months had passed and he hadn't done anything to repay Sing Lee for the wonderful party in his big, fine home.

■ Context should help you understand the meaning. If not, remember that the prefix re- can mean "back."

"Did you and your father catch a lot of fish last night?"

"Not too many." If only he lived in a real house the way Sing Lee did, a place he wouldn't be ashamed to invite Sing Lee to. But instead, he lived in an old kelong,[cg] which was really just a fish trap built on tall poles out in the sea.

"Bet it's exciting, hauling up fish."

"I suppose." Ah Kum climbed up to the pier. Sticking one hand into the pocket of his blue shorts, he felt the coins his father had given him to buy line for mending their fishnets. But he just had to do something for Sing Lee. "Say, would you like to have a soda pop?"

Later, as Ah Kum was putt-putting back to his kelong, he did not feel at all happy. He had not bought cord for the nets, and Sing Lee hadn't seemed very pleased with the pop.

His father was angry, at least at first. When Ah Kum explained why he had spent the money on Sing Lee, the anger went out of his father's dark eyes. A sadness came to them. "My son, it is not good to be ashamed of one's home." He stood up then, straight and tall, and walked off to set the fish trap for the night.

Ah Kum went into the palm-thatched hut atop the kelong. Sinking down on the floor, he buried his face against his knees. He had made his father unhappy. He had not squared[cg] things with Sing Lee. If only he lived in a proper home on land.

That night, as usual, Ah Kum helped his father turn the windlasses<sup>cg</sup> to haul up the net. They sorted out the various kinds of fish, putting them into shallow baskets. There were a few larger fish, but most of them were tiny, silver anchovies.<sup>cg</sup>

Then Ah Kum fired up the gas stove. A large kettle of water started to boil. He threw in chunks of rock salt and stirred the water to make the salt melt.

His father swirled the baskets of anchovies into the kettle of boiling water. After a few seconds the purified[9] baskets were removed and the tiny fish were left to cook for several minutes. Then they were scooped back into the baskets. Ah Kum and his father worked in silence.

Next morning they loaded the fish into their boat and his father took them to market while he went to school.

His father hardly spoke as he picked him up that afternoon and they went back to the kelong.

Ah Kum usually slept each afternoon in order to be wide awake for the night's work. That afternoon, however, he lay on his mat with his eyes open, staring up at the thatch[9] of palm leaves.

Among the leaves he kept seeing that sad look in his father's dark eyes. After a while he knew what he must do. Actually he had known it in his heart the minute his father had said, "It is not good to be ashamed of one's home." Now, though it would mean losing Sing Lee's friendship forever, he must do it.

He found his father lowering the net into the square trap below the kelong deck. "There is something I would like to do."

"And what is that?" asked his father.

"I would like to have a party for Sing Lee and some of the others who were at his party."

His father was silent. At last he said, "When would you like to have this party?"

"Next week."

Fourteen boys and girls, including Sing Lee, came to the party. Ah Kum made two boat trips to bring them all out to the kelong. The day before, he and his father had scrubbed their place with seawater, stacked baskets ready for use, and made strings of sweet-smelling plumeria[9] blossoms to festoon[9] the palm-thatched walls.

"Oh, it is beautiful!" exclaimed one of the girls.

When everybody had climbed the ladder onto the kelong, somebody said, "What is that row of poles for? They march out to sea, but there is nothing at the end."

■ Can poles really march? Or is this figurative language?

Sing Lee, his eyes shining with interest, cried, "Tell us, Ah Kum, how the kelong works."

"Well, that row of poles may look useless, but it is not. It crosses the ocean current which brings the fish. When they get to it, they follow along beside it to the kelong."

"Why?"

"Nobody knows exactly. Perhaps they are curious."

Everybody laughed. Ah Kum wasn't sure whether they were laughing at him or at the curious fish, but taking a deep breath, he continued, "The line of poles leads to a big V shape of more poles. The fish swim into the wide end and from there into a fenced-in square below the deck."

"But how do you haul them up here?"

"There is a net at the bottom, and every two hours during the night we haul it up by these windlasses."

"May we help?"

Promptly at six o'clock, Ah Kum and his father began turning the windlasses. Everyone crowded around, watching for the first sight of fish.

Suddenly, there was a stirring in the dark water. A flash of silver. Another. Everybody talked at once as the bulging netful of writhing,[9] twisting fish came into sight.

Windlass lines were made fast, and everybody helped scoop fish out onto the deck. They put the larger ones into sacks of ice and the anchovies into the boiling water. Ah Kum explained everything.

"You have to know a lot to catch fish," said one girl.

"Of course, silly," said Sing Lee. "Fishing is a business. To make a living, you have to know what to do. Just like my father and his hotel."

Ah Kum glanced quickly at Sing Lee. Was he making fun of him?

Ah Kum's father saved out enough fish to roll in meal and fry in hot oil. They were crisp and brown on the outside, white and flaky inside. They were served with rice, flavored with bits of chili pepper and soy sauce. There was hot tea and a bowl of hard candy for dessert.

One of the girls had a guitar. After dinner they all clustered around her, singing as she played song after song. Too soon the time came to take his guests back to shore.

Sing Lee was among the boys and girls of the last load. As he climbed up onto the pier, he turned back. "You know, Ah Kum, when you took such a long time to invite me out to your home, I thought you didn't like me." He grinned. "See you around."

# Check the Skills

### Understanding the Selection

1.  Is this story make-believe or realistic? Do you think this story would be more likely to appear in a book of tall tales with "Pecos Bill" or in a realistic fiction collection with "Woman Chief"? Why do you think as you do?

### Vocabulary Development Skills Word Structure

2.  The prefix *re-* can help you figure out the word *repay*, as the first marginal note showed you. Why can't *re-* help you figure out the word *reality*?

### Literary Appreciation Skills Figurative Language

3.  Look back at the marginal note on page 17. Is this figurative or literal language? How do you know?

# Selection 4

# Use the Skills

### Understanding the Selection

1.  The following selection is about a tough old mountain man named Jim Bridger, who really lived. Shortly after you begin reading, however, you'll know that this is a tall tale, much more make-believe than real. Compare Jim Bridger with Pecos Bill.

### Vocabulary Development Skills Word Structure

2.  By now prefixes are familiar to you. You should be able to whiz past words that include them. But if you need help, look back to page 3.

### Literary Appreciation Skills Figurative Language

3.  Note similes, metaphors, and personification, and how they are used to "spice up" the story.

# JIM BRIDGER'S ALARM CLOCK

Sid Fleischman

Jim Bridger was a ramshackle,[9] sharp-eyed, long-haired mountain man. He wore fringed buckskins and Indian moccasins and carried a musket.[9] He wandered through the Old West before almost anyone else, and in time they named a fort and a forest after him, and a pass and a creek and a mountain or two.

By then he'd been out west so long he once pointed to a mountain in the distance, flat-topped and red as a Navajo[9] blanket. "Stranger," he said. (Jim liked to talk to strangers; they were few and far between in the wilderness.) "Stranger, look how that mountain has grown! When I first came out here, it was nothing but a red ant hill."

That's what Jim Bridger's famous for. That mountain. He made an alarm clock out of it.

The way it happened, Jim was out in the wilderness, as usual, when a blizzard whipped down out of Canada. He traveled south through the snow for days and nights. And though he was all tuckered[c9] out, he didn't dare to stop and rest. He knew a man could sleep himself to death in the blizzard and bitter cold. Finally, when he figured he couldn't go much farther, he caught sight of that red flat-topped mountain in the distance. It was slab-sided,[9] too, and Jim had bounced echoes off it many a time. He reckoned that from where he now stood, it would take about eight hours for the echo to return.

Jim Bridger gave a yip of joy and made camp. He laid out his bedroll on the snow. Then he gave an ear-quivering yell. "WAKE UP! WAKE UP, JIM BRIDGER, YOU FROST-BIT, NO-ACCOUNT RASCAL!"

After that, he climbed into his bedroll, clamped his eyes shut, and fell away to snoring. Oh, he snored thunderbolts, and he dreamed of hot biscuits and gravy.

Exactly seven hours and fifty-six minutes later, Jim

■ A metaphor here gives a livelier description than would the literal phrase "he snored loudly."

Bridger's Alarm Clock went off. "*Wake up!*" roared the echo. "*Wake up, Jim Bridger, you frost-bit, no-account rascal!*"

■ The prefix *re-* can help you scoot right past this word with not a second thought to its meaning.

Jim roused from his bedroll all refreshed. It was a week before he reached Fort Bridger, where the sun was shining, and no one believed his story.

But a trapper came straggling in and said, "It's true, every word. I found the coals of Jim's campfire and bundled up in furs to catch some shut-eye. Next thing I knew that mountain commenced<sup>cg</sup> booming. I didn't get a wink of sleep. Jim, you snore loud enough to drive pigs to market!"

■ Do you think this is literal language or figurative language?

A few months later, when Jim Bridger was coming back from exploring Yellowstone Park, he bumped into a brand-new town. It stood smack-dab on the spot where he'd camped the day of the big blizzard. But folks didn't know he'd been there first, so they didn't name the place after him. They called it Blue Horizon.

Blue Horizon didn't amount to much, but it did have a general store, a stable, a blacksmith, and a funeral parlor.

Jim said his howdies,<sup>cg</sup> but everyone he met had the grumbles.<sup>cg</sup> "Something bothering you?" he asked the folks sitting around the stove in the general store.

The mayor nodded. "We got to call off the barn dance tonight. The fiddler won't fiddle."

Now Jim Bridger loved a frolic and it had been a long time since he'd kicked his heels to a jolly tune. "Who's the fiddler?" he asked.

■ Can the prefix *un-* help you with this word?

"Buryin' John Potter, the undertaker. He's hornet-mad because folks didn't elect him mayor instead of me."

The more Jim Bridger thought about it, the more his feet hankered[9] for fiddle music. So he went across the street to the undertaker's parlor. "You can't fool me, Buryin' John Potter," said Jim. "I see your fiddle on the wall, but that don't mean you can play a note."

"Can, but won't," grumbled the undertaker.

"No, sir," Jim said. "If you was to saw your fiddling bow across those strings, I'll bet you couldn't hit two notes out of five."

"Haw," said the undertaker.

"Reckon you don't even know 'Chicken in the Bread Tray Pickin' Up Dough.'"

"By heart," said the undertaker, sourly. "But I'm not fiddlin' tonight. Don't think you can sweet-word me into changing my mind."

"Wouldn't think of it," Jim replied. "But I'm a powerful fine judge of fiddle music. Once heard Jingle-Bob Earl play a frolic back in Missouri, and I guess you'll agree he's the mightiest fiddler who ever was."

"Faw," snorted Buryin' John Potter.

And Jim said, "I brought a gourd plugged full of hot steam from the Yellowstone, and it's still perishin' hot. That Yellowstone steam takes years to cool off. I figure to use that gourd as a foot warmer. Buryin' John, that Yellowstone foot warmer is yours if you can play the screech box half as clever as Jingle-Bob Earl. Come outside and prove it."

The undertaker took down his fiddle, and the two men rode out to a distant spot west of town. Buryin' John tuned his strings and ripped out "Turkey in the Straw."

Jim thought he'd never heard it played so sweet, but he said, "Won't do. Jingle-Bob Earl played louder'n that. Do you know 'Scooping Up Pawpaws' or 'Have You Seen My New Shoes'?"

"Both," Buryin' John muttered and commenced sawing away twice as loud as before.

Then the undertaker lifted his chin from the fiddle and said, "Reckon that gourd foot warmer is mine," he declared.

"Not so hasty," said Jim. "You call that a contest? Why Jingle-Bob Earl could fiddle all night without playing the same tune twice."

The undertaker tucked the fiddle back under his jaw and scraped away. Hour after hour the bow cut wild figures in the air.

Finally the sun began to dive for home. Jim jumped up, stomped his feet to the music, and sang out.

> *You can fiddle down a possum from a mile-high tree,*
> *You can fiddle up a whale from the bottom of the sea.*

Then he said, "Buryin' John, you win! You're the mightiest fiddler that ever was! The Yellowstone foot warmer is yours."

When Jim got back to the general store, it was falling dark. "Grab your women and head for the barn!" he exclaimed. "The frolic's about to commence!"

The barn filled up in no time, and folks stood around waiting for Buryin' John.

Finally the mayor said, "Can't be a frolic without a fiddler. We might as well go home."

"Keep your hair on, mayor, and the barn doors wide open. All the windows, too," said Jim, cupping an ear. "Coming this way is the grandest, mightiest fiddling you ever heard. Caller, clear your throat!"

Suddenly, bouncing back from Jim's slab–sided echo mountain, came the first notes of "Turkey in the Straw." The folks in the barn were so taken by surprise that they stood like bird dogs on point. Then Jim leaped to the center of the floor with hours of stored–up frolic in his feet. He kicked his heels, and the dance was on.

■ Which word tells you this is a simile?

# Check the Skills

### Understanding the Selection

1. How do you know that this tale is make-believe? How are Jim Bridger and Pecos Bill alike?

### Vocabulary Development Skills Word Structure

2. How can you determine the meaning of *refreshed* by using the prefix *re-*? Why doesn't *un-* help you with *undertaker*?

### Literary Appreciation Skills Figurative Language

3. a. How do you know that the following sentence is a simile? What does it mean?

   They stood like bird dogs on point.

   b. How do you know that the sentence below is figurative language and not literal language?

   Jim, you snore loud enough to drive pigs to market!

# Selection 5

## Use the Skills

Although the following poem is make-believe and fun to read, there is some truth to it. Think about the message of the poem as you read. Be on the lookout for words with prefixes, but remember that this skill does not always work. You may have to refer to the glossary. See if you can find any examples of figurative language. But mainly read and enjoy the poem.

# DON'T EVER STRIKE
# A RHINOCEROS

Martin Steinberg

I met an old man in Manhattan;
His age was one hundred and three.
And these are the secrets of living
That he sat and imparted[9] to me.

"Don't ever strike a rhinoceros
Or tickle a Man-Eater's gill.
And don't hold a rod in a rainstorm
Unless you have written your will.

You must shun[cg] every sort of a landslide
And beware of the head-hunter's wiles.
Never shake hands with a grizzly,
No matter how broadly he smiles.

Don't ever swim in the Arctic
Or spit in a crocodile's eye.
Move to the side when a laser
Is aimed at an object nearby.

Insulting[9] an angry gorilla
Is thought to be rather bad form.
Stay out of a cannibal's stewpot;
It gets most distressingly[9] warm.

Jumping off bridges is frowned on,
And teasing of tigers, as well.
If you ever run into a meat-eating plant,
Be sure you don't fall for its smell."

With this, he had finished his statement.
I thanked him sincerely, and then,
For all of the wisdom he'd taught me,
I thanked him sincerely again.

The end of my story is tragic,
How he came to the end of his days.
In the rush hour in midtown Manhattan,
He crossed without looking both ways.

# Check the Skills

## Understanding the Selection

1. Can you condense the old man's message down to one sentence? What is it? Even though the poem is silly, do you think the old man's advice is sound? Why do you think as you do?

## Vocabulary Development Skills Word Structure

2. The following words appear in the poem. Why can't your skill with prefixes help you to figure out their meanings? How else can you find their meanings?

   imparted          beware
   distressingly     insulting

## Literary Appreciation Skills Figurative Language

3. Would you consider the entire poem a form of exaggeration? Why or why not? In the third verse, has the poet made use of personification about the bear? How do you know?

# Apply What You Learned in Unit 1

## The Theme

### Real and Make-Believe

1.    In this unit you read about two completely unbelievable characters, Jim Bridger and Pecos Bill. And you can be pretty sure that the man from Manhattan is only make-believe. But Woman Chief and Ah Kum seem like real people. Which type of story did you enjoy more, the ones that seemed real or those that you knew were make-believe? Why?

•    What kinds of things can you think of that young children consider to be real but you know are only make-believe?

# The Skills

## Vocabulary Development Skills Word Structure

2.  Knowing the meaning of prefixes can help you determine the meanings of words. But it doesn't work all the time. If this skill isn't working for you, you may try using context clues or look the word up in a dictionary.

## Literary Appreciation Figurative Language

3.  You learned that figurative language helps to make reading more interesting, more fun, and more picturesque. As you read, make sure you know whether the language used is figurative language or literal language.

# Unit **2**

# Human Abilities

## Overview and Purposes for Reading

### The Theme

### Human Abilities

1. People, unlike animals, can act out of intelligence rather than just instinct. We can think and talk and read and learn. We also have hands that move in many ways. What kinds of things can people do because of our special abilities?

### The Skills

### Vocabulary Development Skills Word Meaning

2. Most words have several different meanings. How can you choose which of these meanings fits what you are reading?

### Study and Research Skills Study Techniques

3. Why is it important to be able to follow directions properly? How can you learn to do this?

# Learn About the Skills

## Vocabulary Development Skills Word Meaning

Have you ever played the game "Password"? In secret you are given a word, such as *pass*. You then give a clue that is a single word to a partner. The clue, of course, cannot be the word *pass*. The points earned by your team depend on how quickly your partner guesses the right word. As clues for *pass*, you might say *throw, free ticket, mountain.*

Yes, *pass* has several meanings. And there are even more. Which clue given above is right for the way the word is used in each of these sentences?

1. In the movie, the army watched from above as the cavalry galloped through the *pass*.
2. *Pass* me the volleyball.
3. I had a *pass* to the concert.

Most words have several meanings. You need to know which one fits best what you are reading. You can do this if you pay close attention to the other words in the sentence or paragraph.

To figure out the right meaning of a word in a sentence or passage, follow these steps.

### Choosing the Right Meaning

1. Pick out the word whose meaning you're unsure of.
2. Ask yourself what is being talked about in the sentence.
3. Decide which meaning of the word makes sense in the sentence.

**Try the Skill.** Follow the three steps above to figure out which meaning of *beat* suits this sentence.

> The baker *beat* the batter in the bowl.

*Beat* has several meanings. It can mean "win" as in *Our team can beat yours.* Or it can mean "hit" as in *Shelly beat the punching bag.* Or it can mean "rhythm." *That song has a nice beat.* None of these meanings fits the sentence about the baker. The baker didn't "win" over the batter or "hit" the batter or "rhythm" the batter. The meaning of *beat* here is "to stir quickly." The baker stirred the batter quickly.

Try another example. Think of the word *compact*. This word can mean several things. It can mean "a small automobile," "an agreement," or "a small case for face powder." What does it mean in this sentence?

> To prevent future problems, the nations entered into a *compact*.

Think what the sentence is about. Choose the meaning that makes sense. You have to choose "an agreement."

Many words like *pass, beat,* and *compact* have several different meanings. But you will not be confused if you think about what the sentence or paragraph is really about. Then choose the meaning of the word that fits.

You'll have a chance to use what you have learned about words with several meanings as you read through the selections in this unit.

## Study and Research Skills Study Techniques

Just about every day, both in school and out of school, you are expected to follow written directions. You must read written directions carefully so that you know what you are expected to do.

Usually, you cannot read directions, then tear them up and expect to remember them. You must keep written directions close at hand as you are following them. Refer to them frequently.

To follow written directions, remember these steps.

---

### Following Directions

1. Read *all* directions before you begin. Understand what the end result will be.
2. Decide what materials you will need and get them ready for use. Not everything may be listed, so you will have to use your common sense.
3. Notice the sequence you should follow—what to do first, next, and so on.
4. Note any special information that you need to remember.
5. If illustrations or diagrams or graphs are included, take note of how they can help you.
6. Reread each step before you actually do it.

---

You'll find some help with using your skill in following directions as you read this unit.

# Selection 1

# Use the Skills

### Understanding the Selection

1.  Performing magic tricks successfully for others is always fun. You will find out how to perform two such tricks when you read this selection. Decide whether humans are the only beings who have the ability to do tricks like these.

### Vocabulary Development Skills Word Meaning

2.  As you read, think how you can choose the correct meanings of the words *fall* and *cross* in the selection.

### Study and Research Skills Study Techniques

3.  Use the steps suggested for following directions as you figure out how to perform these tricks. Marginal notes will help.

# TWO TRICKS

Martin Gardner

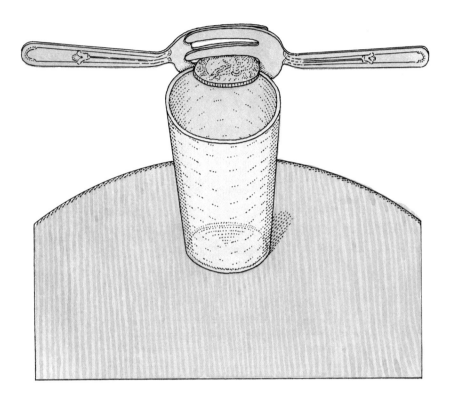

## The Precarious⁹ Forks

If you overlap the prongs⁹ of two table forks, then insert a half dollar between the prongs so that it holds both forks, you'll be able to balance the coin and forks on the rim of a glass as shown.

This is extremely baffling⁹ to most people because the entire weight of both forks is on the outer portion of the coin. Why don't the forks and coin fall?

The explanation is that the heavy handles of the forks curve toward the glass. This shifts the center of gravity⁹ of the entire structure to a point directly beneath the spot where the coin rests on the glass, putting the forks and coin in a state of balance.

■ Materials needed: 2 forks, 1 half dollar, 1 glass. Common sense tells you that you also need a flat surface. Note sequence of steps and end result.

■ You know *fall* does not refer to a time of year. Here it means "to drop."

## A Knotty Problem

Lay a piece of rope or cord out straight on a table. Challenge anyone to seize one end in each hand and tie a knot without letting go of either end.

It seems physically impossible, yet it can be done easily. The trick is to fold your arms first and then bend over and pick up the rope as shown. When you unfold your arms, an overhand knot will form in the center of the rope. It is interesting to note that two different types of knots can be tied in this manner, depending on whether you <u>cross</u> your right arm over the left or left over the right. The resulting knots are mirror images of each other.

■ You can tell that this means "to place one over the other," not "in a bad temper."

# Check the Skills

## Understanding the Selection

1. As you were reading how to do "The Precarious Forks" trick, did you wonder why the forks don't fall? Do you think these are clever tricks that people would like to see? Why or why not? Do you think only people are able to do these tricks?

## Vocabulary Development Skills Word Meaning

2. Look back at the marginal note on page 37. How does the sentence help you know that *fall* means "to drop"?

## Study and Research Skills Study Techniques

3. If you wanted to do "The Precarious Forks" trick, you would first read all the directions. What materials would you need? What steps would you follow? What would be the end result of following the directions?

# Selection 2

# Use the Skills

### Understanding the Selection

1.  Sometimes animals react in such a manner that people be-
    lieve they can think. This is a fascinating story of a horse who
    appears to be much wiser than her master. Find out how
    Pablita's sense helps her become a hero in her village. What
    instinct do you think helps Pablita do what she does? Do you
    suppose human beings might have this instinct?

### Vocabulary Development Skills Word Meaning

2.  Watch for the word *root*. Decide which of its meanings fits.

### Study and Research Skills Study Techniques

3.  This selection contains no directions. Think about whether a
    person could direct a horse to act as Pablita did.

# PABLITA

Sam Savitt

Not long ago in a small mountain village in Spain near the Pass of Pancorbo, there was a celebration being held for a horse. The guest of honor was an old mare named Pablita. Why would a whole town give a fiesta for an old draft[9] horse? Well, let me tell you her story, and you can judge for yourself whether the honor was merited.[9]

■ You know from context that this must be a mountain pass.

For years this little mare pulled a cart filled with fruits and vegetables between two villages which were in the Asturias,[c] a rugged mountain chain of jagged peaks and rock towers. Every morning her master drove her to the local market and loaded up. Then he peddled his produce in both villages—one in the morning and one in the afternoon. The pair would walk slowly through the narrow, winding streets. The peddler led the way. His cheerful call, "Apples, peaches, tomatoes," was familiar to all. His mare followed him faithfully, pulling the cartful of fruits and vegetables. Pablita knew her job and did it well. Not once in their many years together did she question her master's judgment.

Now, between the two villages was a tall, boulder-strewn mountain. Some years before, a tunnel had been constructed through it. From morning until night, automobiles, wagons, trucks, bicycles, carts—everything went through this tunnel.

Late in the morning of July 2, 1968, old Pablita was on the road as usual. Her master drowsed[9] on the high wooden seat behind her. He had had a good morning, and now he catnapped[9] as the wagon creaked along. Soon they would be in the next village. If business was as good there, he would get home early. He was smiling at the thought when, without warning, the cart came to a halt. He sat up, jolted into sharp wakefulness. Why had his horse stopped close to the entrance of the tunnel? He could see no obstruction.[9] He slapped the reins across Pablita's back and urged, "Come on, we haven't got all day." She moved forward a couple of steps, then stopped again. The peddler climbed down from the wagon and walked around Pablita, picking up each foot and examining it closely. Maybe a stone was lodged in a hoof. But there was no sign of any. He climbed back into the wagon, picked up the reins, and tapped the mare with his whip. She trotted ahead a few paces but, when she reached the entrance of the tunnel, Pablita stopped dead. There was no hesitation[9] in her now. She had made up her mind—this was as far as she was going.

Her master got down again, caught hold of her bridle[9] and tried pulling her forward. But Pablita was not going anywhere. Her legs were planted like four posts. Behind them, the traffic quickly piled up. There was much yelling and blowing of horns, but the mare would not be moved. The tunnel was narrow, and the cars and carts that went through it took turns. A signal flag, carried by the last member of one group and handed to the last member of the group going in the opposite direction, kept the traffic in motion. Now the horse and cart blocked the entrance and nothing on wheels could get by. Someone ran through to the other side, about two hundred yards or so, to explain the situation, since it was impossible for anything to turn around once it was inside the tunnel.

The peddler was really a gentle man, but because of the pressure behind, he was forced to use his whip. Still the mare would not budge. A police officer came riding up. When told about the problem, the officer quickly took over. "Let's get some volunteers," the officer ordered. "You, you, you!" Six or eight people were assembled around the mare, and together they tried to lift her off the ground. She didn't fight them, but her feet seemed to have taken root.

■ *Root* here does not mean "underground part of a plant" or "source," but rather "to become firmly fixed."

"Unhook the wagon!" someone cried.

The peddler unhitched the wagon, and it was rolled off to the side of the road. Pablita was still anchored[9] in place. The people gathered around her again, took hold of the leather harness trailing down her sides, and pulled. Pablita sat back on her haunches,[c9] braced for battle. As the tug of war began, suddenly a strange vibration could be felt. Everyone stopped.

There was an eerie[9] stillness in the air, almost as if the day were holding its breath. The distant vibration began again, but this time it rapidly grew stronger and stronger. The earth shook beneath their feet. Then right before their very eyes, the inside of the tunnel seemed to explode with a giant roar. The collapsing roof sent great clouds of dust swirling out of both ends of the tunnel, quickly enveloping the horse and the scores[9] of people and vehicles lined up. The pounding continued; it rolled and boomed. Then it gradually subsided to a rumble, like distant thunder. As the dust settled, the mare and the people gathered around her could be seen still standing there, shocked but alive. And in front of them was no sign of the tunnel anywhere.

Did Pablita know that cave-in was coming? I'm sure she did. It was this awareness, this sixth sense of impending[cg] danger, and her refusal to enter the tunnel, that saved the lives of so many. Can you think of a better reason for a celebration in honor of a horse?

■ Could directions be given about how to have this "sixth sense"?

# Check the Skills

### Understanding the Selection

1.  Do you think Pablita acted instinctively or was she thinking? Could humans do what she did? Why do you think as you do?

### Vocabulary Development Skills Word Meaning

2.  What clues in the sentence could help you know which meaning of *root* was meant on page 42? The note in the margin can help you find it again.

### Study and Research Skills Study Techniques

3.  Do you think it is possible to follow directions to do what Pablita did? Why or why not?

# Selection 3

# Use the Skills

### Understanding the Selection

1. Almost everyone likes to eat sweets now and then. In this selection you will find out how to produce a dessert fit for a gourmet, an expert judge of fine cooking. What abilities help people cook?

### Vocabulary Development Skills Word Meaning

2. Decide what the appropriate meaning of *claims* is in the selection.

### Study and Research Skills Study Techniques

3. Think about why following directions is important with recipes.

# EASY GOURMET[9] DESSERT

Bernice Kohn

You can make a gourmet dessert the first time you try, even if you have never made one before. It that sounds suspiciously like one of those claims that you can play the Brahms Violin Concerto[9] the first time you pick up a violin, it isn't. The difference is that making a gourmet dessert, unlike playing a violin concerto, does not require any skill or experience. All it takes is the ability to follow directions.

■ This could mean "requires," "deserves," "declarations of something as fact," or "pieces of public land people mark out for themselves." Which seems to fit best here?

## Apple Crunch

*Ingredients*

4 medium or 6 small apples
3 tablespoons white sugar
½ cup brown sugar

1 cup flour
½ cup (1 stick) butter
  or margarine
½ teaspoon cinnamon

■ Labels, pictures, and a list of ingredients tell the materials needed for the end result.

## Procedure

1. Turn on oven to 400° F.
2. Break off a small piece of butter, and grease the inside of the baking dish with it.
3. Pare[9] the apples.
4. Slice the apples by cutting off the four sides around the core, then cutting each of the four pieces into ¼-inch-thick slices. Put them into the baking dish.
5. Sprinkle the white sugar over the apples and mix it through.
6. Put the brown sugar, flour, butter, and cinnamon into the mixing bowl and mix it with your fingertips until it is well blended and crumbly.
7. Scatter the mixture over the top of the apples and pat it down slightly.
8. Put the pan into the oven. Bake for about ½ hour or until the apples feel tender when you stick them with a fork.
9. Serve warm or cool, plain or with milk, cream or ice cream.

# Check the Skills

## Understanding the Selection

1.  Do you think this dessert would be easy to make? Why or why not? Do you have a pretty good idea how the dessert would taste? What special abilities do we have that make us able to cook? Why do you suppose animals don't cook their food?

## Vocabulary Development Skills Word Meaning

2.  How do you know *claims* in this selection does not mean "requires" or "deserves," or "pieces of public land people mark out for themselves"?

## Study and Research Skills Study Techniques

3.  Why is it important to carry out the steps as they are listed rather than in another order? Why is it necessary to follow directions with recipes? What could happen if directions were not followed carefully?

# Selection 4

# Use the Skills

### Understanding the Selection

1. The Senecas were a Native American tribe who lived in the forests of what is now the northeastern part of the United States. This selection tells how and why the Senecas grew corn, beans, and squash. As you read, note how the planting was carried out. How did human intelligence make this possible?

### Vocabulary Development Skills Word Meaning

2. Decide what the correct meanings are for *flat* and *cast* in this selection.

### Study and Research Skills Study Techniques

3. You could plant a garden like the one described in this selection. See if you think you would need more detailed directions.

# A SENECA GARDEN

Geraldine M. Guidetti

A young Seneca girl followed her mother to the field where they planted their crops each year. Her feet sank softly into the earth as she walked, for the soil was warm and moist from the heat and gentle rains of late spring. It was planting time.

When they reached the field, her mother began to scrape out a shallow furrow[cg] in the earth with a long stick. Following her, the girl dropped corn kernels, one by one, into the furrow and covered them over with warm soil.

"Now the squash," said the older woman when all the kernels had been planted. Between the rows of corn the two dug small circular[9] furrows for the squash seeds. "When the young corn seedlings are up," her mother said, "we will plant beans by each of them. Corn, squash, and beans must always be planted together. Never forget that."

■ Could you use this description as directions to follow?

For as long as she could remember, the girl had heard this lesson repeated over and over again—corn, squash, and beans together. On cold winter nights her grandfather would tell the tale that explained how these three plants had become the main food of the Senecas, the "life sustainers."[cg]

Like the Senecas, many other tribes grew and ate the "life sustainers." Corn, beans, and squash were very important to them.

Today we realize how wise these early farmers were. They saw how tall and straight the corn plants grew, as if they were reaching for the sun. And they knew that bean plants grew in long, twisting vines that were always searching for something to climb on. It seemed reasonable, then, to plant bean seeds next to the corn so the vines could twist themselves higher and higher up the strong, straight stalks. And it was much easier to pick bean pods that no longer lay on the muddy soil.

The first farmers also saw that squash plants spread across the earth many feet from where they were planted. Greedily[9] gobbling up sunshine, their large, flat leaves cast such big shadows on the soil that there was no sun left for the weeds and grasses. By planting squash seeds between their corn rows, the first farmers could blanket the earth with a living cover that made tiresome weeding almost unnecessary.

■ *Flat* does not mean "apartment" here. What does it mean? What other meaning of *cast* is not correct here?

A good fall harvest meant hunger would not plague[9] the Senecas that winter. Corn, beans, and squash could all be kept for months without spoiling. Ears of yellow, pink, and even blue corn were hung throughout Indian homes in the fall. During the cold winter months some of the dried kernels were used to make hot soups and chowders,[9] while

■ Could this picture help you understand how to grow your own Seneca garden?

others were ground into flour for making bread. Beans were removed from their dry, leathery pods and cooked alone or in corn soup.

Corn and beans, when eaten together, are excellent sources of protein. Your body needs protein to build muscles to make substances that help fight germs, and to produce chemicals called enzymes,[cg] which enable your body to run smoothly. Protein is also needed to build hair, nails, skin, bones, and even blood.

And the tough-shelled squashes, grown by the Senecas for winter eating, are rich in vitamins and minerals that help maintain growth, keep skin and eyes healthy, and aid in the healing of wounds. It's no wonder the three vegetables were called "life sustainers"!

# Check the Skills

### Understanding the Selection

1.  Do you think it would be a simple or difficult task to plant and care for a Seneca garden? Why do you think as you do? How does human intelligence make this possible?

### Vocabulary Development Skills Word Meaning

2.  What is the meaning of *flat* on page 50? Of *cast*? How did you figure out the suitable meaning of each word?

### Study and Research Skills Study Techniques

3.  What are some of the advantages of planting your own Seneca garden? Does the description in the selection tell you enough to do it without more directions?

# Use the Skills

When people have trouble moving their bodies, they often see a therapist. A therapist is a person who has been specially trained to help. This selection tells you what physical and occupational therapists do to help people strengthen their bodies.

You'll need to remember how to choose the best meaning of some words. As you read you might ask yourself how a patient can benefit from following therapists' directions.

No marginal notes accompany this selection. You are on your own.

# THE THERAPISTS

Joy Schaleben-Lewis

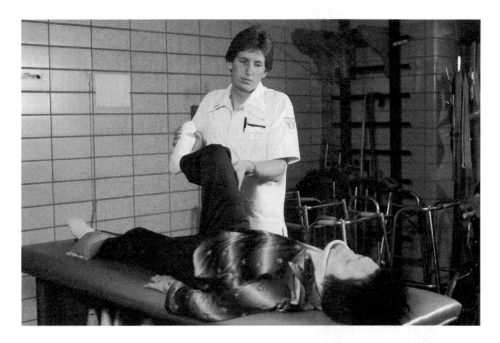

Did you ever see anyone who had lost an arm or leg? Or had an arm or leg that was weak or stiff or wouldn't move? Such people need the help of a physical therapist.[cg] Physical therapists try to bring back all possible movement, strength, and coordination[g] to arms and legs. They also teach people to make the best use of the movement they have. To do this, physical therapists learn about muscles. And about bones and joints—ankles, knees, wrists, elbows, hips, and shoulders.

Physical therapists do not use medicine. They use exercise and special equipment to help patients. A therapist might have a patient with a weak leg soak in a whirlpool bath. This helps to get the blood moving and it relaxes the leg muscles. A therapist might use parallel[cg] bars, hand rails placed side by side to support someone learning to walk again. Next, the therapist might show the patient how to use crutches—on a flat surface and on stairs.

The occupational therapist also gives extra help, usually to people who have trouble using their arms, hands, and fingers. A person might have fingers that are too weak to hold a pencil or a fork. The therapist plans activities to strengthen the fingers.

Another important goal of occupational therapists is to help patients learn to care for themselves. Learn to get out of bed. Comb their hair. Tie their shoelaces. Cook. Clean.

There are certain adaptive[9] devices[cg] that help people who have trouble using their arms or hands. One such device is a cuff that straps around the fingers to help the person hold a fork or pencil. The occupational therapist teaches people to use such adaptive devices.

Occupational therapists must have a great deal of patience. It may take weeks for a patient to improve, even a little. The therapist finds it rewarding to help people become stronger, and to help them learn to master their daily tasks and the activities necessary for independence.

Here, a therapist is helping restore blood circulation to a patient's feet and legs. This must be done before the patient can stand up and learn to walk again.

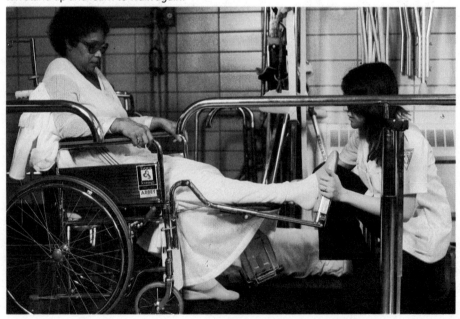

A therapist helps a patient walk down the hall.

# Check the Skills

## Understanding the Selection

1. When a person is physically handicapped, how can a physical therapist help? an occupational therapist? Is this something only human beings can do?

## Vocabulary Development Skills Word Meaning

2. *Patient* can mean "calm and understanding" or "someone under medical care." Which meaning fits the following sentence from the selection?

   > A therapist might have a patient with a weak leg soak in a whirlpool bath.

## Study and Research Skills Study Techniques

3. Why do you think it is important for a patient to follow directions given by a therapist?

# Apply What You Learned in Unit 2

## The Theme

### Human Abilities

1. In this unit you found out about some of the things people can do that animals can't. You saw how we can use our minds and our hands. You also learned from Pablito that human capabilities are not always enough to deal with certain situations. Do you think that people, like animals, sometimes react instinctively in certain situations—that they automatically know what to do without thinking about it? Why do you think as you do?

• Do you think that animals are capable of thinking through a situation? Why or why not?

# The Skills

## Vocabulary Development Skills Word Meaning

2. How can you figure out which meaning of a word fits in a sentence if that word has many meanings?

## Study and Research Skills Study Techniques

3. You have read different types of directions. Remember, you must follow directions carefully to get the desired final results. Follow directions carefully in all your classes, especially when you take tests. It's important!

# Finding Solutions

## Overview and Purposes for Reading

### The Theme

**Finding Solutions**

1.  How do people find solutions to the problems they meet in life? Why is it important to try to solve these problems?

### The Skills

**Vocabulary Development Skills** Context Clues

2.  Why it is important to use the clues around a word whose meaning you don't know?

3.  How can you do this?

**Literary Appreciation Skills** Types of Literature

4.  How can you tell if a selection is fiction or non-fiction? Why is it important to know?

# Learn About the Skills

## Vocabulary Development Skills Context Clues

When you are reading, you often meet words whose meanings you don't know. When this happens, you should first see if there are hints in the words and sentences around the word. These hints are called **context clues**.

Sometimes a word is defined in the same sentence. For example, you may not know what the word *mosque* means. But in this sentence it is easy to figure out.

> The mosque, a Moslem church, had open sides and a tall tower.

The word *mosque* is directly defined in the sentence. With this type of context clue, a phrase defining the word is given in the same sentence or in one nearby. Note how this kind of context clue helps you with the meaning of the word *junk* in this sentence:

> In the harbor was a junk. This type of sailing boat is found on many rivers in China.

The sentence that follows defines *junk* for you.

However, you will not always find such clear context clues. Sometimes you must search for other clues to the meaning of a word. You need to look at the words around the unknown word and think about your own experiences with similar situations. This will help you to make a good guess about what the word means. For instance, check the word *obliged* in the following sentence.

> Because he had damaged Mary's radio, John felt obliged to have it repaired.

You may not be certain what *obliged* means, but you do know from your experience how John probably felt. So to guess the meaning of *obliged* you think of what you would do in the same situation. The meaning you guess will probably be pretty close to the actual meaning of the word.

See if your experience with similar situations can help you figure out the meaning of *fumed* in the following sentence:

Aunt Ann fumed when she saw how high the gas bill was.

If you guessed that *fumed* means "showed anger or irritation," you are right. Remember to use context clues to guess the meanings of words you don't know. Clues like those described above are contained in the following selections. You'll see how to use your skills to figure out some words you don't know.

# Literary Appreciation Skills Types of Literature

Fiction and nonfiction are the two main types of literature. It is often important to know which you are reading.

Fiction is based on imagination, though it may contain some facts. Usually characters and events have been made up by the author. Short stories, novels, poems, folk tales, and plays are fiction.

Nonfiction is what you read usually for information. Nonfiction materials are about the real world—real people, animals, things, or events. These selections are not imaginary. They are based on facts. There are many types of nonfiction. Among them are essays, reports, encyclopedia articles, biographies, and autobiographies.

Often, if you glance through a selection before reading it, you can tell if it is fiction or nonfiction. One clue may be the title. For example, which of these titles would probably be fiction? nonfiction?

The Life of Martin Luther King, Jr.

The Ghost of Oaktree Manor

An additional clue might be the art included with the selection. Photographs, diagrams, or factual illustrations might tell you a selection is nonfiction. Humorous pictures might be a clue that it is fiction.

Sometimes the characters and events in a story seem so real that you cannot tell whether the selection is nonfiction or fiction. This doesn't matter if you're reading for fun. Deciding whether it is nonfiction is important only if you are depending on it for factual information.

Plays and poetry are easily identified just by the way they look. The way the sentences and lines appear on the page is a clue.

# Use the Skills

### Understanding the Selection

1.  Billy has been helping Martha and Jim Riley on their farm. In this story, all three struggle to find a solution to a problem. It seems impossible for a while. See if you think the solution is a good one.

### Vocabulary Development Skills Context Clues

2.  You may meet several words you don't know. Look for context clues that tell their meanings. Or use your own personal experiences to help you figure them out. Notes in the margin will help you with several. Remember that, in this book, words for which there are context clues to meaning are followed by a small letter $c$, like this.$^c$

### Literary Appreciation Skills Types of Literature

3.  This story seems so real that you can't know just from reading it whether it is fiction or nonfiction. The author did make it up, however, so it is fiction.

# ALL SHADED UP

Peggy Simson Curry

Billy wakened with an uneasy feeling that morning. He told himself that Jim and Martha Riley were stubborn. Their place here on the mountain was a burden they could no longer afford. They would have plenty of money if they would only sell their run-down cabins, barn, and 200 acres to Hal Ketchum. Only yesterday the land developer had offered Billy a bonus if he could talk the couple into selling.

Billy felt close to the mountain, the couple, and their two old horses—the only livestock[c] left on the place. *But they can't stay*, he thought now, *not when the only money they have comes from social security*[g] *checks*.

The morning air felt good. In the pasture were the old horses, Doc and Dolly. When they ran, they were stiff and awkward but trying to be free—like colts before a storm.

The clanging of the iron triangle that hung before the main cabin told Billy breakfast was ready. He smiled. The smell of frying bacon told him that the social security checks had come.

He stepped into the kitchen. Martha smiled at him.

"Every day you look more like you belonged on the mountain," she said. "The way Jim did when I married him. Now he looks like a barrel—all belly."

Jim Riley grinned. "Hey," he said, "don't complain about my figure. I've still got the most beautiful piece of land on the mountain for you."

A shadow came over her face. "But how long can we keep it, Jim? All the cabins going up on this mountain! Sometimes I think half the town's moved up here."

"Hal Ketchum will give you lots of money for the place," Billy said. Right away he felt like a traitor.[c] He couldn't look at either of them while he thought about the bonus.

■ Your past experience with situations like this may help you figure out that *traitor* means "someone who is not loyal to a friend."

"Yeah, he's offered us lots of money," Jim said bitterly. "And for what? So he can build houses jammed up against one another so people live like sardines."

Billy could hear Hal Ketchum. "Work on Martha Riley, Billy. She'll have the say when the chips are down."

Martha said to Billy, "You've been just like a son since the first day you came to work for us. What do you think?"

His mind shouted, *Tell her to sell it!* But his throat was suddenly tight. "I have to think about it."

He was still thinking about it that afternoon. He was fixing a length of fence around the pasture. Suddenly he threw down the hammer and a handful of spikes. No use, nothing was any use. They were going to lose the land, he thought. Was it wrong for him to insist they take Ketchum's money, and that he get paid for it?

Jim lumbered[9] toward him. "What's the trouble, Billy?"

"The whole fence is rotten!" he shouted. "I couldn't fix it if I worked all summer. Why don't you get a wire fence?"

"The deer don't like wire fences," Jim said calmly. "Antelope don't either, and sometimes a few drift up here." He turned and stared at the two old horses in the pasture. "Look over there, Billy."

Billy looked. Doc had his neck stretched across Dolly's.

"They do that lots of times," Billy said. "Maybe trying to make up to one another."

"No," Jim continued. "They're shaded up. It's an old western term—means when one horse tries to shade the other from the sun when it gets too hot. Sometimes she puts her neck over his. It's kinda like Martha and me—looking after one another."

Billy's eyes blurred. Was life going to be better for Martha and Jim Riley because Hal Ketchum gave them a lot of money? *Is my life going to be better because I use the bonus*

*to buy a new car, have money for college?*

"Money ought to be kept out of this," he said, more to himself than to Jim. "This land ought to be protected. If someone could watch over it, keep it natural, even after you and Martha . . ." Then he felt Jim's hand grasp his arm.

"That gives me an idea! Come on. Let's talk to Martha."

They talked while supper was cooked. They talked while they got into Billy's old car and drove to the mountain park superintendent.[9] There, they talked late into the night.

When they got back to the cabin they were too excited to sleep. They baked up a batch of cookies to celebrate and Jim ate most of them. Then Martha kissed Billy and told him that, just this once, breakfast would be late.

When the sun came up, Billy walked down to the pasture.

"It's all fixed up," he told Doc and Dolly. "The taxes will be paid. The pasture fence will be fixed. No cars will raise the dust or bother the deer. The cabin, the old furniture—it will all stay as it is. Even after they're gone. You see, Doc and Dolly, they gave the land to the county for a park."

He put an arm across the neck of each of the old horses. "Jim and Martha."

He laughed softly and added, "We're all shaded up."

# Check the Skills

## Understanding the Selection

1. What problem did Billy have to solve? What problem did Martha and Jim have? What solution did they find? How did Billy benefit from the solution? How did Martha and Jim benefit? Do you think the solution of what to do with the land was a good one? Why or why not?

## Vocabulary Development Skills Context Clues

2. How did context clues help you determine the meaning of *traitor*? *shaded up*?

## Literary Appreciation Skills Types of Literature

3. Would you have guessed that this was fiction if you hadn't been told? Why or why not?

## Use the Skills

### Understanding the Selection

1.    If you have a sister or brother, you might understand the feelings in the next selection. Is the possible solution to the problem funny or real?

### Vocabulary Development Skills Context Clues

2.    How do context clues help you decide what *bidding* means in this selection?

### Literary Appreciation Skills Types of Literature

3.    Take a quick glance at the next page. What type of literature do you think this is?

# FOR SALE

Shel Silverstein

One sister for sale!
One sister for sale!
One crying and spying young sister for sale!
I'm really not kidding,
So who'll start the bidding?
Do I hear a dollar?
A nickel?
A penny?
Oh, isn't there, isn't there, isn't there any
One kid who will buy this old sister for sale,
This crying and spying young sister for sale?

■ The way the lines look on the page tells you right away that this is a poem. It is fiction.

■ Your experience and the next three lines are strong enough context clues for the meaning of this word.

## Check the Skills

### Understanding the Selection

1.  What is the problem in the poem? Is the possible solution meant to be funny or real? Why do you think as you do?

### Vocabulary Development Skills Context Clues

2.  What context clues helped you decide that *bidding* means "offering to buy"?

### Literary Appreciation Skills Types of Literature

3.  How could you tell that this is a poem?

Gail Harris

# Use the Skills

### Understanding the Selection

1. Have you ever wanted to be a television reporter? What problems do you think TV reporters face in their work? The next selection describes some of the ways they find solutions to several of these problems.

### Vocabulary Development Skills Context Clues

2. See if you can figure out meanings of several words from the context clues around them.

### Literary Appreciation Skills Types of Literature

3. Look for clues that tell you if this is fiction or nonfiction.

# TV REPORTING IS A SPLIT-SECOND BUSINESS

Dana Lynn Wilson

■ The photograph and the title are clues that this is nonfiction.

A TV reporter's mind is geared[9] to presenting the news in units of seconds. Ninety seconds to two minutes is an average-length story. Five minutes is a full feature.

"TV reporters don't think in words, they think in seconds," according to Gail Harris, TV political reporter, and Charles Austin, TV crime reporter, for a Boston station.

"It's like stuffing 50,000 pounds of information into a 50-pound bag," says Austin.

"And making sure the information is accurate, informative and understandable the first time," says Harris. "A viewer, unlike a reader, has to grasp[c] the meaning of your story the first time around. It can't be reread."

■ Can you get the meaning from context clues?

The two reporters agree that TV reporting isn't as easy as it looks. You might be on the air for only one or two minutes a day, but you're chasing, talking, listening, thinking, writing and scrambling the other 7 hours and 58 minutes of the work day at a hectic[9] pace. The information you gather is usually much more than you can use.

As a TV reporter you are usually assigned to a special area of the news such as crime, politics, sports, or consumer[9] affairs.

As a political reporter, Harris covers the State House and legislature, including everything that goes on in the state government and political campaigns.

"Pressure is hitting the door at 4:30 with two pieces that have to be on the 5:30 news." It can take a half-hour to two hours just to process[9] the filmed report, after which she must edit[9] and coordinate[9] it with words.

Often, she writes her story in her notebook in the cab going back to the station to co-anchor[9] the 5:30 news.

To be good at TV reporting "you have to have physical stamina,[9]" emphasizes Harris. "You have to think and function under constant pressure."

A TV reporter is expected to produce something every day whether or not the news show producer uses it. Usually you write one to three stories, depending on whether it's a slow or fast news day.

As a TV reporter you're dealing with facts *and* feelings in order to tell what happened and how it affected the people involved. That means both your head and your heart and sometimes your soul are on the line. And you have to be able to perform whether it's good news or bad news.

Both Austin and Harris agree that human tragedies are the toughest assignments in TV reporting. "You feel tremendous sympathy," says Harris. "But you also have a job to do."

Despite the pressures and competition, "One of the real charms of reporting is that it gives you a front-row seat on history," says Harris. "If you're a curious person, being given the license<sup>c</sup> to be there as things are happening and to ask all sorts of people questions is a real thrill."

■ Use your experience to decide the meaning of this word here.

Austin agrees with Harris "there are the immense satisfactions. When you go out and do a difficult story well, when you tell people things that are going on and they react, you're doing your job. It's very satisfying."

## Some Questions and Answers from Gail Harris

**Q.** Are opportunities in hiring equal for men and women?

**A.** Pretty much. I think women in non-traditional fields have a real obligation to do a good job so that other women can come in.

**Q.** How about opportunities for ethnic minorities?

**A.** Good.

**Q.** Do you have to be physically attractive?

**A.** You have to be neat and well groomed, so your appearance doesn't distract the viewer from what you are saying. But what you have to say is more important than having a pretty face.

**Q.** Do you have to have a good voice?

**A.** Looking nice and reading smoothly isn't what it's all about. You have to train yourself to read a script and grasp what's important in a story immediately, so you can emphasize the words to give each story meaning. I underline the key words as visual cues.

**Q.** How can I prepare for TV reporting now?

**A.** Read as much as possible about the profession. Read information books and journalism texts. Watch news programs on TV; read about the news in print; compare how each medium covers the same news. Check into college journalism and broadcasting programs to see if they offer internships in television stations.

Look into jobs as a teen correspondent reporting on your high school for the local press. Read the publications TV reporters read, several major newspapers a day, news magazines, *Columbia Journalism Review*. You can't expect to be telling people what's happening if you don't know.

# Check the Skills

### Understanding the Selection

1. No career is without problems. What are some problems TV reporters face? What solutions do they find?

### Vocabulary Development Skills Context Clues

2. How do context clues help you determine the meaning of *grasp* on page 69 and *license* on page 70? Marginal notes can help you find the words again if you need to.

### Literary Appreciation Skills Types of Literature

3. How did you know that this selection is nonfiction?

# Use the Skills

### Understanding the Selection

1.    The next selection tells about some fascinating animals and their life in the wild. It also tells about the life of one particular giraffe. Find out what problems giraffes have in their struggle for survival and what solutions some of them find.

### Vocabulary Development Skills Context Clues

2.    Be on the lookout for context clues that can help you with some words you may not know.

### Literary Appreciation Skills Types of Literature

3.    How can you tell if this selection is fiction or nonfiction?

# BIOGRAPHY OF A GIRAFFE

Alice L. Hopf

■ A clue to the type of literature is in the title.

The mother giraffe had found a safe hiding place. She was hidden among the trees that dotted the vast⁹ African plain on which she lived. Her long neck allowed her to look over the tops of the branches to see if an enemy was approaching. She knew she must stay hidden here until her baby was safely born.

As the giraffe stood quietly among the trees, another giraffe from the herd found her. Then another came, and another. Soon there were six females standing around her, forming a strong wall of legs and swinging necks. This would protect her from the attack of any <u>predator</u>,ᶜ a hungry enemy eager to attack.

■ Use the definition context clue here.

Soon her calf was born. It was a male calf, almost six feet tall and weighing about 150 pounds.

Giraffes have five different spot patterns. Often there are several patterns in the same herd. Most of the giraffes in this herd had large, dark brown spots, separated by thin white or yellow lines. But the new baby had little leaf-shaped spots all over his body. The spots were pale on the baby's woolly hair, but they would darken as he grew older.

There were twelve giraffes in the herd, spread out over a wide area. Giraffes can stay farther apart from one another than most herd animals because their height and keen eyes allow them to see far across the plain and keep in touch with other members of the herd. In times of danger they can run 35 miles an hour.

The little leaf-spotted giraffe soon learned to know all the members of his herd. He recognized the huge bull giraffe who was the leader. He was eighteen feet tall and weighed over 2,000 pounds. When the bull came near, the leaf-spotted baby got out of the way. The big bull chased away the lurking⁹ hyenas.⁹ One blow from that heavy head could knock them flying. One kick could break their backs.

Although the giraffes lived on the grassy plains, they did

not eat grass. Their legs were too long for them to reach the ground with their heads. Instead, they ate the leaves of trees.

■ The whole paragraph contains context clues for the meaning of this word.

Giraffes are ruminants.$^c$ They have four stomachs. When they are browsing, they eat quickly, not stopping to chew. Later, when they are resting in a safe place, they bring the food back into their mouths and chew it over again. Like cows, they chew their cud. When the leaves are well chewed the second time, they go down into the other stomachs to be digested.$^9$

At night, the giraffes came closer together. Now hearing and smell were more important in looking out for an enemy. Only rarely did they lie down and sleep, for they could easily be attacked in that position. When the mother giraffe lay down, she first knelt with her forelegs, then the rest of her body sank to the ground. She rested with her forelegs tucked up on one side or folded under her body. The calf slept beside her with his neck turned around so that his head rested on his back.

One night something alerted$^9$ the herd. A menacing$^9$ sound came to them. It was a low gurgle that rose into the shrill laugh of the hyena. It was answered from another direction. A pack of hyenas was out hunting! When the giraffes began to move away, the leaf-spotted calf jumped up quickly. Only the mother giraffe was still lying down. She began to get to her feet, but it was difficult. First she pulled her long neck back as far as she could and then she thrust it forward. This motion got her to her front knees. Again her neck jerked back and forth as she got her hind legs up. A final jerk got her onto her front feet.

But now the hyenas were closer. The young giraffe did not know what to do. He wanted to stay close to his mother, but he also wanted to run from the attacking beasts. Suddenly the big bull giraffe stood between the mother giraffe and the hyenas. He swung his long neck, hitting one attacker and sending it flying a dozen yards away. The hyena landed in a bush and limped painfully off. As the big bull turned to follow the herd, he gave a mighty kick at a hyena that had come too close. The predator lay howling in the dust with a broken leg. The mother giraffe escaped, with her half-grown calf close behind her.

As the leaf-spotted giraffe grew older, he began to spend more time with other young males. They played at fighting, copying the things the big bull was doing. The young giraffe was no longer a calf—he was almost as big as his father. He swung his head at the other young bulls in mock[9] combat.[9] He was especially friendly with the young bull that had grown up with him in his herd.

One day the two young giraffes left the rest of their group and wandered across the plain until they came to an area of farms. There were roads with scattered houses along them and fields of grain and vegetables. The giraffes were curious about these things and walked across the road.

To the giraffes it looked as if vines grew between the trees that bordered the road. The leaf-spotted giraffe knew all about trees and vines. He pushed through them but found his neck blocked. This wasn't like anything he had seen before. The other giraffe ducked his head to get under the strange vine, but the leaf-spotted giraffe was caught. He pushed and pushed.

Tearing noises frightened him. He pushed harder. Soon

he had pulled all the telephone wires down from their poles! He was angry at this strange vine that had caught him and would not let him pass. He trampled the ground. Then he backed up and escaped into the road. Telephone service was broken down and workers were sent to make repairs. When they arrived at the break, they saw what had happened. They were familiar with this situation.

The two giraffes galloped away across the plain. They wandered for several days before they came upon a female giraffe who had broken away from her herd and was alone with her young calf. The two bulls stayed with the cow, forming a little herd, and helped protect her baby. From time to time other giraffes appeared and joined the herd.

# Check the Skills

### Understanding the Selection

1. What solutions do giraffes come up with for some of their problems?

### Vocabulary Development Skills Context Clues

2. How did context clues help you figure out the meaning of *predator*? of *ruminant*? What do the words mean?

### Literary Appreciation Skills Types of Literature

3. What one word in the title tells you that this is nonfiction?

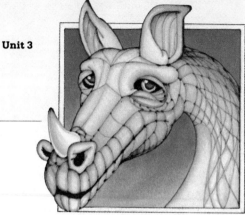

# Use the Skills

Some problems are real and some are imaginary. In this humorous selection an unusual problem requires an unusual solution. Find out what you think the problem is. Also decide *who* solves the problem, *how* it is solved, and *why* it is solved when it is. Try your skills with context clues if you meet a word you don't know. Chances are that you will have no difficulty deciding whether this is fiction or nonfiction. The title gives you a good clue. Part of the fun of reading this story is finding out what the word *discreet* in the title means.

No marginal notes will help you this time. You are on your own.

# DRAGONS HATE
# TO BE DISCREET

Winifred Rosen

Inside this story is a dragon. But don't worry. She won't bite unless I tell her to, and I promise I won't tell her to bite you.

Only just please remember to stand back when she breathes her fire. Except when she's breathing fire, she isn't even too dangerous.

You probably want to know how I got her, but if I told you the truth you wouldn't believe it. Because the truth is, I didn't get her. The truth is, she got me. Anyhow, now we've got each other.

Most of the time my dragon is invisible to most people. Oh, it's not that she's some kind of fake, made-up or *pretend* dragon. It's just that my dragon can make herself into any shape you can think of and stay that way for as long as you like.

Even my mother sometimes forgets she's around. But she always is—wound around some piece of the furniture—appearing to be part of the decor.⁹ Waiting . . .

If you want to know what she's waiting for, I'll tell you. She's waiting for the Right Moment to come along. Whenever the Right Moment comes along, she becomes the True Dragon that she really is.

It is disturbing to most people when a True Dragon explodes into life, breathing fire. But that's what happens.

Here's how. We're having breakfast, and I'm annoyed because we've run out of the only cereal I happen to feel like eating.

My father's annoyed because he's reading the morning paper. The paper always annoys him, which must be the reason he reads it.

My mother's annoyed because nobody's helping her with anything, and the cat's clawed a run in her stocking. She says several of those words you're not ever supposed to say, especially in front of the children, and glares at the cat.

I giggle. "Even the cat's in a crummy mood."

"What kind of way is that to talk?" asks my father. "And what do you mean, '*even* the cat'?"

"Nothing," I say.

My father looks at me and shakes open his newspaper to turn the page. The newspaper knocks over my glass of milk. The milk spills onto the table.

My mother groans. My father says all the words my mother said plus some more. The cat jumps up on the table. Since it isn't *my* fault, I find it funny.

"Margaret!" my mother says. "Get the cat off the table and stop it!"

"But I didn't do—"

"Do what your mother tells you," my dad says. "Or leave the table."

The Right Moment has arrived. Posing as part of a pillar, my dragon has been waiting. Now with an ear-shattering screech, she leaps onto the chandelier, breathing fire. It is wonderful! Those green scales, the red with gold-tipped feathered wings, her purple eyes, the jet-black smoke. I *love* my dragon.

"*Do* something!" my mother implores.[9]

"Now, Margaret," my father begins, "won't you be *reasonable?*"

There is a blast of heat and dragon-laughter from above.

"Please don't make such a big fuss!" he says.

Loud snorts and lots of oily-black smoke come from my dragon. The chandelier is swaying back and forth. Pieces of plaster from the ceiling are raining down on my favorite jam, which is really a shame.

When they say, "*We surrender!*" my dragon stops screeching, hops onto the refrigerator, and ruffles her feathers.

"I wish you wouldn't *do* that," my father says, sitting down.

I try telling them that *I* didn't do anything, my *dragon* did.

"Go and get some fresh air, Margaret," my mother advises. "*Now.*"

The fresh air we go out in is foggy. Foggy fresh air is my dragon's favorite since it reminds her of Eastern Tibet where she was born. Tibet is where the highest mountains in the world are. Dragons are born there because the highest mountains are closest to the sun. The dragons, in case you didn't know it, live on light. Which is how come they breathe fire, you see.

My dragon has been living on light and breathing fire ever since she was born in Eastern Tibet where dragons don't have to be invisible since there is hardly anyone around to see them.

Here, of course, it's different. People are everywhere, watching everything—if not live, at least on television. So dragons have to be discreet.[cg] Discreet means hiding your True Self until the Right Moment comes along.

After the Right Moment has come and gone, my dragon fades discreetly into the fog. Passing by, people do not see her. Either they have something in their eye or their glasses need wiping, they think. They go on their way, rubbing their eyes or wiping their glasses, shaking their heads and muttering.

People can't see what they aren't looking for. Everyone can see the sidewalk, and nobody's bumping into garbage cans or trees or me. But since they aren't looking for a dragon, they don't see one. If they do, they tell themselves it's something else.

Something funny has been happening to my dragon lately. Before I even know what's going on, she is flying into frenzies.°g If I don't control this behavior immediately, my mother says, there will be no TV for a week.

I can't control it immediately. There is no TV for a week. With no TV my dragon is bored. Her tail is constantly twitching, and puffs of smoke keep curling out of her nostrils.°g

My dragon has been around for quite a long time now, and it is getting on my mother's nerves. Also, she is unhappy because everything is dusty, due to the smoke always curling out of my dragon's nostrils.

If you want to know what I think, the curly smoke my dragon breathes is better to watch than television. But my mother doesn't see it this way. What she sees is all the dust all over the furniture all the time.

The dust all over the furniture is making my father sneeze. Sneezing all the time makes my father uncomfortable. Also, our house is hot. The wallpaper is puckering on the walls. Candles are melting. My goldfish died.

The truth is, she's never *been* like this before. She is shaking all over, rattling her scales so sparks fly, and believe it or not, she is *humming*.

Here's what I think. The last Right Moment has arrived!

With a shriek, I leap on my dragon and rocket around the room.

I'm hanging on with all my might as my dragon swoops to avoid a lamp and knocks into a table so that a vase filled with daisies spills. Sounding like a jet, she soars through an archway and starts circling the dining room.

Sneezing, my father follows and screams at the cat, who, with her hair standing on end, resembles a porcupine clinging to the curtains.

Through a roar in my ears I hear dishes crashing and my mother yelling.

I want to tell them not to be angry, that it will all be over in a moment, but my dragon is flying so fast it would be dangerous to do.

They do not even see her stop. Or notice how she hovers in midair—flames flowering from her nostrils, thunder rumbling in her throat. Nobody sees me slide off her back or land on the mantle. They do not watch us wave good-bye.

I stand by the window watching my dragon disappear until I'm so tired they have to carry me to bed. Nobody is angry any more. When they wonder what happened, I explain that my dragon is gone for good.

"Because," I say, "even though Tibet is far away, waiting for the Right Moment to arrive isn't nearly as good as being your True Self all the time. Especially if you're a dragon. Dragons *hate* to be discreet."

# Check the Skills

### Understanding the Selection

1. What do you think is the problem? Who actually finds the solution? What is the solution? Why do you think it is solved at that particular time?

### Vocabulary Development Skills Context Clues

2. In the story you read the following sentence.

   Discreet means hiding your True Self until the Right Moment comes along.

   What do context clues tell you *discreet* means here? Do you think this is close to the real meaning of the word? Check the glossary or a dictionary to see if you're right.

### Literary Appreciation Skills Types of Literature

3. How do you know that this selection is fiction?

# Apply What You Learned in Unit 3

## The Theme

### Finding Solutions

1.  In this unit you read about solutions found by people and by animals, some real and some imaginary. Do you think it's true that "everybody has problems"? Why do you think as you do? Do you think all problems can be solved? Why or why not? "All Shaded Up" and "TV Reporting Is a Split-Second Business" dealt with realistic problems. How might reading about the solutions other people have found to their problems help you?

# The Skills

## Vocabulary Development Skills Context Clues

2.  Sometimes you meet words in your reading whose meaning you are unsure of. You need to know some of the best and fastest ways to figure them out. Using context clues is one of the best ways.

3.  In this unit you became aware of context clues that define the words. You also discovered that your personal experience can help you figure out their meanings. Use your skills with context clues in all of your reading.

## Literary Appreciation Skills Types of Literature

4.  In this unit you have learned how to tell the difference between fiction and nonfiction. Why do you think you often need to decide?

# Unit 4

# Freedom

## Overview and Purposes for Reading

### The Theme

**Freedom**

1.  Do you think freedom is important and precious? Why or why not? What situations can cause people, animals, or living things to have to fight for their freedom? Do you think freedom can be lost forever? Are there different kinds of freedom?

### The Skills

**Vocabulary Development Skills** Dictionary

2.  How can you use a dictionary to find the meaning of a word that fits what you are reading?

**Comprehension Skills** Interpretive Reading

3.  What can you do to help yourself get the most out of your reading? How can you make your reading more valuable to yourself?

# Learn About the Skills

## Vocabulary Development Skills Dictionary

When you read, do you ever have trouble knowing what a word means? Everyone does. You hear over and over, "Use context clues to figure out the meaning." But sometimes that is not completely possible. Sometimes there just are not enough good context clues. So what do you do? Right, you use a dictionary.

For example, can you determine the meaning of *slip* in this sentence?

Captain Aries wedged the tug into the slip.

Context doesn't help much. So, you need to look up *slip* in a dictionary.

You know that words are listed in alphabetical order in the dictionary. You also know that *s* is near the end of the alphabet. So you turn in the dictionary to the last quarter of the book and find the *s*'s. The two guide words in dark print at the top of each page help you find the page that *slip* is on. The first guide word is the first entry word on the page. The second guide word is the last entry word.

Perhaps you find the guide words *sling* and *smog*. You know that *slip* will be on that page because it comes between those words alphabetically. How can you decide which definition fits from the entry below?

**sling**                                                    **smog**

> **slip** (slip), v. 1. to go or move quietly, smoothly, easily, or quickly. 2. to move out of place, 3. to get loose from; escape. 4. to let go; release; unfasten. n. 1. covering: pillows are covered by slips. 2. a sleeveless garment worn under a dress. 3. mistake; error. 4. space for ships between wharves or in a dock. 5. leash for a dog.

From the dictionary you see that *slip* can be a verb or a noun. Now you need to use context clues again. The context clues in the sentence tell you that *slip* is used as a noun. Next you note that *slip* has more than one meaning when used as a noun. You must decide which meaning is the correct one. Each meaning has a separate number. You need to do some more detective work with context clues. Go back to the sentence. *Captain Aries* and *tug* help you decide this *slip* must have something to do with boats since *tug* is short for *tugboat* and a captain often is the head of a boat or ship. Which is the appropriate definition for this sentence?

**Try the Skill.** Now use the same dictionary entry to decide which meaning is correct for *slip* in the following sentences. Be careful. Check parts of speech.

1. I *slipped* the knot in the rope.
2. I made a funny *slip* as I was talking.

As you read this unit, you'll have a chance to use these dictionary skills to determine meanings of words as used in sentences. You'll do this by using the glossary. Remember, many words have several meanings. You must decide which meaning is the suitable one. Remember to try context clues first. Depend on the glossary or a dictionary when context clues are not helpful enough.

## Comprehension Skills Interpretive Reading

During your lifetime you will read many things. How can you make your reading work for you? You need to get involved. You need to ask yourself how you feel about it. You'll get more from your reading if you do this.

In addition to involving yourself, you may want to find out what your friends or family would think about it. You may want to talk it over with them. These discussions can also help you decide how you feel about what you have read.

You may feel that you want to learn more about the subject. If so, decide how you could find more information. Ask yourself how you can use the information you have learned. How can it help you as a person?

These are some of the ways you can help yourself by reacting to your reading.

While reading selections in this unit, be aware of your feelings about what you are reading. Think what further information you might wish to gather. How can you benefit from what you are reading?

# Selection 1

# Use the Skills

### Understanding the Selection

1.  The next selection is the beginning of the novel *The Black Stallion* by Walter Farley. Ask yourself why the Black Stallion fights so fiercely for his freedom.

### Vocabulary Development Skills Dictionary

2.  Remember to try context clues first if you meet a word whose meaning you don't know. If you need to, be sure to use the glossary or a dictionary. Remember that words followed by the small letter [g] are in the glossary.

### Comprehension Skills Interpretive Reading

3.  As you read, decide how you can make the story more important or exciting to yourself.

# THE BLACK STALLION

Walter Farley

As the gangplank went down with a bang, Alec could see that it wasn't the ship itself that was attracting all the attention. People were crowding toward the center of the landing. Alec heard a whistle—shrill, loud, clear, unlike anything he had ever heard before. He saw a mighty black horse rear on its hind legs, its forelegs striking out into the air. A white scarf was tied across its eyes. The crowd broke and ran.

White lather[9] ran from the horse's body. His mouth was open, his teeth bared. He was a giant of a horse, glistening black—too big to be pure Arabian. His mane was like a crest, mounting, then falling low. His neck was long, slender, and arched to the small, savagely beautiful head. The head was that of the wildest of all wild creatures—a stallion born wild. It was beautiful, savage, splendid. A stallion with a wonderful physical perfection that matched his savage, ruthless spirit.

■ Think about what's happening to this wild stallion. Decide how you feel about it.

Once again the horse screamed and rose on his hind legs. Alec could hardly believe his eyes and ears—a stallion, a wild stallion—unbroken, such as he had read and dreamed about!

Two ropes led from the halter on the horse's head. Four men were attempting to pull the stallion toward the gangplank.[9] They were going to put him on the ship! Alec saw a man, wearing European dress and a high, white turban,[cg] giving directions. In his hand he held a whip. He gave his orders tersely[9] in a language unknown to Alec. Suddenly he walked to the rear of the horse and let the hard whip fall. The stallion bolted so fast that he struck one of the men holding the rope. Down the man went and lay still. The horse snorted and plunged. If ever Alec saw hate expressed by a horse, he saw it then. They had him halfway up the plank. Alec wondered where they would put him if they ever did succeed in getting him on the boat.

■ Here, *stern* is a noun, not an adjective. Only one definition for the noun form is given in the glossary. Also, *boat* in the last paragraph helps to clue you to the right meaning.

■ Here, *hold* is a noun. This helps you find its right meaning in the glossary.

Then he was on! Alec saw Captain Watson waving his arms frantically, motioning and shouting for the men to pull the stallion toward the stern.[g] The boy followed at a safe distance. Now he saw the makeshift[cg] stall into which they were attempting to get the horse—it had once been a good-sized cabin. The ship had little accommodation for transporting animals. Its hold[g] was already heavily laden with cargo.

Finally they had the horse in front of the stall. One of the men clambered to the top of the cabin, reached down and pulled the scarf away from the stallion's eyes. At the same time, the man wearing the turban again hit the horse on the hindquarters and he bolted inside. Alec thought the stall would never be strong enough to hold him. The stallion tore into the wood and sent it flying. Thunder rolled from under his hooves. His powerful legs crashed into the sides of the cabin. His wild, shrill, high-pitched whistle sent shivers up and down Alec's spine. He felt a deep pity steal over him, for here was a wild stallion used to the open range imprisoned in a stall in which he was hardly able to turn.

Captain Watson was conversing angrily with the turbaned man. The captain had probably never expected to ship a cargo such as this! Then the man pulled a thick wallet from inside his coat. He counted the bills off and handed them to the captain. Captain Watson looked at the bills and then at the stall. He took the money, shrugged his shoulders, and walked away. The man gathered the people around who had helped bring the stallion aboard, gave them bills from his wallet, and they departed down the gangplank.

Soon the ship was again under way. Alec gazed back at the port, watching the group gathered around the inert[9] form of the native who had gone down under the horse's mighty hooves. Then he turned to the stall. The owner had gone to his cabin. Only the excited passengers were standing around outside the stall. The black horse was still fighting madly inside.

The days that followed were hectic ones for Alec, passengers, and crew. He had never dreamed a horse could have such spirit, be so untamable.

# Check the Skills

### Understanding the Selection

1. Why do you think the horse fought so hard?

### Vocabulary Development Skills Dictionary

2. Use the marginal notes to help you find the words *stern* and *hold* again in the story. What is the best glossary definition for each one as it is used here?

### Comprehension Skills Interpretive Reading

3. How did you feel about what happened to the black stallion? You might enjoy reading the rest of the book to find out what happens. It is *The Black Stallion* by Walter Farley, published by Random House in 1968.

# Use the Skills

### Understanding the Selection

Most physically healthy people take for granted their freedom to participate in sports. But for those who are physically disabled, taking part in sports is not such an easy matter. Special adjustments have to be made. The blind skiers above, for instance, wear brightly-colored fluorescent vests so other skiers can watch out for them.

1.   As you read the next selection, think about that lack of one kind of freedom. See how hard some people fight to have the freedom to ski.

### Vocabulary Development Skills Dictionary

2.   Remember to use a dictionary or the glossary for meanings of some words you may not know. Let context clues help you decide which are the suitable meanings.

### Comprehension Skills Interpretive Reading

3.   Imagine what it might be like to be one of these skiers. How can doing this help you be a more understanding person?

# SKI CHAMPS

Curt Casewit

In February every year, an amazing ski race takes place in Winter Park, Colorado. The mountain slopes come alive with multi-colored pairs of flags. Through these gates descend[9] many young skiers. In a downhill race they're clocked at 50 miles an hour.

Is that unusual? Not for the ordinary racer.

But these kids are not ordinary. Many of them have only one leg. Others have only one arm. A few have no hands. The rest fly down the Colorado mountain despite[cg] paralyzed joints, missing kneecaps, absent toes, or rigid backs. The skiers are all physically handicapped—the result of diseases, accidents, or conditions at birth.

Yet these skiers prove that human beings can conquer almost any barrier.[9] Eyes shining, cheeks glowing, the racers speed across the finish line.

The victory is not always an easy one.

Skiing requires perfect coordination[9] and good balance. To hurtle down a snowy slope, two-legged skiers use all their limbs. Feet direct the two skis, hands and arms hold the ski poles, which act as stabilizers.[9]

The loss of an arm throws the body out of kilter.[9] With only one ski pole, it is more difficult to make turns, or to walk up a hill. Yet, where there's a will, there's a way. Practice, determination and good training will make a one-armed skier as good as a two-armed one.

The sudden loss of a leg is more serious. Yet, even that can be overcome. At first, there is pain and lack of balance. Then come weeks of learning to use crutches. The remaining leg must be strengthened. The muscles will ache a while. There's also the self-consciousness to deal with, but only at first. A positive mental attitude helps to get on the right track within a few weeks. People can do many things even with an incomplete body.

■ Both glossary definitions of this word are nouns. Only the first definition fits this context.

Some of the best things are sports. And the right track for some people is the ski track.

Other handicapped youths turn to this winter sport for the first time with their special equipment. And why not? If you set your mind to it, you really can do anything.

One good example is Larry Kunz, who was born with a condition that gave him little muscle control from the knees down. Larry was introduced to Hal O'Leary, a coach who specializes in disabled kids.

Coach O'Leary recalls, "At first Larry couldn't even walk. He crawled on his hands and knees. But in a week he was able to use his crutch skis and get around in heavy ski boots. Today he soars down the slopes despite his hand-icap."

Perhaps the best proof of great will power has been shown by a young woman named Tomi Keitlen. She still

Specially attached poles make it possible for these physically handicapped people to ski.

has both legs and both arms. But she is blind. Tomi lost her sight after a series of operations. But she believed in herself, and decided to conquer her handicap. Today she swims, plays golf, and takes care of a house.

She even climbs mountains by having the guide dictate her route into a tape recorder, which he passes down to her. Tied to the guide by a rope, she will follow his directions: "Move your right foot about four inches to the left—now up until you feel a ledge—now shift your weight—move your left foot out and up as far as you can go."

■ Think how it must feel to do this.

But, most amazing of all, Tomi learned to ski. Her instructor simply rings a little bell at every dip in the mountain. Other blind skiers come down the mountain sharing an instructor's bamboo pole.

These blind people are handicapped, too, but they didn't give up. Instead, they gave sports a try!

# Check the Skills

### Understanding the Selection

1. Why do you suppose many disabled people fight to be able to ski?

### Vocabulary Development Skills Dictionary

2. Look up *stabilizer* in the glossary. What context clues help you know that the first definition fits its use on page 95?

### Comprehension Skills Interpretive Reading

3. How do you think it might feel to be one of the disabled skiers? Using your imagination in this way can make reading this selection much more personal and useful to you. Why do you think this is so?

## Use the Skills

### Understanding the Selection

1. The poem on the next page is about a special kind of freedom. Find out what it is.

### Vocabulary Development Skills Dictionary

2. You may know that a groom is a person who takes care of horses. See if you think that's the meaning of *groom* in the poem. Check the glossary if you need to.

### Comprehension Skills Interpretive Reading

3. The ideas in this poem are probably new to you. Ask yourself if you like them.

# THE WONDERFUL WORDS

Mary O'Neill

Never let a thought shrivel and die
For want of a way to say it,
For English is a wonderful game
And all of you can play it.
All that you do is match the words
To the brightest thoughts in your head
So that they come out clear and true
And handsomely groomed⁹ and fed—
For many of the loveliest things
Have never yet been said.
Words are the food and dress of thought,
They give it its body and swing,
And everyone's longing today to hear
Some fresh and beautiful thing.
But only words can free a thought
From its prison behind your eyes.
Maybe your mind is holding now
A marvelous new surprise!

■ Which is the suitable glossary definition?

■ What's your opinion of this idea?

## Check the Skills

### Understanding the Selection

1. What freedom is the poem about?

### Vocabulary Development Skills Dictionary

2. What does *groom* mean in the poem? How do context clues help you decide which glossary definition is the right one?

### Comprehension Skills Interpretive Reading

3. Do you like the ideas in the poem? Why or why not?

# Selection 4

# Use the Skills

### Understanding the Selection

We generally don't think of trees or plants as being free in the same way a person is. Freedom for plants means they are free to grow and develop naturally. But the survival of some kinds of trees has been threatened by people who cut down too many for lumber. This selection tells of a special kind of tree whose freedom to survive is being protected.

1.    As you read this article about the tallest trees in the world, ask yourself why people need to help them keep that freedom.

### Vocabulary Development Skills Dictionary

2.    If necessary, turn to the glossary or dictionary for definitions. The photograph above shows a *burl* on a redwood tree. Find out what this word means in this selection.

### Comprehension Skills Interpretive Reading

3.    Decide why the existence of the redwoods should be protected. If you wanted to help, what could you do?

# REDWOODS ARE THE TALLEST TREES

David A. Adler

The tree near my house is so tall that I can't even reach the lowest branch, and the top of it is higher than my house. It is the tallest tree on our street. But this summer I saw trees in California that are much taller. I saw the redwoods. They are the tallest trees in the world.

Redwoods need a lot of sunlight and water. They grow best where it does not get too hot or too cold, and where there is a lot of moisture in the air. The climate on the northern coast of California and in southern Oregon is just right. The redwoods there grow about ninety meters[cg] high—that's over three hundred feet. The tree near my house is only about fifteen meters (fifty feet) high.

■ You may know this word's definition from your work in math. If not, how might you find its meaning?

Redwoods are evergreens. They have small needles that stay green all year. At the end of the redwood branches there are small round cones. Each cone is about the size of a large grape and holds about fifty seeds. Each seed can grow into a tall redwood tree, but few of them do. Most young redwoods grow from the roots of either living trees or those that have been recently chopped down. The old roots take water and minerals from the ground and help the young tree grow more quickly. Many young trees may grow from the roots of just one old tree.

New branches grow at the tops of young trees. This new growth—and the branches of other trees—keeps sunlight from reaching the redwood's lower branches, which then die. Some very old redwood trees have no branches at all on the first thirty meters (about one hundred feet) of their trunks.

It takes about five hundred years for a redwood to grow to its full height, but some live much longer than that. Some live for more than a thousand years. After that the tree begins to die slowly from the top. Sometimes its branches are killed by wind or lightning. Sometimes the tree is weakened by age or fire, and is no longer able to send water all the way up to the top branches.

When a tree has been cut down, you can see the rings in the stump. Tree rings tell us how old a tree is. The width of each ring shows how much the tree grew during that year. Sometimes the weather is so bad that a tree grows very little, and then there is no ring for a whole year. At other times, when the weather is very good, two rings may form in a single year. But years like that are unusual. The number of rings almost always tells us the age of a tree. The width of the ring tells us whether the tree grew rapidly or slowly.

A park ranger showed us the stump of a redwood tree. It was about three meters (ten feet) across. This tree started to grow over one thousand years ago. It was more than five hundred years old when Columbus came to America! Branches have rings, too, and you can also count them and see how many years the branch grew.

The bark of a redwood tree is sometimes almost thirty centimeters (nearly a foot) thick. It's this bark that helps a redwood live for such a long time. The roots of a tree collect water and minerals which then travel up through layers in the tree trunk to feed the branches and the leaves. The bark protects these layers and helps guard the growing part of the tree from fire. The redwood bark contains tannic acid, which also protects the tree from insects and disease.

■ Context clues tell the meaning. No need for a glossary or dictionary here.

On the bark of some redwood trees I saw big bumps that I learned are called burls.ᶜ Burls do not harm the tree. They are really just redwood buds that did not grow into branches. The burl is hard and beautiful. Some of it is used to make jewelry.

The wood of a redwood tree is very strong, and anything made from it lasts a long time. Redwood lumber is used to build houses, to make indoor and outdoor furniture, railroad ties, and much more. Because redwood trees are so tall and straight, there is a lot of valuable wood in each one—sometimes enough to build four houses.

People are afraid that too many tall redwood trees will be

cut down to be used as lumber. To protect these trees, the Save-the-Redwoods League buys redwood forests and turns them into parks.

■ What could you do to help?

Redwoods are the tallest living things in the whole world. I have a photograph of myself standing in a redwood forest, but you can hardly see me. Beside a redwood almost anything looks small. If you ever see one, you will know what I mean.

# Check the Skills

### Understanding the Selection

1.  How can people help to preserve the redwoods' freedom to exist? Why do you think they should?

### Vocabulary Development Skills Dictionary

2.  What is a meter? Did you need to use a dictionary or the glossary to find out? Why or why not?

### Comprehension Skills Interpretive Reading

3.  How does thinking about the survival of the redwoods make this selection have more meaning for you?

# Use the Skills

Do you recall the first time your mother or father decided you were old enough to do something on your own? The next story is about a boy who for the first time is allowed the freedom of going fishing alone. Find out what excitement, disappointment, concern, and fear this adventure brought.

If you need to check the meaning of a word in the glossary, remember to use context clues to help choose the correct definition. As you read, think how you would have felt if you were Lee.

No marginal notes are included to help you use the skills. You're on your own this time.

# THE DAY OF THE GOLDEN EAGLE

Jonathan T. Stratman

"Lee? Lee, it's time to wake up—Lee?" He heard his mother call.

"Okay, Ma—I'm awake." He slowly sat up. Today was the day.

"Lee?" his mother called. "Happy birthday."

His father smiled as Lee walked into the kitchen. "How does it feel to be twelve?" he asked.

"It feels fine," he said.

They went over it all again as he ate, sipping their black coffee and asking their questions until they knew he had it right.

"Where are you going?" (his mother).

"West—toward Heron Island."

"When do you plan to return?" (his father).

"Before sundown."

"How many days' supplies are you carrying?" (his mother again).

"Three."

"How . . ." his father paused, "how many minutes can you stay alive swimming in these waters?"

"About twenty minutes. Don't worry, Dad." He thought about the fishing trip. They'd been going out for years, he and his father. Now it was time for him to try it alone and show what he'd learned. That was the deal for this birthday.

Within the half hour he and his father were down at the landing. It was a pure August morning.

"Castcg off?" his father called. He stood at the bow line.

Lee looked around once more. "Cast off," he called. "I'll be sure to bring home a big one."

"The only big one we need at home is you," his father said, "on time."

The gentle swell outside the breakwater always caught him unexpectedly, though he'd rowed out here hundreds of times with friends. Ahead of him—misty, still gray in the shadow of the mountains— were the islands. There were probably a hundred of them, deserted, wooded with easy beaches, or rocky with the piling surf.

Lee settled into a strong smooth pull on the oars, and the skiff cut through the water. Just for an instant he caught sight of his destination—the humped bulge of Heron Island, farthest out of these near islands.

Twelve years old, the difference between one day and the next. Yesterday he was forbidden to make an all-day run without his father. Today he was alone on the early swells.

Lee ate lunch and went over his tackle.<sup>cg</sup> He reckoned it was about ten-thirty—still early—but he'd already done a four-hour row, and he was hungry. He replaced the tackle and started to close the box when something caught his eye. It was a folded piece of paper, tucked tight against the plastic box that held his lures.<sup>cg</sup> As he pulled it out, he saw his father's handwriting and felt the weight and the telltale bulge between the folds. "It couldn't be . . ." he said aloud, but it was—the Golden Eagle.

It went back a long way, this thing about Heron Island and the Golden Eagle. Others might fish for salmon or red snapper, even halibut, near here. But for years Lee's father had fished for sea-run cut-throat trout off these waters. And for years he had come home with a dry basket. Even so, he was sure they were there.

A long time ago Lee had decided, "I'm going to take a cut-throat out of there." But when he told his parents, his father just laughed and shook his head. "We'll both be eating mush," he said. "Still, I know they're out there." That was where the Golden Eagle came in.

Through the long cold winter months, Lee's father was busy drawing the perfect cut-throat lure. He drew one big lure after another, varying the color and design.

Then one night, very late, Lee awakened to his father's voice close by his ear. "I've finished drawing," he whispered. "This is it—The Golden Eagle. This is the lure that will catch a cut-throat."

Now, with the Golden Eagle double-knotted to a forty-pound test line, Lee trolled<sup>9</sup> into a cove along Heron Island. "Come on in, cut-throat," he said aloud. "Time for lunch." He poked about in the stream outlet for the first hours—casting and reeling, casting and reeling— letting the Golden Eagle strut its stuff. But nothing happened.

Suddenly there was a silver flash, and the Eagle was gone. "A fish?" he asked himself, already beginning to reel in.

One fish—the only lousy bite of the whole afternoon—but a silver fish! Could it be? Lee could imagine his father's face if he brought home a cut-throat. It was too much to hope for. The pole dipped. Lee slacked[9] off and then reeled in some more. Again and again, he cautiously played the fish toward the boat. Suddenly it leaped. Lee shouted. It was a trout! Not a big trout, but proof that there were trout, and that the lure really worked. There, it flashed again. Lee found himself laughing and whooping and shouting. He was right in the middle of a laugh or a whoop or a shout when he felt a terrible weight on the line.

"A snag," cried Lee. But the line still traveled, so he knew it wasn't caught. He struggled to play it smoothly, all the while searching the deep green water for another glimpse of the silver trout. There was no sign of it. Instead he saw a large, dark shadow near the end of his line. What was happening? It came to him suddenly. A big fish or a seal was after his trout. He came back on the line hard, bracing himself and pulling with his full weight. He had to raise the trout out of the water, out of the reach of that dark shadow.

As Lee half stood in the skiff,[c9] the line suddenly broke. He tumbled backward over the seat and into the bottom of the boat. In startled silence he twirled the reel handle, flashing the line aboard. Empty. Swivels, weights, leader, and the Golden Eagle—all gone. Lee struggled up and searched the water for a glimpse of a seal. There was no seal. What had stolen his trout?

"I had that cut-throat," he shouted. He couldn't have broken the line. What was the use of being twelve now? "I was so sure . . ." He slammed his fist into his open palm till it stung.

Lee reckoned it was about four now; five hours until dark—one hour to fish and four to row home with the wind and tide in his direction. But what for? The whole thing made him want to cry. He sat for awhile, almost stunned. Then, mechanically, he set up for salmon.

The hour seemed to go on and on. He had never seen so few fish or had so few bites in his entire life. Finally, when it was five o'clock, he turned the boat. Still trolling, he began to row for home.

As soon as he was about to clear the cove,[9] Lee turned for one last look at Heron Island. "What a birthday," he shouted. Out of the corner of his eye he saw his line jerk taut. Then he heard the reel begin to whine. Startled, he snatched the pole from the holder and began to play the fish. From time to time he caught sight of a broad pink underbelly. "A king salmon, it looks like a king salmon." It wasn't a cut-throat, but he could see that it was a beautiful fish, and the biggest he had ever hooked into. He knew his gear was too light. Even so, he set out to play it for as long as he had to. In forty minutes, somehow the fish was his, flopping about in the bottom of the skiff.

But he couldn't take much pleasure in his catch. The loss of the Golden Eagle gnawed at him all the way home. "I lost the lure—I lost the Golden Eagle." The words drummed in his head. He recalled his father hunched over the dining room table with his tools, paints, and magnifying glass. "I'd hate to have to do this again," his father had said.

He rounded the breakwater. His father was at the landing. In silence, they pulled the skiff up together and stowed the gear in the back of the truck.

"What did you get?" his father asked finally.

Lee shook his head in the darkness. "Only a salmon."

"Only a salmon," his father repeated. "You must be hard to please."

"Dad, I lost it. I lost the lure."

His father halted in surprise. Lee was suddenly afraid. All the way home he had been imagining his father's disappointment. Now if he was angry . . . .

"That happens," his father said, a familiar, easy voice in the darkness. "Not worth bothering about—we won't make you eleven again for it."

Eleven again. That didn't seem like such a bad idea. If he hadn't had a birthday and turned twelve, he wouldn't have gone out by himself. He wouldn't have tried out the Golden Eagle. He wouldn't have fed it to a trout that was likely meant for his father to catch anyway.

They talked slightly on the way home.

Later, his father said, "Happy birthday. You did just fine, just the way I taught you, just the way I knew you would. Now why don't you go on and hit the sack—I'll clean up this fish."

He awoke to his father's voice rumbling at his elbow. Then he half-walked, and his father half-carried him down the narrow stairway, through the kitchen, and out onto the chilly porch under the yellow light. There was the salmon—cut and cleaned, ready to freeze.

Laid out alongside was a small cut-throat trout, almost too small to keep, but just the right-sized meal for a king salmon. In the trout's lip was a magnificent, handcrafted bronze lure. The Golden Eagle.

# Check the Skills

### Understanding the Selection

1. Do you think the freedom to do something on your own is important? Why or why not? Was it important to Lee? How do you know?

### Vocabulary Development Skills Dictionary

2. In the sentence *Lee ate lunch and went over his tackle*, which is the correct definition of *tackle*?

   *a.* a football player. *b.* equipment. *c.* to try to deal with. *d.* to seize and stop by bringing to the ground.

### Comprehension Skills Interpretive Reading

3. How would you have felt if you were Lee? Have you ever lost something that someone else owned and valued highly? If so, how did you feel? Do you think Lee should have used the Golden Eagle? Why or why not? Try to understand how Lee's father must have felt at various times throughout the story.

# Apply What You Learned in Unit 4

## The Theme

### Freedom

1.  There are different types of freedom. Certain kinds of human freedoms come only with age and taking responsibility. Certain freedoms are taken for granted. Some people must overcome obstacles to get physical or mental freedom. Think of freedoms you have. Are they important to you?

# The Skills

## Vocabulary Development Skills Dictionary

2.  You know how to use a dictionary. Remember to use context clues to help you choose the definition that fits what you are reading.

## Comprehension Skills Interpretive Reading

3.  In this unit, you found a few ideas about how to get more involved with your reading. Whenever you meet an interesting idea in your reading, try it out on your friends and family. Think about your own point of view. Also, remember that research can expand your knowledge of a topic you find interesting.

# Apply the
# Vocabulary Development Skills
## You Have Learned

### Apply the Skills As You Do Your Schoolwork

The vocabulary development skills you have learned in this section will be helpful to you in all subjects in school. For instance, the selection on the next page is from a textbook you might read in a history class. Read it to find out about some of the conveniences we take for granted today that were lacking during colonial days in America.

The vocabulary development skills you have learned will help you read this selection more effectively. You can see how the skills work with the following questions. Read them. Then read the selection, keeping the questions in mind. Afterward answer the questions.

1. **Prefixes.** Can knowing about prefixes help you figure out the word *impossible*? What is the prefix in the word? What is the base word? What does *impossible* mean?

2. **Multiple meanings.** The word *fare* has several meanings. As you read, ask yourself what is being talked about in the sentence. Then decide if *fare* as used means 1. a sum of money paid to ride on public transportation, such as a train, carriage, or bus; 2. a passenger on such public transportation; 3. food provided. How does the meaning of the sentence help you decide the meaning of the word?

3. **Experience and definition context clues.** What context clues help you determine the meaning of *contaminated* in the fourth sentence?

4. **Dictionary definitions.** How would you use a dictionary to find the meaning of *hominy*?

# Life in Colonial America

Within even the grandest of colonial houses there were few conveniences judged by present-day standards. The fireplaces rarely provided enough heat for comfort in severe winter weather and there were no furnaces. Adequate screening against flies and insects in summer was impossible. Such items as stoves, refrigerators, and bathtubs were totally unknown. As few houses had running water, people got water from springs or wells that were easily contaminated. This caused many diseases. Candles usually furnished light at night, although whale-oil lamps were common in fashionable circles. People could get food everywhere in great amounts and at very low prices, but often the fare was severely plain. Corn bread, hominy, and salt pork made up the chief food items for poorer people.

## Apply the Skills As You Deal with the World

You will also use your vocabulary development skills when you read materials outside of school. Here is an advertisement you might see in a newspaper. Read the questions below first so you can see how vocabulary development skills can help you read ads, too. Then keep the questions in mind as you read the selection. Afterward, answer the questions.

1.  **Prefixes.** In the ad for the bicycle you'll read the word *precision*. Can what you know about the prefix *pre-* help you figure out this word? Why not?

2.  **Multiple meanings.** In the bike ad is the word *finish*. *Finish* has more than one meaning. It can mean 1. to complete; 2. the end; 3. the way in which the surface is painted, or smoothed, or polished. How do context clues help you decide which meaning is the right one here?

3.  **Experience and definition context clues.** How does your past experience help you decide what is meant by the word *saddle*?

4.  **Dictionary definitions.** To figure out the meaning of *derailleur*, you may have to use a dictionary. Could the dictionary help you figure out how to pronounce the word?

# SAVE $20 on 10-speeds
## 24 or 26-inch bikes

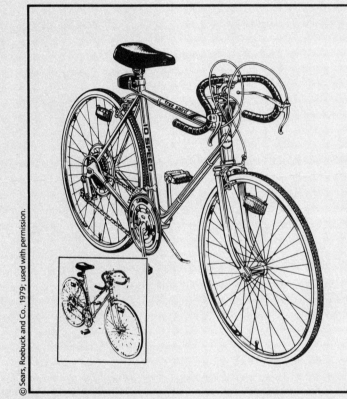

Regular $99.99

# 79⁹⁹ each

A wonderful gift for anyone in the family. 10-speed precision derailleur with dual-position side-pull hand brakes. Yellow finish, racing handlebar with tape kit, padded racing saddle. Amber-wall tires, more! Men's, women's, or youths'.

- Sports Center sale prices thru Dec. 1

# Section 2    Comprehension Skills

# Land and Sea

## Overview and Purposes for Reading

### The Theme

### Land and Sea

1.  People's lives are deeply affected by geography. The places we live in and travel in are important to us. Why do you think this is so?

### The Skills

### Comprehension Skills Literal Meaning

2.  Why is it important to know the main idea of something you're reading?

3.  How can you tell what the main idea is?

### Study and Research Skills Parts of a Book

4.  How do you get information from a map? How can maps sometimes help you understand more about what you are reading?

# Learn About the Skills

## Comprehension Skills Literal Meaning

You need to know what the **main idea** is in whatever you're reading. Why? Because then you understand what is most important.

Every story has a main idea. So does every article, and even every poem. Most paragraphs have main ideas, too.

Sometimes a main idea is clearly stated by the author. Such a statement of the main idea is called a **topic sentence**. The word *topic* means "subject" or "main idea."

Read the paragraph below. The main idea is clearly stated. The topic sentence is the first one in the paragraph.

> Long before submarines and rockets and space ships were in use, Jules Verne was writing about them in his books. In *Twenty Thousand Leagues under the Sea*, he wrote about a long trip in a submarine. This was in 1870, many years before people were traveling under the sea. *From the Earth to the Moon* was written in 1865. That was more than a hundred years before the first moon landings were made in 1969. Jules Verne truly was the father of science fiction, one of the most popular kinds of writing in our own time.

The other sentences in the paragraph give supporting details, or more information, about the topic sentence.

The topic sentence, which states the main idea, is often the first or the last sentence in the paragraph. See which you think it is in the following.

Karen must have been daydreaming. Suddenly she looked around and realized she didn't know where she was. She must have been walking for an hour. She was in a part of the city that was completely unknown to her. She gazed into the window of a flower shop. Perhaps she could ask how to get home. But the door was locked and the shop was empty. There was no one on the street. "What do I do now?" she thought. "I'm lost!"

The main idea of this paragraph is that Karen is lost. It is stated in the last sentence. Notice that all the details about that idea are presented first.

**Try the Skill.** What is the main idea in this paragraph?

In the central African country of Zambia, children make a clever push-along toy from old wires. Many wires are pieced together in the shape of a car. Shoe-polish cans are added for wheels. A long, heavy wire is attached so that the Zambian child can steer the car while walking behind it. Some of the models are quite complicated. No tools are used in making them. Today, in the capital city of Zambia, you may see dozens of boys and girls pushing their handmade cars along the sidewalks.

You're right if you decided that the main idea is stated in the first sentence. The rest of the paragraph gives details about the push-along toy.

As you read the selections in this unit, you will find more help in identifying main ideas.

## Study and Research Skills Parts of a Book

When you think of reading, you probably think of reading words and sentences. Reading, however, includes every-thing else that is on a printed page. For example, you need to learn to read **maps, charts,** and **graphs**. These may use words as labels. But you have to read the information that is not in the words, too.

The secret to being able to read a map is the map's **key**, also called the **legend**. The key explains what the sym-bols, or signs, on the map mean. For instance, examine the legend on this map. The meaning of each kind of symbol follows that symbol.

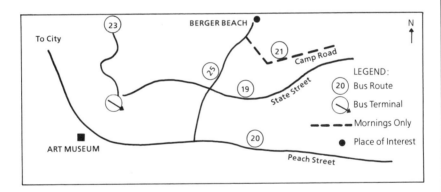

You know from the legend that each circled number is the number of the bus on that route. Find the symbol for the bus terminal in the key, then on the map. You can also use the key the other way around. Find Berger Beach near the top of the map. What does the symbol near it tell you about that beach? Check the key to find out.

You will find out more about using your skill with maps as you read this unit.

# Selection 1

# Use the Skills

### Understanding the Selection

1.  Our knowledge of the world we live in has grown over the years. The next selection explains that ancient people referred to the Seven Seas of the world. See why this term now means something different.

### Comprehension Skills Literal Meaning

2.  This article is full of information. Nonfiction like this often includes clearly stated main ideas. Be on the lookout for topic sentences. Remember, chances are that the first or the last sentence in a paragraph will be the topic sentence. Notes in the margins will help.

3.  Also, see if you can decide what the main idea of the entire article is.

### Study and Research Skills Parts of a Book

4.  Notice how the map helps you understand the selection better.

# THE SEVEN SEAS

Marie Dahlgren Nunn

When asked to locate the Seven Seas, many people say they can't. Some say they once knew but have forgotten. Can you name the Seven Seas?

■ The main idea of the entire article is stated in the title.

In ancient times, before the fall of Constantinople, the people of the Mohammedan world called the following the Seven Seas—Bay of Bengal, South China Sea, Arabian Sea, Persian Gulf, Red Sea, Mediterranean Sea, and Atlantic Ocean.

The largest of all bodies of water, the Pacific Ocean, was not included. Neither were the Indian Ocean, the Arctic, or the Antarctic.

Today we must find a different answer.

If you were taking a long voyage on a passenger ship or freighter,⁹ you might sail more than one of the seas. You cross from one to another unknowingly, as there are no boundary$^{cg}$ lines and naturally no seamarks.$^{c}$ You keep posted by checking a large map displayed in one of the lounges. You will find the names of seas and oceans printed there. Each day the navigator⁹ moves a pin to show the location of your ship. Looking at the map, you find the Atlantic Ocean, Pacific Ocean, Indian Ocean, Arctic Ocean, and Antarctic Ocean.

■ This paragraph is the first one in the selection that has a clearly stated main idea. It is in the first sentence.

"But that is only five," you say.

So you search all over the world and you can't find two more oceans. Then you look at the seas. There are many more than seven. Therefore, the so-called seas are not considered the Seven Seas.

The answer is simple, once you know the equator$^{cg}$ is a boundary line through the Pacific and Atlantic Oceans. On the ship, as you cross the equator, a hilarious⁹ ceremony takes place. You are initiated⁹ into the solemn mysteries of

The map shows continents and oceans with labels:

Arctic Ocean

NORTH

EUROPE

ASIA

AMERICA

North Atlantic Ocean

North Pacific Ocean

Equator

AFRICA

SOUTH

AMERICA

South Atlantic Ocean

Indian Ocean

South Pacific Ocean

Antarctic Ocean

■ This world map has no key. None is necessary. The labels printed on the map tell you all you need to know.

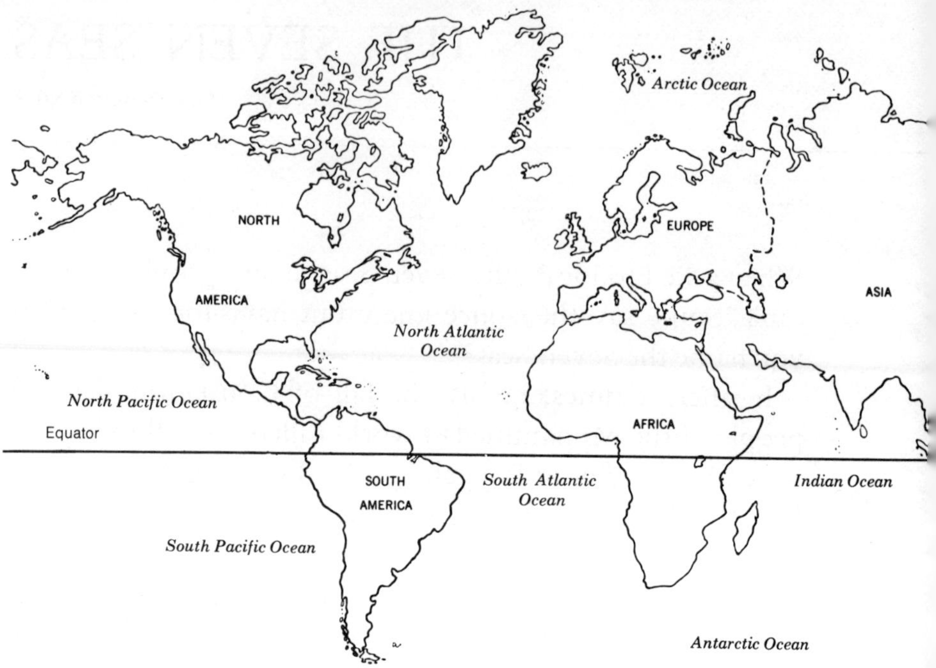

the Ancient Order of the Deep, and you receive a certificate.[9] When this happens, you have crossed from one sea to another.

The equator divides the North Atlantic and South Atlantic, also the North Pacific and South Pacific. In these two

■ The main idea is stated in the last sentence. It is the topic sentence of this paragraph. It is also the main idea of the selection.

oceans are four distinct circulatory[9] systems. These four, added to the Indian Ocean, the Arctic, and the Antarctic, complete the seven. So today the seven systems of water circulation within the world's oceans are considered the Seven Seas.

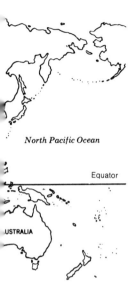

*North Pacific Ocean*

Equator

USTRALIA

# Check the Skills

## Understanding the Selection

1. Are the Seven Seas the same ones now as they were in ancient times? Why has the meaning of the term Seven Seas changed?

## Comprehension Skills Literal Meaning

2. The second marginal note on page 123 pointed out the main idea in the paragraph next to it. Read the last sentence in that paragraph again. How would you figure out that it was *not* the topic sentence of the paragraph?

3. Do you agree that the last sentence tells the main idea of the whole selection? Why or why not?

## Study and Research Skills Parts of a Book

4. Why is there no need for a key with the map on page 124? How does the map help you understand this selection?

# Use the Skills

### Understanding the Selection

1. It's always fun to visit different places. Perhaps you are curious about New York City. Pretend you are a tourist there. The next selection tells how you might find your way around. How can the geography of New York City affect your behavior as a tourist?

### Comprehension Skills Literal Meaning

2. Marginal notes point out the main ideas stated in two paragraphs.

3. The main idea of the whole selection is not stated anywhere, even in the title. Even so, you can probably make a good guess about what it is. Do this by asking yourself what the selection is about.

### Study and Research Skills Parts of a Book

4. There is a map with this selection. Ask yourself how the map adds to the written information. Decide when you would really use a map like this one.

# TOURIST IN THE BIG APPLE

Your plane to New York City has landed at Kennedy International Airport. You're off the plane, and the whole city is before you. But before you run off to see the numerous sights, you should know a little about the geography of the city and the best means of getting around town.

New York City is divided into five boroughs, or districts. Manhattan is the best known. The Bronx is to the north. Brooklyn is to the south and east. Queens, where the airports are, is to the east. Richmond, or Staten Island, is south and west of Manhattan.

You'll probably spend most of your vacation time in Manhattan, so here are a few facts about it. Manhattan is an island, and a rather small one at that. It is twelve miles long and two and a half miles across at its widest point. Its varied neighborhoods, such as the Battery, Greenwich Village, and the Lower East Side, are easy to get to. The center of things is Midtown, an area that runs, roughly, from 34th Street to 59th Street, and all the way across the island. Within this crowded and exciting area, you'll find such famous places as the United Nations, the Empire State Building, Rockefeller Center, and Madison Square Garden. This is the city's heart.

■ Here is the main idea of this paragraph.

If you can count and you know east from west, you can find your way around Manhattan. Getting around is, in fact, so simple that an eight-year-old can easily give directions. All you have to remember is that in Midtown Manhattan, the streets called "streets" run east and west and are numbered consecutively.[9] The streets called "avenues" (like Park, Madison, Fifth, and Tenth Avenues) run north and south. Broadway (neither a street nor an avenue, just "Broadway") rambles from the southern tip of the island, sometimes straight north and sometimes northwest. Except where Broadway crosses while it is slanting northwest, the streets and avenues usually cross each other at right angles.

■ The main idea of this paragraph is stated in the first sentence, too.

New York is one of the few cities left in this country where walking is not only encouraged, but is the most reasonable way to get around. Many places a visitor wants to see are close together, and transportation is slow. So walking is often the quickest way to get somewhere. When you visit New York, put your walking shoes on and wander along the streets and avenues to see the many colorful, delightful sights of the city.

■ The map can help you understand the descriptions in the article.

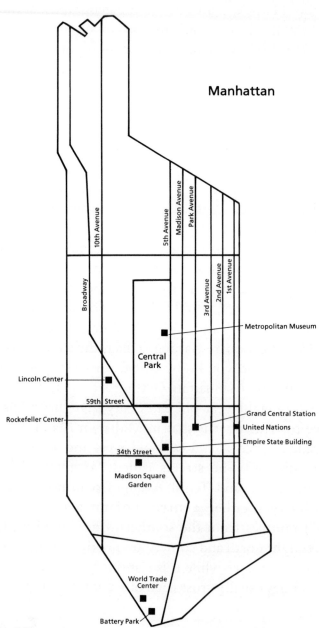

Manhattan

10th Avenue

5th Avenue

Madison Avenue

Park Avenue

Broadway

3rd Avenue

2nd Avenue

1st Avenue

Metropolitan Museum

Central Park

Lincoln Center

59th Street

Rockefeller Center

Grand Central Station

United Nations

Empire State Building

34th Street

Madison Square Garden

World Trade Center

Battery Park

# Check the Skills

### Understanding the Selection

1.  a. Getting around Manhattan is easy because the city has a simple plan. Do you think all cities are so simple? Why do you think as you do?

    b. How easy is it for strangers to find their way around the town or city you know best? Why do you think as you do?

### Comprehension Skills Literal Meaning

2.  Look back at the first two marginal notes and read again the paragraphs next to them. How could you tell that the first sentence in each paragraph was its main idea if the marginal notes weren't there?

3.  Do you agree that the main idea of the whole selection is that it is easy to find your way around Manhattan?

### Study and Research Skills Parts of a Book

4.  Does the map make the information in the article clearer? When would you really use a map like this one?

# Use the Skills

## Understanding the Selection

1.   The desert seems to be an odd place to many people who are used to green trees and grass. But the desert is home for some, as the following poem tells you.

## Comprehension Skills Literal Meaning

2.   A poem always has a main idea. Sometimes it is not so clearly stated as this one is. A marginal note will help you find it.

## Study and Research Skills Parts of a Book

3.   You don't need a map to help you understand this poem, even though you may not know exactly where the desert is. Decide why you think this is so.

# THE DESERT IS THEIRS

Byrd Baylor

This is no place
for anyone
who wants
soft hills
and meadows
and everything
green
green
green . . .

This is for hawks
that like only
the loneliest canyons
and lizards
that run
in the hottest sand
and
coyotes
that choose
the rockiest trails.

It's for them.

■ This is the
main idea of
the poem.

And for
birds
that nest
in cactus
and sing out over
a thousand thorns
because
they're where
they want to be.

It's for them.

And for
hard skinny plants
that do without water
for months
at a time.

And it's for
strong brown Desert People
who call the earth
their mother.

They *have* to see
mountains
and *have* to see
deserts
every day . . .
or they don't feel right.

They wouldn't leave
even for rivers
or flowers
or bending grass.
They'd miss
the sand too much.
They'd miss
the sun.

So
it's for them.

Talk to Papago Indians.
They're
Desert People.

They know
desert secrets
that no one else
knows.

Ask
how they live
in a place
so harsh and dry.

They'll say
they *like*
the land they live on
so they treat it well—
the way you'd treat
an old friend.
They sing it songs.
They never hurt it.

And the land knows.

# Check the
# Skills

### Understanding the Selection

1.  Many people live in the desert areas of the southwestern United States. Do you think their lives are different because of the place they live? Do you know or can you imagine what it is like to move from an area where there are trees, grass, and snow to a desert area?

### Comprehension Skills Literal Meaning

2.  Do you agree that the main idea of the poem is stated in the beginning? Why or why not?

### Study and Research Skills Parts of a Book

3.  Why don't you need a map to help you understand the poem?

# Use the
# Skills

### Understanding the Selection

1.  Puerto Rico is an island in the West Indies, about 1,000 miles south and east of the coast of Florida. Read the next selection to learn about Puerto Ricans who move to the mainland of the United States.

### Comprehension Skills Literal Meaning

2.  Watch for the main idea of the selection.

### Study and Research Skills Parts of a Book

3.  A map with the selection adds additional information about Puerto Rico. Compare the distance between Puerto Rico and the eastern United States to the distance between Puerto Rico and England.

# PUERTO RICAN AMERICANS

Stuart J. Brahs

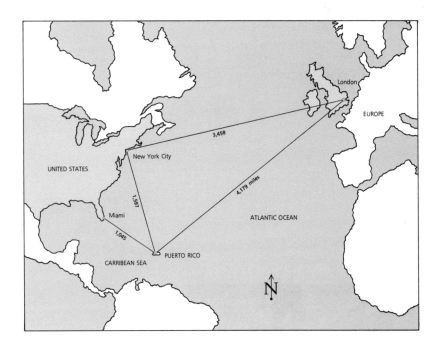

The story of Puerto Rican Americans is concerned partly with the movement of people from a small, warm, Spanish-speaking island in the Caribbean[9] Sea to the crowded, busy streets of the cities of mainland America. Through much of its history, the United States has seen large groups of people arrive on that mainland. However, the Puerto Ricans are in many ways unlike all the other groups. First, they are already American citizens. Second, whereas most of the other peoples arrived at their new home by ship, most Puerto Ricans come by plane. Third, most immigrants[cg] arrived in America during the last part of the nineteenth century or the early part of the twentieth. But the biggest wave of migration[cg] from Puerto Rico to the mainland has taken place in the past thirty years. And yet Puerto Ricans do not yet have full political, economic,[9] or social equality with other American citizens.

■ See if you think this is the main idea of the selection.

In a short time Puerto Ricans have made important contributions to American life and have won a unique[9] status[9] on the mainland. For over seventy years, the United States has maintained a legal relationship with the island of Puerto Rico. Its people have become an integral[9] part of America.

# Check the Skills

### Understanding the Selection

1. Probably more of the Puerto Ricans who move from their homeland go to the United States than go to England. Do you think the reason for this is that England is farther away? Why do you think as you do?

### Comprehension Skills Literal Meaning

2. Do you think the underlined sentence in the first paragraph is the main idea of the selection? Why or why not?

### Study and Research Skills Parts of a Book

3. How did the map help you answer the first question above?

# Use the Skills

Eagle Scout Mark Leinmiller was selected from more than 2,200 applicants to be part of a three-month Antarctic expedition. He was the third Eagle Scout to work in Antarctica. In 1928 Scout Paul Siple went to the South Pole with Commander Richard E. Byrd. In the late 1950s Scout Richard Chappell went on a similar trip.

The explorers Mark Leinmiller traveled with returned home in February, 1979. In the selection, Mark tells about the adventure.

Use your skills with identifying main ideas. You may want to try out your map reading skills by checking an atlas or an encyclopedia for a map of Antarctica. You're on your own this time. There are no marginal notes to help.

# REPORT FROM
# THE ANTARCTIC

Mark Leinmiller
as told to Scott Daniels

"I don't think the helicopters will be able to get up this morning," said my tentmate, Peter Wolcott, as he listened to the fierce Antarctic wind buffet[cg] our tent. "The wind is just too high."

The Navy helicopters were used to carry teams of scientists between the Darwin Glacier base camp and their work site on the Byrd Glacier.

"I guess that means we will have to walk to the glacier," I said.

My friend nodded his head. "It's only about eight miles. If we're lucky, we should make it there in about three hours."

Still huddled inside my down sleeping bag, I reached over for the thermometer. It read −25 degrees. Combined with a wind speed of 30 miles per hour, the cold would feel like −85 degrees outside. And this was summertime. I could only imagine what winter might be like.

I looked at the wind-up alarm clock. It was 7:30 A.M., time to clean up the breakfast dishes and get dressed. The ordeal[cg] of leaving a warm sleeping bag is the same whether you are camping in the Rocky Mountains or on a frozen continent. The only difference is that it takes a lot longer to dress for work in the Antarctic.

I layered on pieces of clothing to shield myself from the cold. I wore a T-shirt covered by thermal underwear, both tops and bottoms. On top of that, I put on a chamois[9] shirt and a pair of woolen pants. A Polarguard vest and down jacket further insulated the top part of my body. A pair of heavy cotton wind pants fitted over my trousers. A toboggan hat, down hood, wool socks, insulated boots, gloves, and ski goggles completed the wardrobe.

Outside, the other scientists had gathered and were preparing to leave. I strapped my backpack onto my shoulders and cinched the hip strap around my bulky parka. Inside the pack were geologist's tools, survival gear, and lunch provisions. Plenty of room was left to carry back rocks and samples of plant life, which we would dig out of the ground.

"Let's all stay close together," the team captain shouted. "It's going to be tough going against the wind." The wind made so much noise that it was difficult to hear anyone speak. We all just nodded to show that we understood.

Our path to the Byrd Glacier passed by towering cliffs of solid ice, light blue in color, their edges sharpened by the cutting wind. There is much more ice on the continent than snow. In some places, it is more than a mile-and-a-half thick. I was surprised to find out that there is less precipitation[9] in Antarctica than in the Sahara.

Leaning forward into the wind, we hiked farther across the frozen landscape. My cheeks began to sting from the icy cold. I wondered how much farther there was to go. Finally, our destination[cg] came into view, and we were soon hard at work.

A glacier is a slow-moving river of solid ice. As it travels forward, it bulldozes an enormous amount of earth and deposits ridges of dirt and rocks alongside its path. These ridges are called *moraines*.

Using picks and shovels, we dug pits in the moraines, sometimes as deep as six feet. We collected soil samples and bits of algae.[9] When measured in the laboratory by a carbon-dating[9] process, the samples would tell scientists how long ago the moraine was formed. These findings, when compared to similar studies on the other side of the continent, could be used to trace the geological history of Antarctica.

The work on the glacier was physically demanding, and the fierce weather robbed a lot of our energies. But it was a strange feeling to know that, no matter where I stood, no one had ever been there before. It was just like the astronauts on the moon.

It wasn't all work and no play, but we had to invent the fun. Pete Wolcott and I began racing down the ice slopes on shovels. We'd sit on the blade and hold onto the handle between our legs. Once, while racing on the wide scoop of a snow shovel, I hit a bump and was suddenly airborne. Somehow I managed to stay on, but when I landed, I had to use a geologist's hammer as a brake dug into the ice to stop my 75-yard glide. It's altogether possible that I may have set the land speed record for the continent that day.

At about 4:30 in the afternoon, the gusting winds finally stopped. It was suddenly strangely peaceful and still. About an hour later, I heard the chopping sound of a helicopter's blades slicing through the air. In the distance was one of the orange Huey helicopters from the Darwin base camp. It had come to ferry us back to camp and save us a three-hour walk.

It was 11:30 that night before I got back into my sleeping bag to go to sleep. Outside, it was as light as it had been at noon time. One of the strangest occurrences in the Antarctic is that for six months out of the year, the sun never sets. Then the next six months are spent in total darkness.

I thought about the things back home that I missed most in Antarctica. Green grass, trees, and unlimited hot showers were just a few.

My work with the scientific expedition was completed in February. As I packed up for the trip home, I realized how valuable my training had been to me in the Antarctic. Backpacking, map reading, and camping skills were second nature to me. They went a long way toward making life a little bit easier.

# Check the Skills

## Understanding the Selection

1.  The land where Mark went was an adventure in itself. Why do you think this is so? What did Mark and the others have to do in order to adapt to the Antarctic?

## Comprehension Skills Literal Meaning

2.  Does the title pretty well state the main idea of this selection? Why do you think as you do?

## Study and Research Skills Parts of a Book

3.  What additional information could you get from a map of Antarctica?

# Apply What You Learned in Unit 5

## The Theme

### Land and Sea

1.  In this unit you read several examples of the effect geography can have on people's lives. Can you think of others? How do you think your life might be different if you lived in a different place? Does visiting different places affect people, too? Why do you think as you do?

# The Skills

## Comprehension Skills Literal Meaning

2.    You need to know the main idea of what you read in order to understand what's important in it. Stated main ideas are most common in nonfiction. So you will find that your skill in recognizing them will be especially helpful as you read materials in your history, science, and math classes.

3.    Remember to look for a topic sentence in a paragraph. If there is one, you can probably recognize it by figuring out that the other sentences in the paragraph tell more details about the idea in the topic sentence.

## Study and Research Skills Parts of a Book

4.    You have seen in this unit that you can get useful information from maps that you can't always get by reading. Depend on this skill as you read newspapers and watch television weather reports, as well as when you do your schoolwork.

# Treasures

## Overview and Purposes for Reading

### The Theme

**Treasures**

1.    When you think of treasure, chances are that you think of old chests full of gold and jewels. But that's not the only kind of treasure. Anything that is loved and especially valued is a treasure. What are some examples?

### The Skills

**Comprehension Skills** Implied Meaning

2.    Understanding how things are alike is an important thinking skill. You often need this skill, called classifying, as you read. How do you classify?

**Literary Appreciation Skills** Story Elements

3.    What are the different points of view from which a story may be written?

# Learn About the Skills

## Comprehension Skills Implied Meaning

Figuring out how things or ideas can be grouped together is called classifying. To classify, you find out how things are alike. For example, what do pens, pencils, and crayons have in common? Yes, they are all writing utensils. So you could label them as "writing utensils" or "things to write with."

It's pretty easy to do that kind of classifying. In the columns below, find the three things that could be labeled "precious stones" or "jewels."

| | | |
|---|---|---|
| book | lifeguard | pearl |
| ruby | newspaper | pool |
| backstroke | magazine | diamond |

Of course you decided that ruby, pearl, and diamond are all jewels. How can you classify the remaining six words in the columns? Can you see that book, newspaper, and magazine are all things to read? How could you label backstroke, lifeguard, and pool?

Classifying ideas can be a little harder. Read the six sentences listed on the next page. See if you can classify them into two groups. Remember to group together the ones that have something in common.

1. A loud cheer rose from the packed stadium as the pitcher hurled the first ball of the season across the plate.
2. Sandy and I packed our gear, climbed into the canoe, and began paddling downstream.
3. The vendors inched their way up and down the aisles selling hotdogs and pop to the audience.
4. As we were pitching our tent, we were caught in a sudden downpour that soaked us to the skin.
5. For dinner we cooked the fish we had caught that afternoon.
6. The batter walloped the first pitched ball over the left-field fence for a home run!

You are right if you classified sentences 1, 3, and 6 together. They deal with the same topic. They describe or could be classified or labeled as "attending a baseball game." Sentences 2, 4, and 5 fit together because they are all about a camping trip.

Grouping ideas together with some logical system is classifying them. You'll find out more about how to use your skill in classifying as you read this unit.

# Literary Appreciation Skills Story Elements

The information you get about a story often depends on who tells the story. This person can be called the narrator. The point of view of the story is the narrator's.

The narrator of the story may be the main character of the story, as in the following example.

> I walked cautiously down the street. John followed me, with fear in his face.

Here the main character tells the story from her own point of view. This is called **first person point of view**. You can recognize it easily because the narrator refers to herself or himself as "I."

The narrator of the story may be someone outside of the story who seems to know everything, even what each character is thinking. Read this example.

> Geraldine walked cautiously down the street. John followed. Both were afraid, but only John showed it.

This is called an **omniscient point of view** because *omniscient* means "knowing everything." This is the point of view used most often by authors.

Figuring out the point of view of a story can help you enjoy it more. It can also help you understand whether there may be things going on that the narrator does not know about.

You'll see how to use this skill as you read this unit.

> Geraldine walked cautiously down the street. I followed her, feeling afraid. She didn't seem fearful at all.

Figuring out the point of view of a story can help you enjoy it more. It can also help you understand whether there may be things going on that the narrator does not know about.

You'll see how to use this skill as you read this unit.

# Selection 1

# Use the Skills

## Understanding the Selection

You be the detective and solve the mystery in the next selection. Watch for a tricky clue. Match wits with Dr. Haledjian, the famous detective.

1. Find out what treasure is involved in this story. Decide if it really is treasure or not.

## Comprehension Skills Implied Meaning

2. Dr. Haledjian solves the mystery by classifying something in the story with things like it that he knows about. See if you can do the same. A note in the margin will give you a clue.

## Literary Appreciation Skills Story Elements

3. See who the narrator of the story is so that you will know the point of view.

# BURIED TREASURE

Donald J. Sobol

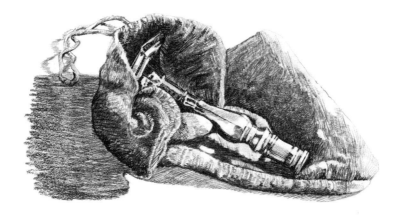

"From the gleam in your eye, I gather you are about to get rich quick," said Dr. Haledjian.

"Clever of you, old chap," said Bertie Tilford, a young Englishman who liked to avoid hard work. "If I had ten thousand I would make a fortune! Do you have ten?"

"What's the game now?" demanded Haledjian. "Pieces⁹ of eight among the corals? Doubloons⁹ from Captain Kidd's chest?"

Bertie opened a sack and triumphantly⁹ produced a shining silver candlestick. "Sterling silver," he sang. "See what's engraved^cg on the bottom."

Haledjian turned over the candlestick and read the name *Lady North*. "Wasn't that the ship that sank in 1956?"

"The *Lady North* sank, but not with all hands as is generally believed," replied Bertie. "Four men got away with a fortune before the ship capsized^c in the storm. They hid their loot in a cave," continued Bertie. "But the storm started an avalanche⁹ and sealed off the entrance, burying three of the sailors inside. The fourth, a chap named Pembroot, escaped. Pembroot has been trying to raise ten thousand to buy the land on which the cave is located."

■ By now you can tell that neither of the characters is the narrator of the story.

"You put up the money, the cave is opened, and the loot is divided two ways instead of four," said Haledjian. "Only how do you know Pembroot isn't a swindler?"

"Earlier tonight he took me to the cave," said Bertie. "This sack was half buried in the bushes. I nearly sprained my ankle on it. I took one look and brought the candlestick here to show you. You've got to agree it's the real thing, old chap."

"It is," admitted Haledjian. "And there's no doubt that Pembroot planted it by the cave for your benefit."

*How did Haledjian know?*

■ The detective classified the shine of the silver with the fact that silver has to be cleaned often to be shiny.

If the sterling silver candlestick had been lying in a sack since 1956, it would have been tarnished and black, not "shining."

# Check the Skills

### Understanding the Selection

1. Was the candlestick really treasure? Why not?

### Comprehension Skills Implied Meaning

2. How did classifying help Dr. Haledjian solve the mystery?

### Literary Appreciation Skills Story Elements

3. How do you know the story is told from an omniscient point of view?

# Selection 2

# Use the Skills

### Understanding the Selection

The next selection takes place in the 1930s during the Great Depression. It was a time when jobs and money were scarce. People had to go where the jobs were. Sometimes that meant that families were separated for long periods of time. The main character in this story has an interesting experience.

1. See if you think the memories of this experience are a treasure to her.

### Comprehension Skills Implied Meaning

2. A note in the margin will help you see how a group of things described can be classified.

### Literary Appreciation Skills Story Elements

3. Note who is telling the story. Be alert to events or happenings that the narrator could not possibly know about.

# TO RIDE AN ELEPHANT

Babs H. Deal

Everyone should, when very young, realize a dream. It gives you a kind of faith to take into the never-never land of the future, a belief in the possibilities of life. It should be a big dream, an important one, and one you believe is impossible. My dream was to ride an elephant.

Small circuses came through our little town only occasionally. Often they didn't have an elephant at all. There was no zoo, so even seeing an elephant was rare. Riding one was clearly impossible.

But I loved elephants. They seemed to me the largest and kindest of creatures. They seemed to be a message from nature that the best things didn't always come in small packages. I needed to believe in this message since I was anything but small myself. The thought of sitting on top of an elephant seemed like magic. From such a lofty[9] perch surely the world would seem beautiful, and so would I.

I needed to believe in something like an elephant ride the year I was nine. My mother had just died and my father had taken a job in another town. I lived with my grandmother. I loved her and was treated well, but the world was strange. Often I would look at the row of little ivory elephants on the living-room mantel and think of real ones, knowing they were beyond me forever.

It was like that the autumn evening I saw the circus posters on the way home from school. We had always gone when a circus came to town, my mother and father and I. But this year, I wasn't sure. I stood in the afternoon light, looking at the clown faces, the acrobats, the elephant with lifted trunk, and I was suddenly lonelier than I'd ever been.

There were to be two performances on Saturday. That afternoon, I sat in the swing in the walnut tree and read a book. I tried not to think of the sawdust up the road, the elephant, the vanished time when Mother and Daddy and I

■ Here is the first clue that the narrator is the main character.

would have gone together into the magic tent.

Then at five o'clock my father's car stopped at the gate. "Hello, honey," he said as I ran towards him. "I heard there was a circus in town, and figured I might persuade you to go."

He had taken the afternoon off from work and driven 60 miles to get me, but I didn't know that then.

■ Here's another clue that the point of view is not omniscient.

■ This group of things could be labeled "circus."

The tent, which was pitched in a lot on the edge of town, was not even half full. There were clowns, a bareback rider and a trapeze performer. There were trained dogs and horses and a juggler. They entertained us and brightened us and lifted us. And then they brought the elephant in.

She was an old elephant. She walked and stood and reared, accepting our applause.

"I wish I could ride her," I whispered. "I wish I could ride an elephant. She's so big and beautiful."

Then the ringmaster announced. "This is Susie, and she likes people." He paused. "We realize that there are some people in the audience who have always wanted to ride an elephant . . ."

I caught my breath.

"Any boy who wants to ride, come forward."

There was a scramble as four boys rushed down off the bleachers. The handler pulled the elephant's ear and she knelt while the ringmaster helped them onto her back.

I could feel the tears in my eyes, but I gritted my teeth. Of course it would be boys. They always got to do everything. Laughing and holding on, they rode Susie around the ring. I watched in resignation.[9] No one ever got to do the thing they wanted most. Life wasn't that way.

Then the ringmaster was talking again. I didn't listen.

"Now's your chance," my father said.

"What?"

"He's calling for girls who want to ride the elephant. That's you, isn't it?"

I stared at my father, and at Susie. I couldn't do it. It was impossible.

"Go on," he urged, "before it's too late."

"I can't," I said. I was so startled that I couldn't get up, go down the bleachers and perch in glory on Susie. I would sit still past the moment of choice. Then the chance would be lost forever. I would know forever that I could have ridden an elephant and hadn't.

But my father was talking again. "Get up, honey, so the ringmaster will see you." Gently, he pushed me to my feet.

"Come on," the ringmaster said.

I walked down the bleachers. My feet felt numb. I stepped across the ring curb. Three more girls followed me. I stood in the center of the ring, smelling the sawdust, and smelling Susie. I was afraid, not of the elephant, or the people watching, or the ride ahead. Instead I was afraid of the enormousness[9] of actually realizing my dream.

We climbed on Susie. Her hide was rough and prickly against my bare legs. I held the harness in front of me and another girl held me around the waist. Then Susie stood up. I was there, high above the world.

That was the last circus my father ever took me to. But I could live without circuses after that. I had ridden an elephant.

And so ever after, whenever something seemed too hard to do, I remembered that moment. I remembered the hard glare of light, the cold wind under the tent, and the bitter thought, *I can't, and it will be too late*. Then I remembered my father's voice and the one small push and the ringmaster. Whenever I don't feel I have the courage to do something, there is in my mind a girl who wanted to ride an elephant—and did—and who therefore knows she can.

# Check the Skills

### Understanding the Selection

1. Is the memory of the elephant ride a treasure to the main character? What else does the memory mean to her besides just an exciting dream come true?

### Comprehension Skills Implied Meaning

2. Suppose you didn't know the story was about a circus. How could classifying clowns, bareback rider, trapeze performer, dogs, horses, and a juggler help you figure it out?

### Literary Appreciation Skills Story Elements

3. How did you know that the story was told from the first person point of view?

# Selection 3

# Use the Skills

### Understanding the Selection

1.  The next selection is a poem about treasures. You may be surprised to discover what the person in the poem thinks a real treasure is. See if you agree.

### Comprehension Skills Implied Meaning

2.  You could classify the things listed in the poem as "treasures" or as "things that grow in the garden." Decide what other label you could give them.

### Literary Appreciation Skills Story Elements

3.  The poem is another example of an omniscient point of view. Look back at page 149 if you need help in deciding why.

# THE GARDEN

Shel Silverstein

Ol' man Simon, planted a diamond,
Grew hisself a garden the likes of none.
Sprouts all growin', comin' up glowin',
Fruit of jewels all shinin' in the sun.
Colors of the rainbow,
See the sun and rain grow
Sapphires and rubies on ivory vines,
Grapes of jade, just
Ripenin' in the shade, just
Ready for the squeezin' into green jade wine.
Pure gold corn there,
Blowin' in the warm air,
Ol' crow nibblin' on the amethyst seeds.
In between the diamonds, ol' man Simon
Crawls about pullin' out platinum weeds.

■ What do the
underlined
words have in
common?

Pink pearl berries,
All you can carry,
Put 'em in a bushel and
Haul 'em into town.
Up in the tree there's
Opal nuts and gold pears—
Hurry quick, grab a stick
And shake some down.
Take a silver tater,
Emerald tomater,
Fresh plump coral melons
Hangin' in reach.

■ There is only
one character in
the poem. Is it
told from his
point of view?

Ol' man Simon,
Diggin' in his diamonds,
Stops and rests and dreams about
One . . . real . . . peach.

# Check the
# Skills

### Understanding the Selection

1.    What does "ol' man Simon" think a real treasure is? Why do
      you suppose he thinks that? Do you agree? Why or why not?

### Comprehension Skills Implied Meaning

2.    How could you classify the underlined words in the poem?

### Literary Appreciation Skills Story Elements

3.    How does the poem fit the definition of an omniscient point
      of view given on page 149?

# Use the Skills

### Understanding the Selection

This selection tells about a real-life sister's feelings toward her older brother who is retarded. Their mother wrote a book about them. In the book the names of the two characters are different from their real ones. So don't get confused when the names of the brother and sister change in the selection.

1. As you read you will see how the retarded boy is a treasure to his family.

### Comprehension Skills Implied Meaning

2. Classifying some words underlined in the first paragraph can help you understand something about the girl.

### Literary Appreciation Skills Story Elements

3. See if the points of view of this selection and of the book it quotes are the same.

# THERE WAS ALWAYS
# LAUGHTER

"My name is Beth. I have a retarded brother, Steven. Mostly I feel happy and I have fun with my friends. There are times that I'm sad or lonely, especially when I feel left out by my friends. There are other times that I feel different from everyone else and sort of strange. Maybe it's because of my brother, Steve."

■ How can you classify the underlined words?

These are the first few sentences from a book, *My Brother Steven is Retarded*, by Harriet Langsam Sobol, Beth's mother.

In the book Beth's brother is a year older than Beth but he's smaller and acts younger. When Beth was little, she says in the book, she thought "retarded" was contagious$^{cg}$ and she was afraid to stand next to him.

"But my mother explained retarded to me and now I know it's not catching," she says.

■ What is the point of view of this selection? Remember to decide who the narrator is.

In real life, Beth is Jennifer Sobol, a high school student in Scarsdale, New York. She takes dancing lessons, plays the piano and enjoys acting. "Steven" is her real-life older brother Greg, who's now a student at a special school.

"I didn't want him to go away," Jenny says. "I was afraid I'd lose him as a brother. But I didn't. We visit him and he seems just as happy to see me as he ever was."

Unlike Steven in the book, Greg can't speak at all. He can't care for himself and never will be able to. But at the school he will be able to learn to do a simple job that he can do when he grows up.

"I know it was difficult for my mother to send him away, but it came down to what was best for him. The most difficult thing about having someone retarded in your family," Jenny says, "is the attitude of other people. They get embarrassed and scared. I understand now but, when I was little, some of my friends would be afraid to come to my house because of the strange noises Greg made or the way he looked. The attitude of my family helped a lot, though. There was a lot of laughter. We weren't afraid to laugh at some of the things Greg did, and that took away some of the tension."

Jenny remembers a babysitter who answered an ad in a local college paper. "She just wanted to earn some money, so she called my mother about the babysitting job. She wasn't put off by Greg and, before long, she grew to love him. She was really good with him. She surprised herself more than anyone else. Now she's the head of a project for blind and deaf children in Oklahoma. She's helping hundreds of kids, all because of Greg. Maybe that's why he was put here.

"What I learned," Jenny continues, "is that things aren't always perfect. You must go along with what you can't

change and make the best of it. Feeling sorry for yourself won't help or change anything."

"Lots of times I feel sorry for Steven," says Beth in the book. "My mother and father say that they feel sorry, too. They say we will always be sad about it, but there really is nothing anyone can do to change it. I hope he will be happy."

■ Who is the narrator of the book?

# Check the Skills

### Understanding the Selection

1.  Perhaps Jennifer and her family consider Greg a treasure because they have learned so much about themselves as they have dealt with him. Do you think this is so? Why or why not?

### Comprehension Skills Implied Meaning

2.  How did you classify "Beth's" feelings described in the first paragraph?

### Literary Appreciation Skills Story Elements

3.  How do you know the selection is written from an omniscient point of view? What clues lead you to believe the book is in the first person point of view?

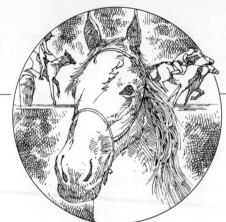

# Selection 5

# Use the Skills

A strong, courageous horse who manages to survive against all odds is the main character of the next selection. As you read, ask yourself if this horse was a treasure.

Use what you know about classifying if you need it as you read. Remember to decide what the point of view of the story is. You're on your own this time, with no marginal notes to help you use your skills.

# MOIFAA

Sam Savitt

This is a story about a New Zealand thoroughbred[g] named Moifaa.

He was a big, brown rangy[g] colt. Even though he won many races in his native country, his appearance always brought hoots of laughter from the crowd. People made comments such as, "He looks like a starved elephant," or "What do you call that thing?"

True enough, Moifaa was not a handsome horse. He was not only awkward and ungainly looking, but he stood over seventeen hands[g] high. Now, a horse that large, especially a race horse, is usually not as well coordinated[g] or as athletic as the more average sixteen-hand horse. But Moifaa's owner, Spencer Golland, had great faith in his horse's capabilities.[cg] One year he decided to send the animal to England to run in the Grand National,[c] the most famous steeplechase[g] race in the world. It is also the most demanding. The course is four miles long. There are thirty fences to be jumped, and they are big and solid. As many as forty horses will start in this race, but perhaps only seven or eight will finish. A Grand National steeplechaser[c] must be a good, bold jumper. The horse must also have a lot of class, speed, and staying power. Except for his looks, Moifaa seemed to have these qualifications, but how much more he had, this story will tell.

The colt was shipped to England several months before the time set for the running of the big race, so he would have plenty of time for conditioning.[cg] Off Capetown, South Africa, the freighter[cg] that was carrying Moifaa ran into a terrific storm. For two days it buffeted[g] the small vessel. The ship began to split apart. The crew lowered lifeboats, and the passengers were taken to safety. Moifaa, however, still locked in his special stall which had been erected on the deck, was left to his fate. As the seas rose and closed in, the trapped horse must have decided it was time to leave. He methodically[g] kicked his way out of the stall and leaped over the side of the doomed freighter.

Once in the water, he instinctively[g] swam for his life. Twenty-foot waves washed over him, then lifted and flung him about. Moifaa was under water more than above, but he wouldn't give up. Probably he didn't know how. There was no panic in him, just the will to reach land. How this horse survived is absolutely incredible. He was in the water for hours. He finally staggered up on the lonely rocky beach of a small island almost a hundred miles from where the ship went down.

Moifaa lay at the water's edge, his heaving sides bruised and bleeding from the awful beating he had taken. But he was alive.

He stayed where he was all night, too exhausted to move. By morning, hunger pains sent him wandering along the shore, foraging[cg] for whatever he could find. And there wasn't enough to feed a rabbit. He turned inland over the dunes and soon came across marsh grass that grew in clumps and tasted quite salty. Afterwards, he found water to drink in little pools and puddles.

Moifaa lived this way for several months, wandering around and around the small island. He grew thin, and his coat lost much of its luster,[9] but his constant search for food kept him on his feet.

A fisherman, coming in with his catch one evening, suddenly thought he saw a movement on the shore of a small island he was sailing past. The sun had already gone down, and the visibility wasn't too good. He peered through the mist at the island he'd thought was uninhabited.[cg] But what was that standing near the shore? It might be a deer but it looked a lot like a horse!

He turned his boat and headed toward the shore. Moifaa had been nibbling on some dry weeds. He raised his head and watched the sailboat approach. Then the fisherman called. Moifaa answered with a shrill whinny[cg] and came galloping down to meet his rescuer.

That's how he was found. After the rescue was completed, Moifaa resumed his interrupted journey to England. He arrived shortly before the Grand National.

Spencer Golland was there to meet the horse and quickly took over his reconditioning.[cg] The day for the running of the great race arrived. The foremost horse racing enthusiasts in the world were there, including King Edward VII, whose own horse also was racing. The New Zealand colt had still not regained[cg] his top form, but the eager look in his eyes was there.

Golland said, "I've seen him in better shape, but this is what we came for, so let's let him run."

Well, Moifaa raced in that Grand National of 1904—and won it by eight lengths. To make the "fairy tale ending" even better, he was purchased by the King and lived happily ever after in royal splendor.

# Check the Skills

### Understanding the Selection

1.  Do you think Moifaa was a treasure? Why do you think as you do?

### Comprehension Skills Implied Meaning

2.  Which three of these sentences would you group together as having something in common?

    a.  The freighter ran into a terrific storm.
    b.  A fisherman thought he saw a movement on the island.
    c.  The day for the running of the great race arrived.
    d.  For two days the storm buffeted the small vessel.
    e.  The ship began to split apart.

### Literary Appreciation Skills Story Elements

3.  What is the point of view of this selection? How do you know?

# Apply What You Learned in Unit 6

## The Theme

### Treasures

1.  In this unit you learned that treasure is not only riches and wealth. It can be a dream realized or a lesson learned as in "To Ride an Elephant." It can be a special human being, as in "There Was Always Laughter." Or it can be an animal as in "Moifaa." What other treasures are there in life?

*   Think about your own treasures—those whose loss or destruction would be especially difficult to accept.

*   What would life be like if people had no treasures? Why do you think as you do?

# The Skills

## Comprehension Skills Implied Meaning

2. Being able to classify helps you organize your ideas. This is important when you read. It is also important when you are completing assignments in your classes at school. Remember to decide how things are alike. Group them together under a label that fits them all.

## Literary Appreciation Skills Story Elements

3. Remember that a story may be written from the point of view of the first person, or from the point of view of an omniscient person. You'll find it helpful to decide the point of view in each story you read.

# Do Something!

## Overview and Purposes for Reading

### The Theme

**Do Something!**

1.    What are some kinds of situations that require quick action? In what kinds of situations is it better to develop a careful plan?

### The Skills

**Comprehension Skills** Critical Reading

2.    What is realism? fantasy?

3.    Why is it important to be able to tell the difference between the two?

**Vocabulary Development Skills** Word Structure

4.    How can knowing about contractions help you when you read?

# Learn About the Skills

## Comprehension Skills Critical Reading

You know that fiction is the kind of writing made up by the author's imagination. Some fiction seems very real. It describes people and events that could happen. You may not be able to tell that it's fiction and not fact, unless the author or someone else tells you so. This kind of fiction writing is called **realism**.

Sometimes the characters and events are totally unbelievable. This is called **fantasy**. How can you tell the difference between realism and fantasy when you read?

Fantasy is so completely imaginary that it could not happen in real life. Look at the following example. Is this fantasy?

> Fred, my pet dog, insists that his pants be the same color as his hat.

Of course, this is fantasy. You know because your experience tells you that pet dogs do not wear pants and hats. They also do not have opinions about colors.

So the secret to telling whether something is realism or fantasy is to think about what you already know about life. Then decide whether what you are reading about could be real.

Look at another example. Use your experience—what you know about life. Could this really happen?

> Margaret likes to play the guitar, and it is usually relaxing for her. But this particular day was an exception. She had a great deal of trouble tuning the instrument. Then a string broke and she couldn't find a replacement string. When she returned from the store, she discovered that her father hadn't noticed the guitar leaning against the wall. He had knocked it over and stepped right through the top.

Have you ever had an experience similar to Margaret's? Could such a chain of events happen in real life? Of course it could. So this writing is realism.

Sometimes it is easy to tell fantasy from realism. However, there are other times when it is hard. A skillful writer can sometimes make fantasy *seem* real. The following paragraph is an example.

> Like all of Napoleon's speeches, it was short and to the point. He too, he said, was happy that the period of misunderstanding was at an end. For a long time there had been rumors. They had been credited with attempting to stir up rebellion among the animals on neighboring farms. Nothing could be further from the truth! Their sole wish, now and in the past, was to live in peace and in normal business relations with their neighbors.

This is from the book *Animal Farm* by George Orwell. You may not be able to tell whether it is realism or fantasy. This paragraph seems real. However, Napoleon is actually a pig who has been the main force in the takeover of an entire farm. Knowing this, it is obvious that the paragraph is fantasy.

To be a good reader, you should always read critically. Ask yourself, "Could this really happen? In my experience with life, does this seem real?" If you do this, you will not fall into the trap of "believing everything you read." Use this skill as you read the selections in this unit.

## Vocabulary Development Skills Word Structure

Sometimes you can figure out words you don't know if you know how words are formed or built.

One way new words are formed in English is by sliding two or more words together to make a shorter word. These are called **contractions**. We all use contractions when we talk. For example, we say *isn't* for *is not* and *we'll* for *we will*.

Sometimes contractions can be confusing when you meet them in your reading. Remember that the letters and sounds that have been left out are replaced by an apostrophe. Think what makes sense in the sentence you are reading. "Listen" in your mind to the way the contraction is pronounced. You should then have no trouble reading contractions.

As you read, be alert for contractions. Make sure you know what words have been combined to make each contraction.

You'll use this skill as you read this unit.

# Selection 1

## Use the Skills

### Understanding the Selection

Esther Morris believed that women, as well as men, should have the right to vote. She also believed in doing something to make that dream come true. She did do something about it, and she was the first woman to cast her ballot in Wyoming in 1870.

1. Find out what Esther Morris did to gain the vote for women.

2. Decide what type of person she was.

### Comprehension Skills Critical Reading

3. This story is true. See if you think there is any fantasy in it.

### Vocabulary Development Skills Word Structure

4. You may need to use what you learned about contractions to help you with some of the words you meet.

# ESTHER MORRIS— MOTHER OF EQUAL RIGHTS

Helen Markley Miller

Wyoming had been newly proclaimed[9] a territory. That fall it was to hold its first territorial election. Although Wyoming claimed a vast spread of lonely land, it had a population of only ten thousand. There were few women in the territory. And those few showed great courage, endurance,[9] and determination. Here in Wyoming Esther Morris was determined to drive her tiny wedge.

That wedge was to be nothing more than a tea party. Who could suspect a tea party of being the start of a movement that might rock the political traditions of America, perhaps of the world? So thought Esther, smiling to herself.

After careful consideration she issued her invitations. First she asked the two men who had been nominated by their parties to serve as representatives to the new territorial legislature. They were her friends, William Bright, Democrat, and Herman Nickerson, Republican. When the Brights and the Nickersons had accepted, Esther gave thought to her other guests. There must be some pretty girls, but intelligent ones. She invited them. There must be thinking older men and women. All the women must be honest, sincere, and solid. Such women would make intelligent voters.

■ These were real people. So was Esther Morris. Therefore, this is not fantasy.

On September 2, 1869, twenty guests assembled[c] for the tea party. There was new snow on the Wind River Range, but Esther's garden was still a glory of pink, purple, and lavender fall asters. The guests walked among the flowers. Soon all of the men were in a happy and receptive mood.

"Do I smell a mouse?" John Morris asked his wife. He knew Esther's dream.

She laughed. "Not a mouse, John. A wedge."

"Of cheese, perhaps?"

"Perhaps. Let us hope the mice will nibble."

■ Although the conversation and events may not have happened exactly in this way, they could have.

Soon she had all the guests inside her miners' shack, made bright with flowers from her garden. She waited until she had served the tea, the squares of homemade bread, the cakes she had frosted. There came a moment's break in the talk. Then Esther spoke out with all her sincere directness the proposition[cg] that had filled her mind for days. The speech that she'd made up sounded a little stilted[9] even to her, and she knew that she was breathless.

■ *She'd* is a contraction of *she had* or of *she would*. The general meaning of the rest of this sentence tells you that here it is *she had*.

"We have with us here two opposing candidates for the first legislature of our newborn territory, Captain Herman Nickerson and Colonel William Bright. One of you gentlemen is to be elected. We women want to have from you both a promise given before all at this tea party. Whichever of you is elected will present to the legislature a bill. It will confer upon the women of our new territory the right of suffrage.[9]"

There was a startled silence for a moment. Then William Bright took a deep breath. He shook his head as if he were coming out from water. Then he pledged his word. During all the summer months he'd been listening to the arguments of Esther and his wife. And he'd been doing some clear thinking. Many of the women he knew were as intelligent, as informed on public affairs as were the men of his acquaintance. Why then should women not be allowed the vote?

Herman Nickerson was in a spot. After his Democratic opponent[c] had given his pledge so readily, what could a Republican do but yield? No doubt he thought easily to himself that such a bill never would pass the legislature anyway. Nowhere in all the world had women been given the right of equal suffrage. Surely the untried legislature of the new territory of Wyoming would not pass such a bill. And so to please his charming hostess, he gave his pledge.

Esther was satisfied that she'd won a first battle. Her wedge was in the wood. Now let it split wide open the block of intolerance.[9]

Colonel Bright was elected. Before he left South Pass City, he told Esther, "I'll do everything I can to give you women the ballot."

From her cabin on the mountain she watched with alternate hope and doubt the progress of her effort to improve the status[cg] of women. Eagerly she scanned the newspapers, always days old before they reached Pass City. Gloating,[g] she read the report of Bright's proposal on November 12. The newspapers called the bill revolutionary.[g]

> That every woman of the age of eighteen years,
> residing in this territory, may, at every election to
> be held under the laws thereof, cast her vote. . . .

The result of Bright's proposal was startling. There was some opposition. But the senate passed the bill with a vote of six in favor, two opposed, one absent.

# Check the Skills

### Understanding the Selection

1. How did Esther Morris help to gain the vote for women? Do you think she planned her strategy carefully? Why do you think as you do?

2. What kind of person do you think Esther Morris was? Was she quiet and undecided, or sociable and determined? Why do you think as you do?

### Comprehension Skills Critical Reading

3. Do you think this selection is an example of realism or fantasy? Why do you think so?

### Vocabulary Development Skills Word Structure

4. Look back at the last marginal note. How could the sense of the sentence tell you that *she'd* meant *she had*?

# Use the Skills

### Understanding the Selection

The coyote is a common character in folk tales of many American Indian tribes in the Southwest. The next selection is one of these tales, as written by a young San Carlos Apache girl.

1.  Decide for yourself whether Coyote did some quick thinking in this situation.

### Comprehension Skills Critical Reading

2.  Remember that realism is writing that could happen in real life. Fantasy could never happen. Think about this as you read the selection. Decide whether it is realism or fantasy.

### Vocabulary Development Skills Word Structure

3.  You should have no difficulty figuring out the contractions in this selection.

# COYOTE AND THE MONEY TREE

Tina Naiche

Coyote had some money, just a few dollars. He was walking down a road trying to figure out how to change those dollars into something more valuable.

■ To decide whether this is realism or fantasy, think about what coyotes can and can't do.

Coming toward him were some American prospectors[9] with their horses and mules and blankets and guns and bags of food.

Coyote had a brilliant[9] thought. He put his money up in the branches of a tree that was growing beside the road. Then he just sat there watching the tree.

When the prospectors rode up, they asked him, "What are you doing?"

"I am watching this tree. It is very valuable," Coyote said.

■ Can coyotes really talk? This should help you decide whether the selection is realism or fantasy.

"Why is it valuable? What is in that tree?" the prospectors asked.

"Money grows on that tree," Coyote said. "When I shake it, money falls out."

The prospectors laughed at him. So Coyote shook the tree a little, and one of his dollars fell out.

Now the men were very interested. "Sell us that tree," they said.

"No," Coyote said, pretending to be angry. "This is the only tree in the world that grows money."

The prospectors said, "We will give you everything we have . . . our horses and mules and everything else. We'll just climb down, and you'll own everything."

Coyote still pretended not to want to, and the prospectors tried to persuade him.

But after a while Coyote let them persuade him. "All right," he said. "I will sell you the tree. There's only one thing."

■ You should know the meaning from the sense of the sentence. It is there is, not there has.

"Anything at all," they said.

"See those blue mountains over there? Well, you will have to wait until I get there. If you shake the tree before that, nothing will come out, and you will spoil it forever."

The prospectors agreed. So Coyote jumped on one of the horses and rode away with everything they had.

When he reached the blue mountains, the men shook the tree. Only one dollar fell out, though they shook and shook and shook. That was the last dollar Coyote had put there.

Over by the blue mountains, Coyote was laughing.

# Check the Skills

### Understanding the Selection

1. Do you think Coyote is a quick thinker? Why do you think as you do? Did his situation require quick action? Why or why not?

### Comprehension Skills Critical Reading

2. Is this selection realism or fantasy? How do you know?

### Vocabulary Development Skills Word Structure

3. The contraction *there's* can stand for *there is* or *there has*. How can you know which is the right one when you see it in your reading?

# Use the Skills

### Understanding the Selection

Skip dreams of being a hero, but he knows he'll never be a great athlete. He finds out something important about himself when a dramatic situation forces him to do something.

1.    See if you agree that the situation requires quick thinking rather than careful planning.

### Comprehension Skills Critical Reading

2.    Remember that it is sometimes difficult to distinguish fantasy from realism. Read critically and ask yourself whether the events in this selection could really happen.

### Vocabulary Development Skills Word Structure

3.    Use what you know about contractions to help figure out several in the selection.

# THE REAL THING

A. R. Swinnerton

I guess every kid has fantasies. Mine are mostly about something physical. I might be an Olympic contender,[cg] in the last heat of the shot-put competition.

I pick up the heavy shot, heft[c] it from hand to hand. I step into the circle, shading my eyes from the sun.

I wind up like a baseball pitcher. I don't heave the shot, I hurl it—300 feet out. It buries itself, *splat!* in the turf. There is a hoarse, ear-shattering roar from the stands.

■ These are some of Skip's fantasies. But don't decide yet that the whole selection is fantasy.

Hands reach out to touch me, voices yell into my ear. One voice above all the rest has the edge of authority. "Drink up your milk, Skip."

My reverie[cg] ends as it usually does, and I say, "Yes, Mom. Next time don't interrupt me, though."

"Doing what?"

"I was just about to accept the gold medal for the United States of America, that's what. I set a new world's shot-put record."

"Oh, excuse me, Skip. I didn't hear the applause. Now hurry up or you'll be late."

As for sports in general, I'm a fair swimmer, but not strong enough for competition. I'm too short for basketball. And baseball makes me nervous.

I've talked it over with my dad. "I know how you feel," he'd say. "Believe me, I do. But you never know about some things, Skip. Be happy that you've got good health. And a quick mind. Use it to the best of your ability, and you'll be enjoying life long after some of these athletes are forgotten."

Sometimes, after school, I hop on my bike and wheel down to the river, which cuts our town in half. Neither deep nor real wide, it meanders[g] peacefully through town on its way to Lake Erie. Except in midwinter or spring, when it's not peaceful. Then the ice jams up and the river floods, going out of its banks just above town and spreading out into an area we've always called the flats.

With federal funds, the city contracted to deepen the channel and build flood walls. This is what I like to watch. I've made friends with a guy named Barney Harper, who operates one of those big shovels. With its scoop it digs into the river muck or raises up and dumps a load, just as easy as you'd scoop up a measure of flour. In action, the thing reminded me of a dinosaur, craning its neck and gobbling up huge bites of river-bottom food.

I usually wait around for quitting time. Barney lets me climb up into the cab and sit in his seat.

This particular day I looked out over the river, green and sluggish under the afternoon sun. From upstream I heard some tinny music. Just under the Monroe Street bridge, I could see a canoe. I turned Barney's field glasses on it. Sure enough, it was Jelly Bean Malloy, a kid I knew. His canoe was drifting slowly. He was sitting down, casting. I could hear his radio louder now. He always had it with him, even in school.

Barney, watching from the front of the tractor, saw him too. "Hope he can swim," he said, rubbing his chin. "Canoes flip mighty easy. You know him?"

■ This means *he has*, not *he is*.

I climbed out beside Barney. "I hope he's got a life jacket," I said. "That kid can't swim a stroke."

I was just about to raise my arm and yell at him to be careful. Jelly Bean stood up in that crazy canoe. He lunged far out for a sweeping cast. He jigged back and forth as if he had a bee in his britches. Then he was in the river.

What I was watching wasn't a dream. It was a nightmare and it was real. My mind was working like crazy, knowing we had only three or four minutes to do something.

■ Use your own experience, and what you know about life, to decide whether the events in the rest of the story could really happen.

Then, cutting across the wall, I saw the thin shadow of the beam. "Barney!" I yelled. "The bucket! Hoist<sup>cg</sup> me over, quick! Maybe we can reach him."

He nodded, knowing I'd be safe enough with him as pilot. I climbed inside the muddy bucket. Then I was out over the water, looking down. I could still see Jelly Bean. I

yelled out to him, ripping off my jacket at the same time. I pointed straight down and the bucket hit the water not three feet from Jelly Bean's splash marks.

I leaned out and flipped out my jacket. He grabbed and missed, then went down. When he came up, he was a little farther away, but the jacket was wet and made a better rope. Eyes filled with terror, he grabbed it.

We both hung on like bulldogs. I got him over to the edge of the bucket but couldn't get him in. I felt the bucket sink and move forward gently. Then both of us were inside, along with a ton of river water which poured out with a

huge, foamy splash. The fire department took over with some oxygen after we'd drained the river out of Jelly Bean.

■ Does this contraction stand for *we had* or *we would*?

Barney tossed my bike into his pickup truck and took me home, wet and shivering. "It was really something," he said to my dad. "Before I could scratch my head, your kid was in that bucket, ready to go. Quick thinking with the chips down tight."

I thought about my fantasies. They had seemed important to me, but probably would never happen. Yet something did happen, and it was real. As my dad said, you never know.

# Check the Skills

## Understanding the Selection

1.   Do you agree that Skip's quick thinking saved Jelly Bean's life? Why or why not? Did the situation require quick thinking? Why?

## Comprehension Skills Critical Reading

2.   Do you think the events in this selection could happen in real life? How did your own experience, and what you know about life, help you decide as you did? Is the selection realism?

## Vocabulary Development Skills Word Structure

3.   Look back at the last marginal note. Does *we'd* stand for *we had* or *we would*? How do you know?

# Selection 4

# Use the Skills

### Understanding the Selection

Anthony is a foster child. His mother is dead, and his father is away—somewhere. Anthony is living with Mr. and Mrs. Diamond and their daughter, Hildy. But he thinks the Diamonds don't want him to live with them any longer. So he has made up stories about going back to live with his father. Now Hildy is trying to find out about Anthony's father and when Anthony is leaving.

1.  Find out how talking with Hildy helps Anthony change his mind about his course of action. Decide if this situation requires careful planning.

2.  Think about why Anthony imagines his own funeral.

### Comprehension Skills Critical Reading

3.  Remember to read critically to decide whether this selection is realism or fantasy.

### Vocabulary Development Skills Word Structure

4.  Your skill with contractions may help you figure out a word or two.

# KEEPING IN TOUCH
# WITH REALITY

Mildred Ames

"I've been perishing[9] to talk to you," Hildy said.

"Perishing?"

"Yes—to find out what happened. Mom said I wasn't to bother you until you felt better. Is your headache gone?"

■ You should be able to figure out the contractions used throughout the conversation.

"Headache? Oh. Oh, I guess."

"Good. Then tell me all about your father."

Anthony crunched down on the celery. "Nothing to tell."

"Was it a secret mission?"

He scowled.[cg] "Yeah, big secret."

"You mean it wasn't? What's he been doing?"

"I can't talk about it."

Hildy chewed on the carrot and regarded him gravely. Finally she said, "You going to live with him?"

■ Could such a conversation take place in real life?

"In the fall."

"Oh," Her voice sounded solemn.[9]

"Yeah. You see, he's got a couple of terrific job possibilities lined up. By fall, everything will break. Then we'll get a house and a housekeeper and it'll be like old times." He concentrated on his plate and became very absorbed in his scrambled eggs.

"Did you ever have a housekeeper?"

"Well, no."

"Then how can it be like old times?"

Irritated, he said, "Well, it just can, that's all."

She was quiet for a moment. Then she said, "I'll miss you."

"You will?"

"Well, sure. I won't have anyone to talk to. And Mom will miss you. And Dad—I don't know what he'll do. He'll never go fly that stuff all by himself."

"It's not stuff—it's a Stuka."[9] With his fork, he piled his eggs into one big mound.

"All during supper that's all we talked about. Did your father have a job? Was he going to take you away? And nobody knowing what to think because you wouldn't tell. Dad's been climbing the walls. He wanted to come right upstairs when he got home, but Mom wouldn't let him."

"Really?" Without thinking, Anthony scooped up a mouthful of eggs and swallowed. They went down hard. "You know, you could always get another foster."

"Maybe. But it's hard to get used to somebody new."

"That's true." And it *was* true. He'd thought he would never get used to Hildy. Yet she didn't even look squinty to him any more. And right now she looked a little sad. She really would miss him. Both Hildy and Mom. And Mr. Diamond would never fly the Stuka again, never test his skill in radio-control.

■ This is Anthony's fantasy. Does this mean the entire selection is fantasy?

A deep rich sadness came over Anthony. He visualized[cg] himself dead, lying in a casket, the way he dimly remembered his mother. The Diamonds were leaning over, looking at his still face. Mrs. Diamond was saying, "They'll be glad to get a nice boy like Tony in heaven." Mr. Diamond was saying, "Nobody could bring in a plane for a three-point landing the way Tony could." Hildy was saying, "He really had a good sense of humor."

That was the way it had been with his mother—neighbors, friends, saying all the nice things they remembered about her. He wanted to say to Hildy now, "You'll get over it—you really will." At first you don't believe it at all. Every morning for a long time he'd kept thinking that his mother would be there in the kitchen when he came downstairs. Then one day he stopped thinking about it, stopped expecting it. The kitchen was no longer a room without his mother. It was only a room.

"When is he coming back?"

Anthony roused[cg] himself to stare at her for a moment. Then he said, "I don't think he's coming back."

"Ever?"

"Ever." The words had popped out of his mouth before he was aware he was even thinking them. Now that he'd said them, he was sure they were true. His dad would never come for him. He felt a big ache inside him, something he knew would be with him for a long time. Yet one day, he supposed, the kitchen would again be only a kitchen.

"I don't understand you," Hildy said. "You mean he's going to send someone else to get you in the fall?"

"No."

"Then how are you going to live with him?"

"I'm not."

"I *really* don't understand you. If you're not going to live with him, where *are* you going to live?"

"Here. As long as you all want me."

"Here? You mean it?"

Hildy helped herself to another carrot stick. "You know something? I'm really thrilled that you're staying."

And Hildy really did look thrilled. That made Anthony feel a little better.

# Check the Skills

## Understanding the Selection

1.  Do you think Anthony acted too quickly when he started to make plans to leave the Diamonds? Why do you think as you do? How did Hildy help Anthony change his course of action?

2.  Anthony imagines the Diamonds saying good things about him at his own funeral. Why do you think he does that? Do you think he really wants to die? Why or why not?

## Comprehension Skills Critical Reading

3.  Do you think this selection is an example of realism or fantasy? Why do you think so?

## Vocabulary Development Skills Word Structure

4.  Contractions are used in speech more than in writing. Do you think this is why there are many contractions in the conversation in this selection?

# Use the Skills

Professor Sherman made careful plans for a balloon trip that was to last a full year. Unfortunately, the trip met with disaster on the seventh day. As you read, you will find out that sometimes you cannot control things, no matter how well you plan.

Decide whether or not Professor Sherman acted in the only way possible. Think about whether the action will probably save his life. Try to figure out if this selection is an example of realism or fantasy. Your skill with contractions may help you with words you don't know.

# UNWELCOME PASSENGER

William Pène du Bois

I shall never forget the seventh day of this voyage of mine for as long as I live. Just about everything went wrong. My dreams of spending a year in a balloon were shattered. The first thing I noticed on the morning of that fateful day was a small speck far off on the horizon. It couldn't possibly be anything else but land. Land on my seventh day out. I had flown straight across the Pacific Ocean at a fabulous rate of speed! I had originally hoped that the winds would blow me first in one direction and then in another. I would spend at least a month without seeing any land, whether it be on the Asiatic side of the ocean or back on the American side. But there in the distance before me was a small speck which was slowly taking on the shape of a little volcanic island. Most of it was a mountain, with a column of smoke slowly rising from it into the blue sky.

Then, seemingly from out of nowhere, appeared sea gulls. They were the same sort of birds that had seen me off from San Francisco. Now they were forming a welcoming committee for an island I hadn't the slightest desire to visit.

At the sight of the gulls, I instantly dumped my garbage overboard. This I thought to be a fine idea. I was not only feeding the gulls but also rising up high enough to clear the island by a wide margin. I'd get away as far as possible from this unwelcome sight of land. However, it didn't work out quite the way I had hoped. The gulls plunged[cg] into the water after my food. One of them grabbed the remains of a carcass[cg] of smoked turkey I'd been living on for most of the week. The gull took it onto the very top of my balloon and settled down to devour[c] it in comfort. The other gulls, after having dived for all of the smaller pieces of food in the ocean, flew back up to where I was. They noticed their comrade[c] comfortably feasting on cold turkey on the top of my balloon. This instantly set off a loud symphony of cawing, and a big fight over the carcass started to shape up at once. This was all out of my reach. All I could do was pace around my small porch, praying that nothing would happen to my balloon. I leaned over the balustrade,[cg] looked up, and saw one lone sea gull gliding very slowly over the *Globe*. Its head was hanging down with that frightening look of a hawk studying his prey.[cg] This was horrible. The gull circled slowly around the balloon once, then dove. It plummeted[cg] straight for the turkey carcass. Whether it got it or not, I'll never know. There was loud and confused sea gull action on top of my balloon. It seemed to me they all flew away at once. Then I heard something ghastly. It was the sound of a sea gull beating his wings and cawing for breath inside the silken bag of my balloon.

On this seventh day of my trip, which was supposed to last a year, I found myself with a hole in my balloon the size of a sea gull.

I was heartbroken. It was impossible for me to get at the hole in order to attempt to mend it. The *Globe* had already begun to lose altitude.[cg] I had only one choice—to try to land on the island. I saw immediately that at the rate I was descending[c] I would be in the ocean long before I reached the island. I started throwing things overboard to make my basket house lighter. Then I would fly above water

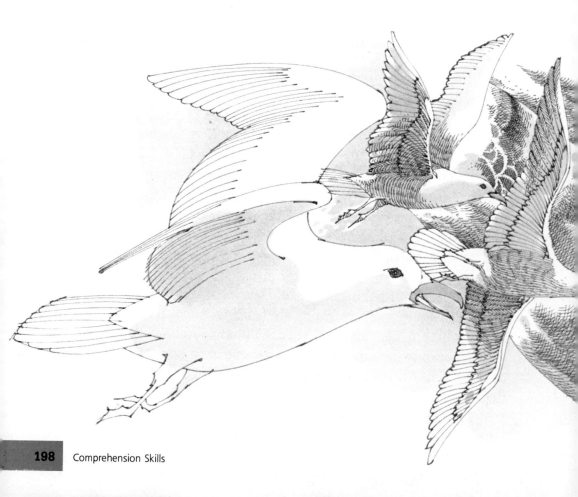

longer. I had no idea of the nature of the island I was approaching. So at first I decided to save all of my food in case I needed it to live on when I landed. I threw chairs, table, books, water-distilling[9] apparatus,[9] water cans, dishes, garbage containers, cups, saucers, charts, globes, coat hangers, clothes—everything noneatable. Clocks, scissors, towels, combs, brushes, soaps, everything I could lay my hands on I threw out through the doors, off the porch, out of the windows. The *Globe* continued to descend at a speed which was far too great if I were to make the island. I had to throw away my food. I threw all of the heavier canned goods first. This wasn't good enough. I threw the fruits, vegetables, smoked meats, everything in my house. I looked overboard. I was but a few hundred feet above water. The island was still over a mile off. Then I discovered something new and worse in the way of horrors. A school of sharks was following me in the water beneath and swallowing the food I threw as soon as it hit the water. This meant that I had to make the island or fall among the sharks. I was desperate.[c]

There was nothing left in the house to throw overboard. I emptied my pockets, saving only my pocket knife. I threw the clothes I was wearing next, all of them except my right shoe. I walked around the porch and, clinging to the window sills with my arms, I kicked the balustrade and uprights off the porch with my right foot. The balloon still had a half mile to go. There was only one thing left to do. I climbed up on the roof of my basket house, pulled the ladder up and threw that overboard. With my pocket knife, I cut four of the ropes which attached the house to the balloon—one from each corner—and tied them securely together. I looped my left arm through these ropes. I then grabbed my knife and slashed all of the other ropes supporting my house. My basket house fell and splashed among the sharks and the *Globe* gave a small leap upward. I dropped my pocket knife, kicked off my right shoe, and prayed.

A minute or two later, I felt my toes hit the water and I shut my eyes, afraid to look and see if any sharks were about. But my toes only skipped once or twice on the water's surface when I found myself being dragged across the beach of the island and the giant deflated[c9] bag of the *Globe* came to rest on top of a tall palm tree.

I was exhausted, burned by the sand, and too weak to crawl out of the sun into the shade. I must have gone to sleep on this beach.

# Check the Skills

### Understanding the Selection

1.   Do you think Professor Sherman's quick action probably saved his life? Why or why not?

### Comprehension Skills Critical Reading

2.   Do you think this selection is realism or fantasy? Why do you think as you do? If you wish to find out what happens to the professor, read the book by William Pène du Bois entitled *Twenty-one Balloons*, published by The Viking Press, New York, 1947.

### Vocabulary Development Skills Word Structure

3.   Did you have any difficulty with contractions as you read? If you did, how did you figure them out?

# Apply What You Learned in Unit 7

## The Theme

### Do Something!

1. In this unit you read about some people who found themselves in situations that required some kind of action. Esther Morris achieved the vote for women through her careful planning. The coyote changed his lot in life with his quick thinking. Skip saved Jelly Bean's life because of his quick action. The professor saved his own life. Anthony had to decide whether he really would leave the Diamonds' home. Do you think each of these characters chose the best course of action? Why or why not?

- Sometimes we must act quickly to correct a situation. Other times it is better to take the time to develop a careful plan. What kinds of situations require quick action? When should you plan your actions carefully?

# The Skills

## Comprehension Skills Critical Reading

2.  In this unit you learned that in fantasy the characters or situations are unbelievable and fantastic. In realism, they are believable and lifelike.

    Remember this as you read so that you will be able to distinguish between the two.

3.  Whatever you read, whether inside or outside of school, remember to read critically. Don't believe everything you read. Ask, "Could this really happen? Is this reasonable?" Rely on what you know of life, and on your own good sense, to decide whether what you are reading is realism or fantasy.

## Vocabulary Development Skills Word Structure

4.  You will come across contractions in much of your reading. Knowing how to figure out their meanings will help you be a better reader.

# Work and Play

## Overview and Purposes for Reading

### The Theme

**Work and Play**

1. What are some different kinds of work that people do? How do some people combine work and play?

### The Skills

**Comprehension Skills** Interpretive Reading

2. What can you do to make your reading more interesting?

3. How can you relate your reading to your own life?

**Study and Research Skills** Reading Techniques

4. Why is it important to understand your purpose for reading and to change your reading rate? How can you do this?

# Learn About the Skills

## Comprehension Skills Interpretive Reading

Perhaps you have read a story about someone your own age and thought, "I know exactly how that person feels." You remember being in a similar situation. You think about what you did and how you felt. You want to keep reading to find out what the character will do. When you do this, you are relating your reading to your own life and experience.

Reading becomes more exciting when you do this. You understand better what the author is trying to say. And you understand yourself better by relating to what you're reading.

Perhaps you have never had the same experiences as the character you are reading about. Or maybe you are reading about a topic you know nothing about. You can still add your own thoughts and feelings.

You may have to dig a little deeper to find something to relate to. The way something is said may bring someone or something to mind. Perhaps you saw a movie or read an article on the same subject. Maybe you know someone who knows about the topic or who is like the main character in the story.

For example, imagine you are reading an article on the pyramids. You have never been to Egypt or seen the pyramids. You certainly were not around at the time they were built. So you couldn't have known anybody who worked on them. But you have seen pictures.

You can see in your mind what's being talked about. You have most likely seen big buildings being constructed and know how much heavy equipment is used. Think about creating such a building without that equipment—mainly by hand. The pyramids are bigger than many modern buildings. Then imagine yourself on a work crew at a pyramid site. Could you work all day in the hot sun, straining to move the huge stones into place? You know how warm and tired you get when you work hard. All these thoughts will make the article more interesting to you, and the situation will seem very real.

Maybe you aren't reading something factual. Maybe you're reading a funny poem. It is funny to you because you are relating it to yourself or to what you know.

Regardless of what you read, you should be able to find something to relate to. Check the following suggestions.

---

**Relating Reading to Your Own Experience**

1. **Fiction, biography, autobiography.** Think about experiences and feelings that you have had that are similar to those of one or more of the characters.
2. **Informational materials.** Think about what you know about the subject. Remember what you have heard about it or seen on TV or in movies. Think about things you have done that might be similar in some way. Compare your thoughts and opinions to those of the writer.

---

As you read the selections in this unit, you will get more suggestions on how to relate your reading to your own experience.

# Study and Research Skills Reading Techniques

Do you read the newspaper comics at the same speed that you read your history textbook? Probably not. Good readers know how to adjust their reading rate to the type of material and their purpose for reading. If you're reading for entertainment, you may read quickly. But you should read somewhat difficult materials more slowly and carefully.

The following suggestions will help you decide what your rate, or speed, should be.

---

### Setting Purposes and Rate

1. **Fun or general interest.** You can read these materials quickly since you are reading for your own pleasure. You don't have to remember everything.

2. **Informational materials.** You may have to change your rate several times. Read quickly or skim to find what you need. Then slow your rate at the important sections.

3. **Directions and how-to articles.** Read through quickly the first time. Go back and read slowly by making certain you understand each step. Then read each step again as you follow the directions.

4. **Study materials.** Your rate should probably be slower than for most other kinds of materials. You will be trying to gain specific information and answer definite questions.

---

Whenever you read, think about why you are reading. Then decide what your reading rate should be. Change your rate when necessary while you are reading. You will get more practice as you read the selections in this unit.

# Use the Skills

### Understanding the Selection

Eva is a young Inuit, which is the proper name for Eskimo. She lives so far north that there are only a few hours of daylight in the winter months. It is so cold that the waves freeze as the water is whipped up on the shore by the wind. The ice keeps building. But the water underneath never freezes completely. When the tide goes out, there are caves underneath the ice. This is where Eva and her mother work, hunting for mussels to feed the family.

1.      Find out how Eva combines her work with play.

### Comprehension Skills Interpretive Reading

2.      Think about the first time you were allowed to do something by yourself that you enjoyed doing. Decide whether you felt the same as Eva does.

### Study and Research Skills Reading Techniques

3.      This selection is fiction. So your reading rate can be fairly quick. Just relax and enjoy the story.

# THE VERY LAST FIRST

Jan Andrews

Eva Padlyat lives in a village on Ungava Bay in the north of Quebec in Canada. She's Inuit,⁹ and for as long as she can remember, she's known how to walk on the bottom of the sea. It's something the people of her village often do, in winter, when they want mussels⁹ to eat. Today, though, something special is going to happen. Today, for the very first time in her life, Eva will walk on the bottom of the sea alone.

Eva and her mother stand in the small, warm kitchen of their home. They put on heavy parkas^c and go out. Then they pull their hoods close to protect their faces from the bitter cold of the wind and the sting of whipped-up snow. It is January, one of the worst months in the long, harsh Ungava winter.

Eva and her mother walk through the village. A hundred or so one-story wooden houses are nestled together at the head of a sheltering bay. Each pulls behind her a small sled loaded with a shovel, a long ice chisel,^cg and a pan for mussels. Snow lies white as far as the eye can see. There is snow, but no trees for miles and miles on the vast northern tundra.⁹ There are no highways, either. The village is off and away by itself. Snowmobile tracks leading away from it disappear into the distance.

■ Have you ever been out in the country when it snows? Then you have some idea of what Eva sees.

The street Eva and her mother are on takes them past the school and down to the seashore. They meet a few friends on the way and stop for a quick greeting. Then they go on to cross the snow-covered beach and step out onto the thick sea ice. They've come at just the right time. The tide has pulled back from the land, and there won't be any water near the shore. So they can go under the ice and wander about on the sea bed quite safely.

"Goodbye," Eva's mother says. "Be careful, and good luck."

Eva grins. "Good luck yourself," she replies.

Eva plods on over bumps and ridges where the cold has caught and frozen the waves once chased by the wind. She looks toward the open sea beyond the bay and sees only ice and more ice, on and on. Finally, she stops in what seems to be a good place, where the ice is raised and swollen. She shovels away a patch of snow. Then she works the sharp end of her chisel under a heaved-up crack in the ice to make a hole. It's hard, because the freeze-up came months ago, and the ice is very thick.

When the hole is about two feet square, Eva lowers herself into the darkness. She stands in the under-ice cavern[c]—proud and excited and alone. She lights a candle and watches the yellow light soften the blackness. The light glistens on the ice shining over her head and on the wet, black stones and pools and seaweed at her feet.

Then, for a moment, she's afraid. It's too dark to see far. She knows it can be dangerous down here. The under-ice world stretches far across the bay to where the sea tide is already beginning to lap back. She'll have to be careful. If she forgets how long she's been down, the tide could catch her. If she goes too far, she could lose her way back. Eva shivers, then laughs to herself.

"I'd better get to work," she says.

Eva carefully wedges[cg] her candle between two stones and starts collecting mussels. She has chosen her spot well. Her candle shows up strings of blue black mussel shells among the stones wherever she turns. Before long, her pan is full.

Eva goes back to the ice hole, sets her pan down, and listens for the sound of the waves. The tide is still quite a way out. There's plenty of time to do what she has always wanted to do. There is time to enjoy being by herself down here in the dark, mysterious, undersea winter world.

Eva sings a tune, quietly at first, then loudly, so the echoes of her singing bounce off the ice. She shouts to herself and is glad. She dances a little dance. She pokes in

rock pools, and makes strange shadows with her candle. She lifts up seaweed in long, flat ribbon strands, then lets them down with a flop.

At last Eva hears a voice. Her mother is calling through the ice hole. "Are you all right down there? Are you nearly done?"

Eva takes her candle, goes back to the hole, and picks up her mussel pan. "Of course I'm all right. I'm coming up now."

She climbs out into the fresh air and feels the cold wind on her face again.

"You've done well," her mother says. "You must have chosen a better place than I did."

They load up the sleds again, and Eva takes her mother's hand. Together they walk over the ice, across the beach,

through the village. Already, twilight has fallen. Daylight lasts only a very few hours this far north in January.

Eva glances back over her shoulder at the mussel shells. She thinks of popping them in boiling water, watching them open, tasting the salty fish in her mouth.

"That's my last very first time," she says sadly. "My very last very first time for walking alone under the sea."

Eva's mother laughs. "You really like it down there, don't you?"

"Yes," Eva answers. "Yes, I do." She thinks of the black, glistening ice and the faint humming of the tide far out to sea. She remembers being frightened when she first stood alone in the huge cavern and then dancing on the sea floor once her mussel pan was full. Eva looks back toward the bay, then up at her mother. "I like it down there. It's fun."

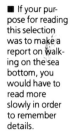

■ If your purpose for reading this selection was to make a report on walking on the sea bottom, you would have to read more slowly in order to remember details.

# Check the Skills

### Understanding the Selection

1.  How did Eva combine play with her work? Do you think she enjoyed the work she was doing? Why or why not?

### Comprehension Skills Interpretive Reading

2.  Can you remember a first time when you were allowed to do something important by yourself? Did you feel the same way Eva does? Could you picture what it was like under the ice?

### Study and Research Skills Reading Techniques

3.  Do you think your reading rate might have been different if this had been an informational article about the Inuit's life style in winter time? Why or why not?

# Selection 2

# Use the Skills

### Understanding the Selection

1.  Some people look at the stars for pleasure. But the Egyptians worked to figure out their pattern. Find out about that pattern as you read.

### Comprehension Skills Interpretive Reading

2.  As you read, think about your experiences with star-gazing.

### Study and Research Skills Reading Techniques

3.  This selection, although short, is technical. Your reading rate will probably be slower than for the first selection.

# LOOKING TOWARD
# THE EQUATOR

If you look directly south, you will see a different major constellation[9] each month. Earth's motion around the sun causes the constellations to appear to move in the same belt of space as do the planets in their orbits.[cg] This belt is called the zodiac.[c] The center line of the zodiac, called the ecliptic,[c] is the apparent path of the sun.

Ancient Egyptian astronomers divided this ecliptic to show the sun's location each day of the year. For convenience they settled on 360 divisions. This led to the division of circles into 360°. Since a different constellation appeared in each of the twelve 30° divisions of the ecliptic, ancient people used the constellations to count the passage of time.

■ You may have to read this slowly and more than one time to grasp what is being said.

■ Think about a pie cut into twelve pieces. Each piece represents a different month and a different constellation. If you were in the center, facing south, you would see Scorpio in August and Pisces in December.

## Check the Skills

### Understanding the Selection

1. How is the pattern that the Egyptians worked out still being used today?

### Comprehension Skills Interpretive Reading

2. Did you realize that the patterns of the stars are as predictable as they are? Did you know you could tell time by them? What have you thought about as you looked at the stars?

### Study and Research Skills Reading Techniques

3. Did you find your reading rate was slower for this selection than for the first selection? Why? Did you have to read any parts more than once?

# Use the Skills

### Understanding the Selection

1.  This article is about certain kinds of work. It gives informa-
    tion about careers in the field of conservation. As you read,
    decide whether such careers would be all work or whether
    there may be some play involved, too.

### Comprehension Skills Interpretive Reading

2.  You probably are not involved in a career in conservation.
    You may not even have thought of the possibility. However,
    you should have no trouble relating your own experiences to
    the information. Its content involves you every day. You drink
    water, breathe air, and use other natural resources. Think
    about it.

### Study and Research Skills Reading Techniques

3.  You may wish to skim this article first to find out about the
    type of information included. Look at the headings first.
    Then go back and read more carefully. Adjust your reading
    speed. You may need to read some parts more slowly than
    others.

# CONSERVATION CAREERS

Conservation[c] is the wise use and management of natural resources. These include the soil, the water, the forests and other plant life, the wildlife, the rich minerals, the very air we breathe.

We must understand these resources. We must know how they work together and how to use them. Otherwise, there is little hope for a healthy environment in the future.

The main job at the National Wildlife Federation is to make the public aware of the need for conservation. One way to do this is to help those who seek a career in conservation.

## What Are Typical Kinds of Conservation Jobs?

This depends on the field of your interest. A forester may direct land surveys, road construction, and the planting and harvesting of trees. Or he or she may be a specialist in protecting trees from insects, disease, and fire. The forester plans forest land uses and practices. The job includes working with people. It may require administering private forest preserves, public land, or lumber company property. There may be time spent in research or in teaching forestry. Just in the category of forestry, you can see how many different kinds of work there are.

■ Have you ever seen a TV news report about fire fighters trying to put out a forest fire? Or a documentary about planning and maintaining forests?

For another example, take the vocational[cg] category called *environmentalist*. Careers related to the environment are found in government (local, state, or federal), private industry, and educational and research institutions.

■ What are the areas of concern of an environmentalist? Think about what you know of the world around you.

**The federal government** is busy setting and enforcing pollution standards, such as those for air and water quality. It is researching the causes, effects, and control of environmental problems. It assists state and local governments. It funds research. It develops and demonstrates new pollution control techniques. Its activities require the services of many highly educated specialists. There is room also for workers with less education: laboratory or instrument technicians, repair and maintenance people, computer specialists.

**Local and state governments** need workers in many areas. Some of these are air pollution control, urban planning, and food protection.

**Private industry** is using more and more pollution control specialists. It needs people who understand how to develop and market equipment to clean air and water or systems to make useful materials from waste.

**Educational and research institutions** need scientists, engineers, and teachers of environmental subjects.

To list all of the subject areas in which you might make a conservation career would require a book.

## How Much Education Is Necessary?

■ If your main purpose for reading was to find out what courses to take in college, you would read this part slowly.

Jobs in conservation are like those in many fields. As a minimum, the professional needs a four-year college degree. A forester, for example, has a bachelor's degree at the least.

Many conservation problems relate both to the natural sciences and to people. Therefore, someone interested in a career in conservation also takes courses such as English and history. A good scientific background and an ability to communicate with people are both necessary.

Degrees are now available from many colleges in such specific areas as conservation, ecology, range science, environmental science, and environmental communications.

But suppose you don't want to spend four years in college. Does that close the door on a conservation career? Not at all. In the field of forestry, not all the work is done by the college-educated forester. A large supporting staff of technicians, aides, skilled workers, clerks, and laborers is needed. For instance, technicians might lead road crews or survey parties. Forestry aides might serve as smoke-jumpers,[9] recreation guards, and so on. Such jobs as carpenter or mechanic require skilled workers who need not have been to college. The same is true of employees who plant trees and work on roads.

For these jobs you could get the education you need in one or two years of college. Then you would get the rest of the knowledge necessary through practical experience.

A suggestion: summer work in a forest, park, or urban planning office is a good way to gain experience, or to find out if you really want a career in conservation. Summer employment of this type, however, is hard to find. Applications should be made well in advance.

# Check the Skills

## Understanding the Selection

1.  Do you think a career in conservation could be both work and play? Why do you think as you do?

## Comprehension Skills Interpretive Reading

2.  Were you able to relate your own experiences—thoughts, feelings, ideas—to the information? In what ways did you do this? Did it help you understand the article better?

## Study and Research Skills Reading Techniques

3.  Look back at the marginal note on page 218. If this was the information you were looking for, would you read the entire article from start to finish? Why or why not? How did your reading rate on this article compare with your rate on the first two selections?

# Use the Skills

### Understanding the Selection

1.   Some people play baseball as their work. This is true of all professional sports players. Think what it must be like to play a game as your work.

### Comprehension Skills Interpretive Reading

2.   Have you ever played baseball? If so, you may be familiar with the frustration and the humor described in this selection. Even if you haven't played baseball, your imagination can help you enjoy this selection.

### Study and Research Skills Reading Techniques

3.   This article provides information, but it is also fun to read. You will have to decide what your reading rate should be.

# BAD-HOP GROUNDERS

Howard Liss

A ground ball that takes a bad hop is an infielder's nightmare. In the 1960 World Series, Tony Kubek of the New York Yankees was hit in the throat by a bad–hop grounder. An important run scored, and Kubek had to leave the game.

But bad–hop grounders aren't always so serious. In September of 1948, the Boston Red Sox were at bat against the Philadelphia Athletics. They had Ted Williams on third and Billy Goodman at bat. Goodman hit a sharp, twisting grounder toward Philadelphia shortstop Eddie Joost.

Joost got in front of the ball, but he couldn't handle it. It hit his glove, ran up his arm, and disappeared into the sleeve of his shirt. Joost dropped his glove and began to search all over for the ball. It was under his shirt!

■ Have you ever had this kind of experience?

He started to unbutton the shirt, but that was too slow. Finally he pulled his shirttail out of his pants. The ball dropped out and rolled away.

Goodman reached first and then stood on the bag, grinning. Williams could have scored easily. But he was still standing on third base, laughing too hard to run.

■ What reading rate did you use to read this selection?

## Check the Skills

### Understanding the Selection

1. Do you think professional baseball players play at the game as well as work at it? Why or why not?

### Comprehension Skills Interpretive Reading

2. Have you ever had an experience like Joost's? What happened? How did you feel? How do you think Joost felt?

### Study and Research Skills Reading Techniques

3. What reading rate did you use for this selection? Why?

# Selection 5

# Use the Skills

Ben Franklin was a remarkable man. He was always busy and had many different interests. He lived to the age of 84, which was very old indeed for the 1700s. In this selection you will find out about some of the things Ben Franklin worked at. As you read, think about the type of person Ben Franklin was. Decide whether he had fun at his work.

Remember to relate your own experiences, thoughts, and ideas to what you read to make it more interesting to you. Think about your reading rate and adjust it to suit the material.

You're on your own this time. There are no marginal notes.

# BENJAMIN FRANKLIN

Nancy Garber

When Ben Franklin was a young boy, he lived with his father and mother and thirteen brothers and sisters in a small house in Boston. Even in a house as full of children as that one was, Ben found a corner for himself. He sat copying articles out of the *Spectator*, a paper from London full of ideas. He loved ideas, and he wanted to know about everything new.

By the time he was fifteen he had been working in his brother James's printshop for three years. He wanted to write articles for the *New England Courant*, the paper they printed. But James said he was too young. So after everyone else had fallen asleep, Ben wrote a letter by candlelight. He signed it with the name of an imaginary woman, "Silence Dogood." It was funny and full of good ideas about what was right and wrong with life in Boston. He slipped it under the door of the printing house in the morning. James printed it in the paper, and all the readers enjoyed it.

People liked it so much that Ben wrote thirteen more Silence Dogood letters. He finally ran out of ideas and confessed that he had written the letters. This added to the already strained relationship between Ben and James. So it was not long before young Ben, then seventeen, got into a sloop⁣ᶜ for New York. Then he walked 50 miles, took another boat, and finally landed in Philadelphia. He had only a few coins in his pocket. But he found work with a printer, since he already knew that trade.

By the time he was twenty-two, he had saved and borrowed enough money to open his own printshop. His paper was called *The Pennsylvania Gazette*.

For the next twenty years he worked six or seven days a week at the *Gazette*. He wanted to pay off his debts as soon as possible. He didn't like to owe money.

Most people at that time had only two printed things in their houses: the Bible and an almanac. The almanac told them about holidays, the weather, and important dates to remember. Ben decided to print his own, which he called *Poor Richard's Almanack*. He put in little sayings about working hard and saving money, and how to get over being poor, as he had been.

Ben Franklin said he didn't make up these sayings. He said he learned them from other ages and nations. He was able to read books from other countries because he had taught himself to understand five languages: French, Spanish, German, Italian, and Latin.

As soon as he started to make some money on his printshop and his paper and his almanac, he gave money to other young people who wanted to start printshops of their own. He also started the first volunteer fire department, the first public library, the first street cleaning department, the first fire insurance company, and the University of Pennsylvania. He was postmaster of Philadelphia and later of all the colonies. He experimented in many different sciences.

Almost everyone knows that Ben Franklin experimented a lot with electricity and invented the lightning rod. He also invented the Franklin stove and bifocals and new kinds of printing presses. But swim fins? Yes, swim fins. Ben was a great swimmer. He made little paddles he could wear on his hands and feet to make himself go faster.

Some of Franklin's inventions—spectacles, the Franklin stove, and an "early electrical machine."

He could have become rich by selling his inventions, but he said that ideas should belong to everyone.

The people sent him to London as the agent for Pennsylvania, New Jersey, Massachusetts, and Georgia. He stayed there for years, working for the colonies.

When he came home again, the American Revolution was starting. He was sixty-nine. It was time for the young men to take over. But they could not let old Ben rest.

Ben Franklin was the only person who signed four of America's first great papers: The Declaration of Independence, the treaty with France, the peace treaty with England, and the Constitution of the United States.

When he was seventy-nine he came home again, after nine years as America's representative in France. And at eighty he became president (governor) of Pennsylvania. Then he wrote his autobiography. People are still reading this great book today for all the funny and important things it says about life and living. The last paper he wrote was against slavery.

# Check the Skills

### Understanding the Selection

1.  Do you think Ben Franklin mixed work and play? Why do you think as you do?

### Comprehension Skills Interpretive Reading

2.  Were you able to find something in this article that related to your own experience? If so, what was it? What kind of person do you think Ben Franklin was? Have you ever known anyone like him?

### Study and Research Skills Reading Techniques

3.  Did you read this selection quickly or slowly or at different rates? How did you choose the rate you did?

# Apply What You Learned in Unit 8

## The Theme

### Work and Play

1. In this unit you learned how some people combined work and play. Doing so made the work seem less like drudgery and more like fun. Do you think most people combine play with their work? Why do you think as you do?

• Can you think of ways that people could make their jobs more fun and still get the work done? Do you think it is important for people to have fun at what they do? Why or why not?

• Do you think most people enjoy the work they do? Why or why not? Is all work fun? Why do you think as you do?

# The Skills

## Comprehension Skills Interpretive Reading

2.  In this unit you learned one way to make your reading more interesting. Trying this is especially important when you think you don't particularly like the material. If you make an effort to find something that you can relate to, you will find that the reading goes more quickly. Try it the next time you have a reading assignment in one of your subjects. You may find that a subject that didn't interest you before has something to offer. Your reading will be easier and you may even like the material!

3.  You learned several ways to relate to your reading. Whatever method you choose, you will find that all your reading will be more interesting if you relate it to your own experience.

## Study and Research Skills Reading Techniques

4.  You learned that good readers adjust their reading rate according to their purpose for reading and to the type of material. You will save yourself a lot of time if you do this. You won't make the mistake of reading an entire article when you could find what you want by skimming. And you won't read important materials too quickly and find that you have missed something and must go back and reread.

# Apply the
# Comprehension Skills
## You Have Learned

**Apply the Skills As You Do Your Schoolwork**

You will find the comprehension skills you have learned in this section will be helpful when you read material assigned in school. You will see that this is true as you read the selection on the next page. It was taken from a textbook used in many language arts classes. It offers some helpful hints on study habits.

As you read, put to use what you've learned about comprehension skills. Keep the following questions in mind as you read. After you finish, answer the questions.

1.  **Main idea.** What is the main idea in each of the five paragraphs? What is the main idea of the entire selection?

2.  **Classification.** What things can be classified under the label "distractions"? What items can be classified under the label "supplies"?

3.  **Fantasy and realism.** The difference between realism and fantasy does not apply here because this is not fiction.

4.  **Relating to previous experience.** Most likely you have a special place at home for studying. How does it compare to the place described here? Can you think of any other supplies you might need for studying? What are they?

# Getting Ready To Study

Your study place should have no distractions. A distraction is anything that takes your mind away from what you are doing. A television program, a telephone call from a friend, or a playful dog can all be distractions.

Distractions for some people are not always distractions for others. Some people find radio music distracting. Others think it helps to drown out noises. Some people find that being near a refrigerator is distracting. They keep wanting to get snacks. Others are not interested in food.

Think about what might take your mind away from studying. Then choose a study place away from these distractions.

When you have decided on a place, you will need to put all your supplies there. Then you won't have to waste time looking for things you need.

Your basic supplies will include: paper, sharpened pencils, one or more pens, an eraser, and useful books such as a dictionary. Get into the habit of keeping your school books in your study place, too. In that way, you will have them there when you are ready to use them.

## Apply the Skills As You Deal with the World

You'll find these comprehension skills useful when you read material outside of school, too. On the next page is the beginning of a story from a popular magazine. It is about two boys who live in Kenya, in eastern Africa. Kilimanjaro, the highest mountain in Africa, is nearby. See how the skills work here by thinking about the following questions as you read. Answer them afterward.

1. **Main idea.** What is the main idea of each paragraph?

2. **Classification.** The story begins with things the boy saw when he woke up. Which are the sentences in the opening paragraph that can be classified as the things he saw?

3. **Fantasy and realism.** Is this story an example of realism or of fantasy? How do you know?

4. **Relating to previous experience.** Have you ever felt, like the boy in this story, that "it was going to be a good day"? Do you think that growing up in Kenya may be similar in many ways to growing up here? Where could you find out more about Kenya?

# The Honey Guide

William Riziki Riwa

The clear view of Mount Kilimanjaro was fading away with the smoky clouds of early morning when I woke up. After a long dry spell, it had rained heavily all night. Everything outside looked wonderfully healthy. Banana and coffee trees and yams all looked as though they were dancing with joy for the rain that had fallen. I had had nothing to eat the night before because the rain had come just as we went out to get firewood. All the wood was wet and would not burn, so nothing was cooked. Even so I felt strong—like the green plants. I wondered if I might be a plant, too, and draw strength from the soil. But I decided that I did not envy the plants. They could not move. It was better to be a boy.

Semali, my friend and neighbor, came running across the ridges. He ran like a gazelle. "Oh, friend," he shouted. "Let's go now! My mother is cooking bananas and maize. Come and have breakfast with me."

It was going to be a good day for us. We did not often get a good breakfast—especially not from Semali's mother. Her husband had left her a shop and a big coffee farm. But even though she was wealthy, she was very stingy—especially with food. She used to hide her food when I came to visit, so that she would not have to offer me anything to eat. One time she hid a pot of boiling food under her bed. I saw the clouds of steam and asked her what it was, but she did not reply. Just then a cat crawled out from under the bed, carrying a big piece of meat. The cat kept dropping the meat because it was very hot. Semali's mother got so mad that she threw a piece of firewood at the cat. Semali and I ran outside before she could throw firewood at us, too. So it was a very good day when she could overcome her stinginess and give us a good breakfast.

# Section 3 Study and Research Skills

# Patterns

## Overview and Purposes for Reading

### The Theme

**Patterns**

1. A pattern is something that happens over and over again in the same way. There is a pattern to your days at school. The day begins and ends at a certain time, and you have a certain number of classes each morning and each afternoon. What other kinds of patterns are there?

### The Skills

**Study and Research Skills** Study Techniques

2. How can study plans help you with your school work?

3. What steps should you follow to make a study plan?

**Comprehension Skills** Implied Meaning

4. When you are reading, why should you note only the details that relate to what you need to know? How can you learn to identify them?

# Learn About the Skills

## Study and Research Skills Study Techniques

Do you sometimes have trouble getting your homework done? Or do you sometimes feel that you are spending too much time studying? If so, you need a study plan to help organize your work.

---

### Making a Study Plan

1. Know exactly what your teacher wants you to find out or do.
2. Determine what you need to read or write or do to complete the assignment.
3. Decide where you can get the necessary information. Will you need to use your textbook? Will you need to look something up in an encyclopedia or some other reference source?
4. Figure out how much time you need.
5. Be sure you know when the assignment is due.

---

**Try the Skill.** Let's see how a study plan works. Suppose your social studies teacher wrote this assignment on the board:

> A week from today, hand in a five-page written report on one of the tribes of Native Americans who lived in the northwestern United States in the 1850s.

The first step is to make sure you understand the assignment. Look again at the directions for the report. They tell you when the report should be done, how long it should be, and what to write about. You would waste time if you wrote more than five pages or if you wrote about Native Americans of today.

Next, think about what you need to do to complete the report. You will need to do research. This means you will find and read material about the tribe you choose. You will take notes on your reading and organize them. After that, you'll write your report.

Your third step is to decide where to find the information you need. Your social studies textbook may give you some information about Native Americans of the Northwest. But you'll need to visit the library and find other reference sources, too.

When you know what needs to be done, decide how much time it will take. How long will your research take? How much time will you need for writing the report?

Finally, think about when the report is due. Decide what to do to make sure it's completed on time. You may want to set up a time schedule with a specific time for completing the research and the writing. Set up your schedule so that you will be able to get all the work done in one week. For example, you might allow two days to find information and take notes on it, and one day to organize them. Then you would have two days left for writing and revising your report.

Start making a study plan for each of your assignments. With a study plan, you will know just what to do and when to do it. Stick to the schedule you set up. You'll get your homework done on time, and you'll spend less time doing it.

You will get more ideas about how to make study plans as you read this unit.

## Comprehension Skills Implied Meaning

People usually have a purpose for reading, especially when reading nonfiction. They may want to find out how to grow flowers, or when the Civil War began. But no matter what the subject, good readers concentrate on finding information that fits their purpose for reading.

Suppose you want to know the length and weight of a fully grown blue whale. Try to pick out that information as you read the following paragraph.

> The blue whale is the largest creature that has ever lived. At birth, the blue whale is almost 25 feet long. It grows to a length of 50 feet by the time it is seven months old. The blue whale often lives 50 years, but it stops growing when it is about 12 years old. A fully grown blue whale is about 100 feet long and weighs about 150 tons.

The last sentence in the paragraph gives you the information you need. The other details are interesting but you don't need to know them.

Now suppose you want to know how long a blue whale lives. Look back at the paragraph to find the information you want. You'll need different facts than you needed before. The figure you are looking for is in the fourth sentence. It's 50 years.

Learn to pick out the details that fit your purpose for reading. Don't be confused or sidetracked by other information that does not relate to that purpose.

You'll use this skill as you go through this unit.

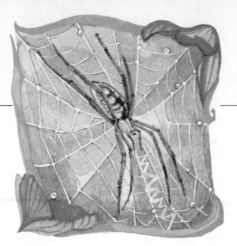

# Use the Skills

### Understanding the Selection

1.  Read this selection to find out about some patterns of behavior in nature.

2.  Does the weather influence certain patterns of action? What patterns do you follow when the weather is very cold? very hot? very wet or windy?

### Study and Research Skills Study Techniques

3.  Imagine that you have one hour to write a short report on how insects are affected by humidity and weather. You will use this selection as your only source of information. Think of a study plan. Decide what you need to do to complete the report. Marginal notes will help you.

### Comprehension Skills Implied Meaning

4.  Remember that your purpose is to write a report about insects. Marginal notes will help you decide which details would be important.

# WEATHER WISDOM

Helen R. Sattler

A long time ago, when people lived mostly out-of-doors, they were close to nature. They noticed that <u>plants, mammals, insects, and birds sensed the coming of a storm sooner than people did.</u> All living things have a natural instinct[g] to save their own lives and so they look for shelter just before a storm. When ancient[c] people saw animals seeking shelter, they did, too.

■ You would probably include the underlined information in your notes for the report.

Weather affects living things in special ways, and their reactions give clues to weather changes. The people of long ago called these clues "weather signs." Those who knew how to read the signs were often just as correct in their predictions[c] as modern meteorologists,[c] the scientists who study weather and collect weather information.

Meteorologists tell us that during fair weather, the air usually contains very little moisture. But just before a rain, the air becomes damp, or humid.[c] Humidity[c] is the amount of moisture (water vapor) in the air.

Today meteorologists use special instruments to measure humidity. In earlier times, people used nature to tell them when it was humid. For example, they often watched spiders in their webs.

Usually, spiders spin their webs between 6 and 7 P.M. During calm, clear weather they don't bother to make large webs. <u>But when there is high humidity and a drop in air pressure, spiders work overtime building more and larger nets.</u> Somehow they seem to know that insects will be easier to catch when the humidity is high. <u>The moisture in the air soaks the insects' wings. This makes it difficult for them to fly.</u>

■ More information suitable for your report is underlined in the next several paragraphs.

However, since a heavy rain would ruin a spider's web and wash away the bugs caught in it, spiders will take down their nets before a storm. An old saying warns:

> When spiders take in their net,
> The ground will soon be wet.

Some people watch ants for weather clues. Anytime you see ants building huge mounds around their holes, prepare for rain. About two hours before a downpour, all kinds of ants—but especially large black or red ants—will break up their caravans,[9] scurry[9] into their nests, and begin building dams around the ant hill. These mounds, which are sometimes several inches high, prevent rainwater from running into the ant hills. The ants will stay inside until the rain is over. An old saying goes:

> When ants build high,
> Rain will fall from the sky.

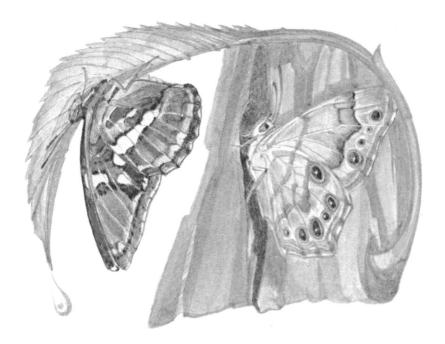

Bees give weather clues, too. They are unusually active several hours before a rain. As the air becomes more humid, they return to their hives. When that happens, you can expect a rain in about two hours. Some American Indians say that the longer the bees' increased activity lasts, the longer the rain will be.

Other insects are also good humidity indicators.[c] Butterflies usually flit from flower to flower all day long. When they suddenly disappear and hide on tree trunks or on the undersides of leaves, they are seeking shelter to protect their fragile wings from a hard rain.

Fireflies fly very low when there is high humidity. But an old saying states:

> When fireflies are about in large numbers,
> The weather will be fair for the next three days.

And if you hear lots of locusts singing, you can be sure the air is dry, because locusts sing only when it is hot and dry. No wonder Benjamin Franklin said, "One little bug knows more about rain than all the almanacs.[9]"

Plants are also handy humidity indicators. They are affected in different ways. Just before a rain, many flowers—like the daisy, morning-glory, dandelion, and tulip—close their blossoms. Clover plants draw their leaves together. Pine cones open in dry weather and close when it is humid.

Many things in and around your home also absorb moisture from humid air. Almost everyone is familiar with lumpy table salt that sticks together and will not shake out. If the air is very damp, there may be drops of water on the salt shaker's lid. Some things just feel damp when they absorb moisture. Others, like the wood in windows and dresser drawers, swell. Absorbed moisture makes them fit tighter so that they are hard to open or close.

Almost everyone knows what humidity does to hair.

Curly hair gets curlier and straight hair gets limp. The reason is that hair absorbs moisture from damp air. Straight hair actually gets longer.

People who have arthritis are often very sensitive to humidity. High humidity causes the fluid in their tissues and joints to increase, making movement difficult and painful. That is why many older people say, "It's going to rain. I can feel it in my bones." They actually can.

By learning to read weather signs, you can get a few hours advance warning if a storm is headed your way. It might keep you from getting your new shoes ruined in the rain or from having a family picnic spoiled or your garden beaten down by a storm. If you are backpacking, camping, boating, or taking part in another outdoor activity, it might even save your life.

# Check the Skills

### Understanding the Selection

1. What are some of the patterns in nature that can let you know a storm is coming? Can you remember some different kinds of examples, involving insects, plants, ordinary household items, or even people?

2. Do you wear more and warmer clothing when it is cold? Do you stay indoors more often? What do you do when it is hot? Do your eating patterns change then? What about when it is rainy?

### Study and Research Skills Study Techniques

3. How long do you think you will need to take notes, organize them, and write the report on insects from this article? Could you get it done in an hour? Why or why not?

### Comprehension Skills Implied Meaning

4. Why would you *not* include the details indicated by the last two marginal notes?

# Selection 2

## Use the Skills

### Understanding the Selection

Here is part of an interview with the famous Olympic ice skater, Tai Babilonia. Tai is a pair skater. That means she skates with a partner. Tai's partner is Randy Gardner.

1.  As you read, think about the patterns Tai followed at the time of the interview. When did she skate? When did she study? How do these patterns differ from the ones you follow?

2.  Decide if there are patterns to the skating Tai and Randy do.

### Study and Research Skills  Study Techniques

3.  Suppose your assignment, due a week from today, is to write a two-page report about recent United States Olympic figure skaters. Think through a study plan for this report. What sources besides this selection would you need for your research? How long do you think your research would take? How long would you guess writing the report would take?

### Comprehension Skills  Implied Meaning

4.  Suppose you were reading this article to find out how Tai started skating. What information would be important?

# TAI BABILONIA

Karen Folger Jacobs

At 9:00 A.M. the refreshingly cool ice skating rink seems like an empty amusement park. The skate shop and food concessions[cg] are locked up. Only the candy machines and the ice are lit up.

At first glance, I recognize Tai Babilonia. Her total concentration draws my eyes. She appears completely alone on the rink. Deliberately, carefully, she stares into the ice as she slowly makes circles with her skates. Her movements are hypnotic.[g]

Tai skates over to where I'm standing at the rail. She whispers, "Now it's time for freestyle.[g] I'm working on a jump. I used to have it, but now I'm having some problems with it, so don't be surprised if I fall."

Off she skates. I can tell by Tai's speed and expression that she is ready to practice the jump. In an open space she takes off, sailing, spinning through the air, and lands on her rear. She slides across the ice until her back slams into the guard rail.

She stands up immediately, brushes off loose ice, and begins skating again, looking even more determined. She circles the rink twice, weaving[cg] between slower skaters and increasing her speed. Again she springs into the air, whirling faster, and lands—on her knees. She tries twice more and falls both times. Then she's up again, standing still and rehearsing the jump in her mind.

Tai's coach, Mr. Nicks, walks over to her, his fingers gesturing[cg] a spin and his legs bending to indicate the footwork. With his hands on his hips, he nods and signals for her to start again. Another coach begins filming Tai with a video[g] camera. She takes off and skates faster than ever, leaning into her turns past the camera and heading toward the place Mr. Nicks has indicated with his hand. At that spot Tai leaps way out, twists in the air, and spins high. This

■ The title of the selection tells you that it is about only one United States figure skater. So you know you'll need to use other sources for a report on United States figure skaters.

■ Further research will probably tell you that all skaters need the determination and hard work that Tai shows here. However, until you do that research, you cannot know that the details this selection gives about Tai also apply to others.

time she lands skatefirst. But a split second later she has fallen again.✓

Tai skates to me, and I ask her, "Have you ever been seriously injured?"

"It depends on what you call serious. One time I frac-tured⁹ my tailbone. Once I was spiked by another skater. Last year my four front teeth were knocked out when Randy dropped me on my face. They rushed me and the four teeth to the dentist, and he rerooted them. He said that if I hadn't been wearing braces, more teeth would have been knocked out, and I probably would have had to wear false teeth. Plastic teeth when you're fourteen?

"A few days after the accident, we had to skate in the world championships. I was afraid I wouldn't skate well— not because of the pain, but from the fear of falling. But we took tenth place, the top Americans. In 1979 we took third.

"Oh, I've got to go back onto the ice!"

While Tai is on the ice, I talk with Mabel Fairbanks, one of her former coaches.

"Tai works," she says. "Were you here when she was trying to iron out a jump? It may take a week or two, but Tai will get it perfect. Mr. Nicks had it videotaped,⁹ so tomorrow they'll go over the tapes before she works it on the ice."

Now out on the ice Tai and Randy glide, threading them-selves through slower skaters. Hand in hand—facing for-ward, backward, or one in each direction with their free hands extended—they look like soaring eagles.

Each time they reach an open patch of ice, he lifts or throws her. What amazes me is the delicacy⁹ of Tai's land-ing. After being thrown, she lands as if she's tiptoeing— gracefully continuing her airborne motion. Or, she touches down in reverse, skates backward in an arabesque,⁹ and then holds the pose. The skating gets faster, the lifts longer, and the jumps higher. It looks like ballet on ice.

After the practice is over, Tai looks totally different. She's wearing jeans and a T-shirt. Her hair is out of a bun and hangs to her waist in a thick braid.

I ask her, "How will you spend the rest of the day, Tai?"

"I've got to go to summer school to make up for the months I took off for the Olympics and the world championships. I go to a special school. Almost all the students at my private school skate at this rink. California requires students to be in school for at least four hours a day, so we're there from two to six."

As we walk, Tai suddenly blurts[cg] out, "Oh, this morning I forgot to tell you one thing about skating—how much I love traveling. We go places to skate, and we get some days off after the competition. You can learn a lot by meeting people from different countries and becoming friends with them."

■ Here's the section that gives the only details you would read if your purpose was to find out how Tai started skating.

"How did you get into skating?" is my next question.

"By accident. When I was five, I went to a birthday party at a skating rink with my godfather. He's Japanese. He's the one who named me. In Japanese, tai[c] means "lovely" or "tranquil."[g]

"At the party, I tried to skate. And I just loved it, right from the first time. I kept asking to go back. Finally my mother took my brother and me to the rink. Then I wanted skates and lessons . . . ."

"How long will you keep skating?" I ask.

"Randy and I made a commitment[cg] to each other. We'll skate together through the 1980 Winter Olympics in Lake Placid, New York. After that, I really can't say. It depends

on so many things and on how we both feel then. Maybe I'll eventually join an ice show. And someday, I'll probably teach skating. But right now, we're training so hard for 1980 that it's all we think about. The most important thing to be said is that skating is a lot of work. And I like work. The better I get at skating, the more I love it."

# Check the Skills

### Understanding the Selection

1.  When did Tai skate and study? What is your pattern of hours in school and hours out of school? What do you do with your out-of-school time?

2.  Are there patterns to the skating routines Tai and Randy do? In the 1980 Olympics, Tai and Randy could not compete because Randy was injured just before they were supposed to skate. How do you suppose this terrible disappointment changed the pattern Tai and Randy expected to follow?

### Study and Research Skills Study Techniques

3.  Your study plan for a report on Olympic figure skaters should include plans to visit the library for information. There have been many such skaters. For this reason, for your two-page report, you should limit yourself to a few skaters from one or two Olympics. An encyclopedia could be a good source. It should take about an hour to find and take notes. You may need another two hours to organize and write your report. Could you do this work in one day?

### Comprehension Skills Implied Meaning

4.  If you only wanted to find out how Tai started skating, would you pay close attention to the description of how she practiced the jump? Why or why not?

# Selection 3

# Use the Skills

## Understanding the Selection

A computer is a machine that works with numbers. It follows patterns, doing the same job over and over. Its job may be to add up food bills at a supermarket or count passengers on an airplane.

1.  Read this article to find out something about how a computer works.

## Study and Research Skills Study Techniques

2.  Suppose your teacher says, "For tomorrow, read the selection on computers on pages 251–254. At the start of class tomorrow, we will have a short test on the most important points in the article." What would you include in your study plan to prepare for this quiz? Marginal notes will help you.

## Comprehension Skills Implied Meaning

3.  Use your skill at picking out information that fits your purpose for reading. As you read, find answers to these questions.

    a. What are the three parts of a computer system?
    b. What does a programmer do?

# MEET THE COMPUTER

Bruce Lewis

A computer is an electronic<sup>c</sup> machine that works with numbers. It is run by electricity and filled with wires, connectors, switches, and electronic devices that it uses to add, subtract, multiply, and divide. It does this so quickly that each step may take as little as a billionth of a second! But a computer is still just a machine—and usually a rather modest-looking one at that. There are computer systems that fill whole rooms. There are computers that are no bigger than a desk. Many are even smaller.

■ Here is a definition of a computer. This is important to know for your test.

Electronic machines are all around us. A television set, a transistor radio, and an amplifier in a record player are some different kinds of electronic machines. But while these machines and a computer may use the same kinds of parts, a computer does its job in a different way. It has more in common with two machines that are not electronic at all—a washing machine and a dishwasher.

■ This sentence, and the paragraph that follows, explain quite simply how a computer works. Do you think you should know this for your test? Watch for other important points as you read.

Both a washing machine and a dishwasher do a certain kind of job in a certain sequence.<sup>c</sup> First, you load them with something to work on—clothes or dishes. Next, you tell them what to do. You set the timer or push the buttons for the kind of wash you want. Then you start them up, and they follow your instructions one at a time—wash, rinse, spin, and so on. They are mechanical servants that follow your orders and work for you.

A computer is an electronic servant. Like the washing machine and the dishwasher, the computer must be given something to work on. It will follow instructions and solve problems—but only if people tell it what to do. Of course, a computer does not work with clothes or dishes. It works with numbers.

To understand the way a computer works with numbers, think of a light bulb with a switch to turn it on or off. Now if you make a rule that the light bulb stands for the number *one* only when it is on, and that it stands for nothing, or *zero*, when it is off, you will have a kind of electrical counter. You can switch it on for *one* and off for *zero*.

This is the way computers use electricity to stand for numbers. But instead of light bulbs, computers today use electronic parts that can be switched on and off.

Inside a computer there can be many thousands of these tiny electronic counters. Because the counters are like switches, they stay the way they are set until the computer is instructed to change them. Setting them to stand for a number is like putting the number away until it is needed. For this reason, the number is said to be put in *storage*.[c]

Other parts of the computer are used to *process*[c] the numbers—to add them, subtract them, multiply, or divide them. Processing means moving the numbers around in storage so that the computer can work with them and solve problems.

The control panel, or *operator's console*,[c] is an important part of the computer, too. It is usually on the front of the machine, where you find the buttons and dials and flashing lights. The operator uses it to find out, and control, what is going on inside the computer.

■ These are the details related to the question about the three parts of a computer system.

In any computer that solves problems for people, there are three different jobs being done—input,[c] processing,[c] and output[c]—the three parts of a computer system. If we want the computer to process numbers for us, we must have a way to put the numbers into the computer. And we must have a way to get the computer's answers out when it is finished processing them. These things are done with input and output machines.

Input machines change our number language into the electronic number language of the computer. Output machines do just the opposite. After the computer has finished its processing, output machines change computer language back to human language so that we can understand and use the work the computer has done.

Who decides on the kinds of input and output and processing systems? The choice is up to the people who are

The computer system shown here is used to design advertisements. The operator's console in front has a special electronic pen called a stylus. A keyboard like a typewriter can be pulled from below the console and used to set the type needed. The operator can check the ad as it is being designed by looking at the screen.

using the computers. Without people to tell it what to do, the biggest computer system in the world would be help-

■ This section tells what a programmer does.

less. The people who use it must spell out every single detail of the job they want it to do. They must write instructions that tell the computer what things it needs for processing, where to get them, and what to do with them. These instructions are called a *computer program*.[c] The people who write the instructions are called *programmers*.[c]

Computer programs are often complicated, because they have so many instructions. But the instructions themselves are usually simple and can even be written in everyday language. Most important, all the instructions in a program must be correct so that the computer will do exactly the same things every time. If some instructions are wrong, the computer will carry them out anyway, because it can only do what it is told to do. Then all its answers will be wrong. The programmers will have to test their programs again and again until all the wrong instructions are found and corrected.

With all the things computers can do, you may believe you could never do anything better than a computer. But you *can*. Every day, you do something that is a lot more complicated than anything a computer will ever do. You can *think*. A computer can't. Not even the biggest, most complicated, most impressive-looking one. You can paint a picture, write a book, or compose a song. You can *enjoy* pictures and books and songs. A computer can't. In fact, a computer can't do anything at all without a program of instructions written by a human being just like you. But with the right instructions and programs and people, a computer can be a marvelous and powerful tool that helps us expand our knowledge and improve our lives.

# Check the
# Skills

**Understanding the Selection**

1.  a. You have seen what a computer is made of and how it works. Do you agree that this article about computers fits very well into a unit about "Patterns"? Are patterns very important in computer operation?

    b. You may have read stories or seen movies in which computers take over the world or otherwise order people around. From what you now know about computer patterns, do you think this could really happen? Why or why not?

**Study and Research Skills** Study Techniques

2.  Would your study plan for your quiz on this selection look something like this?

    Assignment: Know enough about the article to answer questions on most important points.

    Read article quickly to get idea what it is all about.

    Read article again, slowly, making short notes on important points.

    Look over points several times to become familiar with them.

    Do this today to be ready for test tomorrow.

**Comprehension Skills** Implied Meaning

3.  a. What are the three parts of a computer system?

    b. What does a programmer do?

# Selection 4

# Use the Skills

### Understanding the Selection

1. You probably know something about the immigration of people moving to the United States from other countries. An important part of our history is this repeated pattern. The next selection includes some information about the pattern of Chinese immigration that may surprise you. See what it is.

### Study and Research Skills Study Techniques

2. Pretend that you were assigned to make a short oral report on the information in this selection. How would you make a study plan?

### Comprehension Skills Implied Meaning

3. Suppose your report was to cover only the role of the Chinese immigrants during the Gold Rush. Which parts of the selection would you *not* include?

# CHINESE FOREBEARS[9]

Betty Lee Sung

When we think about the birth of this nation, we think about Christopher Columbus, the Mayflower landing, and the pilgrims. We tend to forget that the United States has a western coast and that this region was settled long before Columbus ever set foot on American soil.

In fact, there is strong evidence that people from China had settled in the Americas over 2,500 years ago. They probably set sail in double canoes, plank boats, or rafts and were carried by strong ocean currents that brought them to these western shores.

Scientists who have studied Indian cultures in the Pacific Northwest, in Mexico, and in Peru see a definite Chinese influence in the calendar, the arts, and the tools of the American Indians.

Few people like to think of the settlement of the American continents this way. There are no exact records, and the settlements established along the West Coast are long gone. Only the ruins of the ancient American Indian civilizations give us some clues.

However, we do know for certain that the Chinese were among the pioneer settlers of the American West. They came to California when gold was discovered in 1848. The news of gold had traveled to Canton, a southern port city in China, almost before word reached the eastern shores of the United States. The Chinese were among the "forty-niners" who rushed here in ships, in the same way as other brave and adventurous people from all over the world. These early pioneers risked life and limb in the hope of finding gold.

The Chinese came in clipper ships with big billowy sails. When there was a good strong wind, the ships moved rapidly through the waters. Even then, the journey across the Pacific Ocean sometimes took as long as three months.

■ Would you include the information in the first four paragraphs in a report centering on the Gold Rush? Would you include it in a general report on the selection?

■ How long do you think it would take you to study this selection in order to make a report on it?

The first Chinese settlers landed near San Francisco, where gold had been discovered. They came from a vast[9] empire with a recorded history of over 4,670 years. China is a country as big as the United States today, but in spite of its vast size, it had more people than it could feed. When the land cannot support the people, some of them have to go elsewhere. Most people do not like to leave their country and go to unknown lands, but the prospect[cg] of getting rich quick was a special reason.

The word *gold* not only attracted the Chinese, but lured[cg] people from all corners of the globe. They came from France, Spain, Mexico, Chile, Peru, Russia, Australia, and, of course, from the eastern states of the United States. Within a few short years, the hills where sheepherders once tended their flocks were swarming with people all hoping to become rich over night. This period in American history is called the Gold Rush.

By the year 1870, one out of every four people who had

flocked[c] to California was Chinese. By and large, these immigrants were young men from the poorer families who lived in and around the region of Canton. They came with the intent[cg] of working hard, saving their money, and going back to China. They did not bring their wives or children with them.

These men came with a dream of finding gold, so it was natural that they would turn to mining. But the burden of a tax on foreign miners fell very heavily upon the Chinese. They looked different—"more foreign" than the other foreigners. Usually they had to pay the tax while white foreign miners escaped payment. As a result, the Chinese turned to fishing, farming, manufacturing, and drainage[g] work. They harvested the land and the sea to provide food for the increasing numbers who continued to stream West. Theirs were the hands that stitched shoes and clothes and provided the services so vitally[g] needed on the western frontier.

# Check the Skills

## Understanding the Selection

1.  Were you surprised that the pattern of Chinese immigration into America goes back as far in time as it does? Why or why not? Why do you suppose most people in the United States are surprised to learn this?

## Study and Research Skills Study Techniques

2.  a. What would your study plan be if you were making a report on this selection?

    b. How long would it take you to study the selection?

## Comprehension Skills Implied Meaning

3.  Which parts would you *not* include if your report centered on the Gold Rush? Why?

# Use the Skills

This is an article about a very small animal that lives near the sea. Read the selection to find out the patterns this creature follows to get food and escape its enemies.

As you read, decide if there is enough information given to write a short report on this animal. Think through a study plan for the report. There are no notes in the margin to help this time. Good luck!

# HASTY DIGGER

James H. Carmichael, Jr.

You are walking barefoot along a beach. Each wave brings grains of sand and bits of broken shells to swirl[cg] around your toes.

As you watch the water, you see something very strange. It is white and looks like a bird's egg with short legs! It scurries[cg] up the beach in the shallow water of an incoming wave.

The wave stops, and the water flows back down the beach toward the sea. This creature now burrows[cg] quickly into the sand. You don't know what kind of animal it is—but it digs so fast, you decide to name it Hasty Digger.

You keep your eyes on the exact spot where Hasty disappeared from sight. For a moment you see only two small feathery things poking up from the sand. But they disappear as soon as another wave rushes over them.

Right away you dig your hands into the wet sand. Holding a handful, you suddenly feel something tickling your fingers. You carefully clear away the sand and are left holding the squirming creature. What in the world is it?

Some people would call Hasty a "sand flea." But it really is a mole crab—a crab without large pinchers or the usual crablike shape. When you study it closely, you see it has a tail shaped like a triangle. On each side of this tail are little fanlike paddles, called uropods.[cg]

If you were to place Hasty in a bucket of sea water, you would see its uropods whirling like tiny propellers. In the sand this movement quickly digs a hole and throws sand on top of the crab. At the same time, the mole crab's strong churning[g] legs help to shove it backward into the sand.

Hasty always faces the sea when digging in. Burrowing backward, the mole crab holds itself in the sand with its tail. Only its short, hairy breathing antennae[g] stick up above the sand. You can also see its tiny eyes on stalks.[g]

Besides antennae for breathing, Hasty has a longer pair on its head, called feeding[c] antennae. These look like little feathers. The crab keeps these rolled up out of sight except when collecting food.

Hasty sticks out its feathery feeding antennae only when water from a wave is rushing back to the sea. Then hundreds of tiny hairs on the antennae act like nets. They gather plankton'—tiny plants and animals—from the water.

Hasty rolls up the antennae, one at a time, and brings them down near its mouth. Special mouth parts will then scrape off the captured plankton.

As the tide⁹ moves in, the water rises slowly over Hasty. So every few minutes the crab crawls out of its burrow. It moves up the beach with a wave and digs into the sand again. When the tide goes out, the water gets too shallow. So now Hasty moves bit by bit down the beach toward deeper water.

Why is it important for Hasty to dig so quickly? Well, many larger animals of the beach know Hasty by another name—Tasty. Certain fish love to eat mole crabs. Other kinds of crabs also eat them. Some shore birds are experts at catching them. Even fishermen collect mole crabs for bait.ᶜ For Hasty, being able to disappear quickly into the sand means survival.ᶜ

Sometimes Hasty may be washed high on the beach by a big wave and left there stranded. By digging very quickly into the wet sand, the crab can keep from drying out in the hot sun.

So Hasty Digger leads a busy life—up the beach with the incoming tide and down again as the tide goes out. Crawling, tumbling, and digging, the mole crab moves quickly to keep from becoming a meal for another hungry creature.

# Check the Skills

### Understanding the Selection

1.  Are there patterns in the mole crab's life? What are some of the patterns? Do these patterns help the tiny creature to survive?

### Study and Research Skills Study Techniques

2.  Could you write a report on the mole crab using only this article? How long would it take to do the report? What would your study plan be?

### Comprehension Skills Implied Meaning

3.  If you needed to know why the mole crab moves up and down the beach with the tide, would you study the description of what the mole crab looks like? Why or why not?

# Apply What You Learned in Unit 9

## The Theme

### Patterns

1.    Living things follow many patterns. You read about several of them in this unit. Usually there are good reasons for these patterns. Think about the article about animals and weather. Spiders, ants, and butterflies act the way they do to protect themselves. The mole crab, too, has patterns for protecting itself. Why did Tai Babilonia follow her pattern of skating in the morning and studying in the afternoon? Could she have become the outstanding athlete that she is if she hadn't followed this pattern? Why do you think as you do?

Think about the patterns you follow. Why do you follow these patterns? Keep your eyes open for patterns in nature. Try to understand how these patterns help living things. You'll learn more about the world around you.

# The Skills

## Study and Research Skills Study Techniques

2. The purpose of a study plan is to help you organize your work. If you plan ahead, you will know just what needs to be done, how to do it, and how long it will take. You will get your work done in less time and with less effort.

3. What steps should you take to make a study plan? Look back at page 235 if you need to.

## Comprehension Skills Implied Meaning

4. You usually have a purpose for reading. Especially when you are studying, remember to find only information that relates to that purpose. Sort out the details that do not relate to that. This will help you with your reading both in and out of school.

# Facts and Figures

## Overview and Purposes for Reading

### The Theme

#### Facts and Figures

1. In this unit you will read facts and figures about plants, animals, and people. As you read, try to think of ways you can use this information.

### The Skills

#### Study and Research Skills Parts of a Book

2. Books that give information usually have several parts. The main part, the text, is the chapters, sentences, and paragraphs of the book. What are some other parts of a book? What information does each part contain? How can you use these other parts of a book?

#### Vocabulary Development Skills Context Clues

3. As you read, you sometimes find words whose meanings you don't know. What are some ways you can figure out the meanings of these words?

# Learn About the Skills

## Study and Research Skills Parts of a Book

The basic text of a book is its sentences, paragraphs, and chapters. Many books include other kinds of information, too. You will find it helpful to know what some of these parts of a book are and how to use them.

**Table of contents.** This is near the front of the book. It is the list of the chapters, or sections, in the book. The chapters are listed in the order in which they appear in the book. The page number where each begins is given. Skim a table of contents to find out generally what topics the book includes.

**Index.** At the back of many informational books is a list of the topics mentioned in the book. Each topic is followed by the numbers of the pages that contain information about that topic. The topics in the index are listed in alphabetical order. An index usually includes more details than a table of contents does. Use the index to find specific information about what is in the book.

**Graphic aids.** Other parts of a book can add to your understanding of the information given in the text. Graphic aids make use of something besides words to give you information. These are illustrations of some kind, with or without words of explanation.

**Maps.** Maps give many different kinds of information. They can show the highways and streets of a city. They can show the places where oranges are grown in California. The information given on a map is usually explained in a legend or key to the map's symbols.

**Graphs, charts, and tables.** Each of these graphic aids organizes detailed information into columns or lists. You can find the information you need quickly and easily by checking the titles of the columns. Graphs, charts, and tables often include keys to their symbols, too. Remember always to study the key carefully. You will then be able to find the information you want.

**Pictures, drawings, and diagrams.** Often pictures have captions that explain them. A diagram is a drawing that shows how something is made or how it works. Be sure to read any captions, titles, or labels.

These special parts of some books can be useful. Remember that you use them as references. You do not need to read or go over everything they contain. Be sure to check carefully any key or other explanation given so that you know how to get the information you want. You will see how to use these skills as you read this unit.

# Vocabulary Development Skills Context Clues

You can't know all the words you might come across in your reading. No one can. What can you do when you come across a word you don't know? One thing you can do is check the words and sentences around the word for clues to its meaning. These are called **context clues**. There are several kinds of context clues you can learn to use.

Sometimes the meaning of the unknown word is given right there. This is a **definition context clue**. Here is an example.

> A *philanthropist* is a person who gives large amounts of money to worthy causes that help people.

The meaning of the word *philanthropist* is given right in the sentence.

You can use what you already know to help yourself figure out some words. This is using **experience context clues**. Read the following sentence and see if you can make a good guess at the meaning of the word *lapping*.

> I could hear the little waves *lapping* gently against the rocks.

You may remember hearing both large, angry waves and small, gentle waves hit the shore. The large waves made a crashing noise, but the small waves made a more gentle splashing sound. If you can guess that *lapping* means "gently splashing," you are right. You will use your skill with these types of context clues as you read the selections in this unit.

# Selection 1

# Use the
# Skills

### Understanding the Selection

1.  Do you know why leaves change color in the fall of the year?
    The following selection will give you some facts about this
    mystery of nature.

### Study and Research Skills Parts of a Book

2.  Before you begin to read this selection, turn back to the table of
    contents in the front of this book. Read the information given
    for Comprehension Skills Unit 10, Facts and Figures. Find the
    title, author's name, and starting page for each of the five
    selections in this unit.

### Vocabulary Development Skills Context Clues

3.  Marginal notes will help you use context clues to figure
    out the meaning of several words.

# WHY LEAVES CHANGE COLOR

E. Lucy Burde

Leaves change color each autumn. Why? What causes the yearly show of scarlets and oranges and yellows?

Even modern science can't fully answer these questions. But researchers[g] in the U.S. Forest Service have found part of the secret in sunshine, temperature, and pigments.[c]

What are pigments? They are chemicals that color almost all living things. Without them, both you and the leaves of a tree would be pale and colorless.

■ This sentence is a definition context clue to the meaning of the word *pigment*.

The leaf is the food maker for the tree. During the spring and summer, it uses a green pigment called chlorophyll[c] to turn moisture[c] and carbon[g] dioxide from the air into sugars and starch. Chlorophyll acts as an antenna[g] to trap energy from the sun. As winter comes, the leaf's work ends. It stops making food, and the chlorophyll begins to dissolve.[c] The green color starts to disappear.

Underneath, once hidden by the green of summer, are the oranges and yellows of fall. They've been there all the time, since the leaf first opened in the spring! The answer to the appearance of the oranges and yellows of fall lies in the disappearance of chlorophyll.

But where do the other colors come from? What causes the reds and purples that make sweetgum[g] and sumac[g] look as if they're on fire?

Unlike the yellow and orange colors, the red pigments don't occur until summer ends. Scientists think that sugars trapped in the leaf may cause the red colors to form. Another pigment makes hickory and walnut leaves shiny brown.

Nature mixes these pigments in just the right amounts to produce fall colors: flashes of scarlet for dogwoods and northern red oaks, yellow for birches, brown for walnut trees. Each kind of tree usually has its own distinctive[9] colors. But trees can differ, too, depending on sunlight, moisture, and the kind of soil in which they're growing. A single tree may have branches of different colored leaves.

Weather and geography also influence autumn displays. "Indian summer"[9] weather—warm sunny days and cool but not freezing nights—brings the best color. In countries such as England, with warm fall nights and cloudy days, the autumn trees are muted[9] and dull.

The northern and eastern forests put on the most spectacular[cg] fall show in the United States. If you live in the desert or in the tropics, you may not even notice when trees change from summer to fall. But in New England and in other northern places, autumn comes with a blaze of color.

Despite their beauty, all the autumn colors are signs of death for the leaves. Even the most brilliant of scarlets will soon tarnish[9] and fade. The beautiful leaves will fall to the ground.

Special layers of cells develop where the leaves are attached to the twig. This gradually cuts the tissue[c] there until the leaves hang by just a whisper. Soon a fall wind brings a shower of color as the leaves fall and close the season's show.

But that's not the end of the leaf—or the mystery.

Even on the ground, the once-brilliant leaves still contain food. Earthworms and other creatures, so tiny you can't even see them, nibble on the leaves. The leaves decompose[c] and return part of their food to the soil to make future mysteries of painted birch and red maple leaves.

■ You may not know the word *tarnish*. There are not enough context clues here to help you. Look it up in the glossary or a dictionary.

■ Your experience with dead leaves on the ground can help you decide that *decompose* means "rot."

# Check the Skills

### Understanding the Selection

1.  What gives leaves their color? Do pigments and other elements have an effect? Does the weather make a difference?

### Study and Research Skills Parts of a Book

2.  When you looked at the table of contents, did you notice that it lists the selections in this unit in order? What other information, besides the titles and authors of the selections, is given in the table of contents?

### Vocabulary Development Skills Context Clues

3.  How could context clues help you figure out the words *pigment* and *decompose*? What can you do if there are not enough context clues for a word you don't know? Use the marginal notes to remind yourself if you need to.

# Selection 2

# Use the Skills

### Understanding the Selection

Thousands of people watch sports programs on television. Have you ever wondered which sports programs are the most popular? The following table lists the top sports programs on TV in 1973.

1. As you study the table, notice what kinds of facts and figures it contains. For one thing, it tells you what were the most popular sports events on TV in 1973. Which events would you have wanted to watch? What event was most popular with viewers?

### Study and Research Skills Parts of a Book

2. The titles across the top of the table tell you what information the table gives. Find out how many million people watched the World Series. A marginal note will help you read the table. There is no need to read every bit of information in the table. You may want to refer to it for certain questions you think it may answer. Read the titles of the columns to find out what information it contains.

### Vocabulary Development Skills Context Clues

3. Look at the event ranked third on the table. Do you know what sport was involved? If you have a lot of sports experience and know who the people are, you can guess the sport. Are these names a context clue?

# SPORTS ON TV

| Rank | Sport or Special | Percent of homes watching | Millions of Viewers | Percent of men, women and non-adult viewers | | |
|------|------------------|---------------------------|---------------------|---|---|---|
| | | | | M | W | N-A |
| 1. | Super Bowl (football) | 41.6 | 50.7 | 48 | 30 | 22 |
| 2. | World Series (baseball) | 30.7 | 34.8 | 45 | 38 | 17 |
| 3. | Billie Jean King— Bobby Riggs Special | 28.5 | 37.2 | 38 | 44 | 18 |
| 4. | Baseball All-Star Game | 23.8 | 27.6 | 48 | 32 | 20 |
| 5. | Football-NFL on ABC | 20.7 | 23.2 | 52 | 30 | 18 |
| 6. | Football College All-Stars/Bowls | 18.3 | 26.6 | 47 | 32 | 21 |
| 7. | Horse Racing's Triple Crown | 16.3 | 17.5 | 41 | 41 | 18 |
| 8. | Football-NFL on CBS | 15.4 | 16.2 | 51 | 27 | 22 |
| 9. | Baseball Pennant Playoffs | 15.0 | 14.7 | 43 | 41 | 16 |
| 10. | Football-NFL on NBC | 14.6 | 15.0 | 54 | 27 | 19 |
| 11. | Football-NCAA on ABC | 12.2 | 12.5 | 50 | 29 | 21 |
| 12. | Auto Racing | 11.1 | 8.7 | 38 | 32 | 30 |
| 13. | Super Stars | 10.9 | 14.3 | 43 | 25 | 32 |
| 14. | Wide World of Sports | 10.7 | 12.6 | 44 | 30 | 26 |
| 15. | NBA Basketball | 10.0 | 11.2 | 50 | 28 | 22 |

■ This is the only line across that you need to read to find out how many people watched the World Series. Read the title of the column about the number of viewers. The answer to the question is found where the line and that column meet.

## Check the Skills

### Understanding the Selection

1. What was the most popular sports event on TV according to the table? Would this have been your first choice to watch? What other events would you have enjoyed? You can use the facts in the table to compare your own first choices with the choices of television viewers across the country.

### Study and Research Skills Parts of a Book

2. How many people watched the World Series? Can you use the table to find out what program was watched by 8.7 million people? Does the table tell you what percentage of the audience watching the Super Bowl was men?

### Vocabulary Development Skills Context Clues

3. If you know that Billie Jean King and Bobby Riggs are tennis players, you can figure out from experience that the third most popular event on the table was a tennis match.

# Selection 3

*Bonsai*

# Use the Skills

### Understanding the Selection

1.   Read this selection for facts about some of the unusual gardens of Japan. Decide which type of Japanese garden you would like best.

### Study and Research Skills Parts of a Book

2.   There are several pictures with captions in this selection. They will help you understand better some of the descriptions in the article. Be sure to pay close attention to them.

### Vocabulary Development Skills Context Clues

3.   Try context clues to figure out the meanings of any words you do not already know. Remember that a small$^c$ after a word tells you that there are clues to its meaning in the surrounding words or sentences.

# JAPANESE GARDENS

You probably live in a country where a garden often consists of flower beds and green plants. In Japan, however, many gardens are quite different.

What would you think of a garden composed entirely of rocks and sand? In Kyoto, Japan, is a type of rock garden known as *kare-san-sui*.<sup>c</sup> This expression means "dry mountain water." The "mountains" in this garden are represented by fifteen rocks of various shapes and sizes. These are carefully arranged in the "water," represented by raked white gravel. No flowers or plants of any kind can be seen in this garden.

■ Here is a definition context clue for the Japanese word *kare-san-sui*.

This kind of rock garden is just one form of Japanese landscape<sup>c</sup> gardening. Another is the moss garden in Kyoto. Here fifty different varieties of moss form a velvet carpet under the ancient trees. Many other beautiful gardens are large enough to have ponds and streams, stone bridges and lanterns, pine trees and flowering shrubs.

But what about people living in huge apartment complexes?<sup>cg</sup> How can they enjoy the pleasure of having their own gardens?

Can you imagine some mountain and sea scenery on a small tray measuring about 20 by 12 inches? This is called *bonkei*,<sup>c</sup> which means "miniature<sup>cg</sup> landscape on a tray." Here is a small rock, some 4 inches high. It is shaped like a mountain and slopes down to rugged cliffs and an island-dotted sea of sand, complete with white-crested waves. There are even boats and fishermen with hair-thin fishing lines.

■ The word *bonkei* is defined here.

Or, the scene may be the famous Mount Fuji, capped with snow. Below it is a miniature house with thatched<sup>g</sup> roof and tiny sliding doors. Another model is a garden complete with lantern, shrubs, and trees about an inch high.

In these tray gardens the seas, rivers, and ponds are made of sand. Yet they are so realistic<sup>c</sup> that the city dweller can

This is the moss garden of a temple in Kyoto, Japan. The bridge with the large rock at the end is a typical feature of a Japanese garden.

This example of *bonkei* illustrates the rhythm of the mountains.

The sand in this dry garden has been raked in straight lines and represents the waves of the ocean. This sand is never walked on, so the design lasts for some time.

enjoy an ocean view or a country scene even in the small front entrance of an apartment.

*Bonsai*<sup>c</sup> is another art in which the Japanese excel.<sup>cg</sup> These are living trees and plants kept to miniature proportions by careful pruning<sup>g</sup> of stems and roots. A grove of maple trees may be growing in a shallow pot small enough to hold in the palm of your hand. Or, a gnarled<sup>cg</sup> pine tree 20 inches high may turn out to be 150 years old. These miniature trees and plants are often handed down from generation to generation and are regarded as family treasures.

■ This sentence defines *bonsai*.

■ If you have seen the twisted trunks of old pine trees, you'll be able to guess the meaning of this word.

The gardens of Japan are beautiful. Perhaps you will visit them some day!

# Check the Skills

### Understanding the Selection

1. You have read about gardens of rock and sand, moss gardens, gardens in a dish, and gardens of miniature trees. Which of these interest you most? Which would you like to visit, if you could go to Japan?

### Study and Research Skills Parts of a Book

2. How did the pictures and their captions help you understand better the things described in the selection? Do you think pictures and captions can be an important part of a book? Why or why not?

### Vocabulary Development Skills Context Clues

3. Did you figure out the meaning of the word *gnarled*? Remember to use a glossary or a dictionary if there are no context clues or if they don't help you understand the meanings of unknown words.

# Selection 4

# Use the Skills

### Understanding the Selection

1.   This article gives you some facts about fishing. It describes three different ways to catch fish. Read the article to find out what the three ways are.

### Study and Research Skills Parts of a Book

2.   Suppose this article is just one chapter in a long book about fishing. What words might you look for in its index, if you want more information about lures?

3.   There are some labeled pictures with the selection. Look at them carefully. Doing so can help you understand some of the things described.

4.   At the end of the selection is a pair of pictures. They show you how one kind of artificial lure compares to the insect it imitates.

### Vocabulary Development Skills Context Clues

5.   Watch for certain words that are defined in the text. Marginal notes will help.

# FRESHWATER FISHING

Jim Arnosky

Have you ever seen a fish jump in the middle of a pond? Do you know what it's doing? It's catching bugs and flies that float on the surface of the water.

If you see a fish tail splash in a shallow stream, you'll know that a trout is feeding on underwater insects that cling to the rocky bottom. A V-shaped wave through the water could be a large fish chasing a smaller one. And a loud glunk in a splashy circle may be a big hungry fish gobbling up a frog or a swimming mouse.

It's always a good idea to watch the water for a while before you begin fishing. If you can figure out what the fish are feeding on, offer it to them on your hook. You'll catch more fish.

## Bait fishing

All you need for bait fishing is a line on a pole, a couple of hooks, and some split-shot sinkers<sup>c</sup> to add weight to your line. Most young people who fish use earthworms as bait. However, fish eat very few worms. They eat the more abundant<sup>g</sup> foods, like the underwater insects living with them in the pond or stream.

The next time you are fishing in a clear stream, turn over some rocks and you will find insects clinging to the undersides. These insects, called nymphs,<sup>c</sup> are good fish bait. Put a nymph on a very small hook and squeeze a split-shot sinker on your line a foot above it. The weight will drift the bait along the bottom of the stream, where the fish normally look for nymphs.

■ There is a definition context clue for the word *nymph* in this sentence.

Fish also eat caterpillars, grasshoppers, and beetles that fall into or swim on the water. And some fish will eat anything they can fit into their mouths.

Whatever bait you choose, remember to make it appear

natural to the fish. If your sandwich leaped off the plate and danced off the table, you would hesitate[cg] to eat it. The same is true of fish. They are wary[c] of any food that doesn't look and act natural.

Always use a hook smaller than your bait, so the fish won't see it. If you want the bait to sink, squeeze a split-shot onto the line. If you want it to float, take off the sinker. Watch the water and see how different insects behave. Then imitate them[cg] with your bait.

When you are fishing, be as quiet as possible. Fish can't hear you talking, but they can feel the slightest movement in the water and the vibrations[g] from any thumping sounds you make on the bank or in a boat. Stay low so the fish won't see you, and try not to make any sudden movements. All of these things will alarm the fish and stop them from feeding.

**Lure fishing**

Artificial[g] lures[cg] are designed to attract fish to your line by imitating the motions or sounds of foods they usually eat. There are metal lures that will wiggle, wobble, and flash

SWIVEL

WOBBLING
SPOON

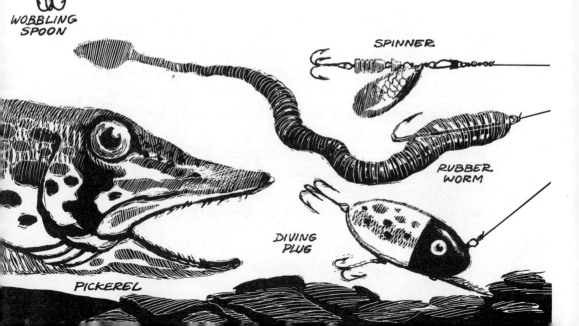

SPINNER

RUBBER
WORM

DIVING
PLUG

PICKEREL

like shiny minnows when pulled through the water. And there are wooden or plastic lures, called plugs,[c] that will float on the water and dive momentarily when you reel[c] them in. A plug acts like an injured fish, and an injured fish is an easy, tempting meal that a hungry fish will rarely pass up.

Some plugs are weighted inside so they'll sink to the bottom and then swim back to the surface as you reel in your line. In this way, they imitate the movements of crayfish, salamanders, and other bottom-dwelling creatures.

Another popular lure is the rubber worm. With only a little practice, you can make it swim through the water like an eel, curl up on the bottom like a drowned night crawler, or slither[cg] over lily pads like a water snake. All of these motions attract fish, so don't be surprised if a huge, toothy pickerel clamps onto your line and nearly pulls you off the bank.

Lures that make sounds are good for fishing at dusk or at night, when the water is still and visibility[g] is low. One of the simplest of these is the popping plug. A popper floats

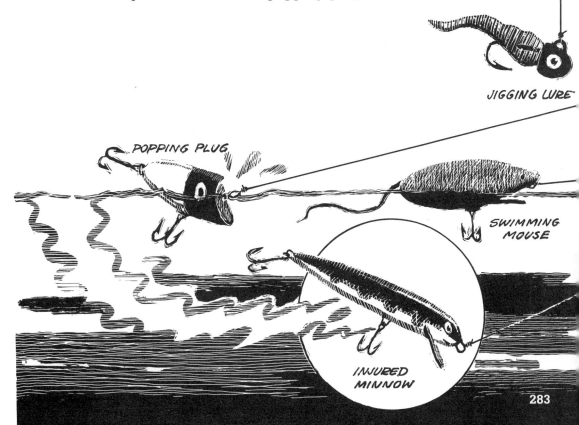

JIGGING LURE

POPPING PLUG

SWIMMING MOUSE

INJURED MINNOW

quietly until you give it a jerk. Then its hollowed front cups the surface water, making a loud pop that sounds like a frog jumping. Nearby fish will inspect the noise every time. And getting a fish's attention is the most important step in catching it.

There are other plugs that are designed to crawl through the water as you pull them in. A crawling plug looks and sounds like a swimming mouse.

Whatever kind of lure you choose, just a fishing pole and string won't do. You'll need a rod and reel. Cast your line and wait ten seconds to let the water calm down. Then reel it in slowly, without stopping. Keep reeling even if you feel a tug on the line. Fish expect their food to try to escape!

Fishing with a lure is like working the strings of a marionette.[9] It's tricky at first. But the more you practice, the better you'll become at making the lure—or the marionette—look like the real thing.

**Fly fishing**

Another way to catch insect-eating fish is to use a lure called a fly. Flies are made of feathers and fur tied on tiny hooks. Tied light and bushy, they will float on the water like winged insects. Fish will jump right out of the water to get them. This is called dry fly fishing. Tied woolly and heavy, they will sink below the surface and swim along like underwater insects. These "wet" flies catch the most fish.

You don't need special equipment just to try fly fishing. You can buy some inexpensive flies at a sports shop and use them on your own pole or rod. Simply tie one to your line and stand by the edge of the water. Lower the fly till it gently touches the surface and let it float along. You'll get a close-up view of the fish if it sips in the fly and tries to swim away with it. Or you can let the fly get waterlogged and sink. A fish will try to swallow it as it drifts to the bottom.

Fishing time is anytime—rain or shine, day or night. You can fish in the spring, when the waters are cold and the fish are scrappy. You can fish in the lazy days of summer under the shade of a willow or in autumn when the big fish are feeding. You can even fish in the winter through a hole in the ice.

Whatever the season, fishing can lead to a deeper understanding of stream or pond life. It can also provide you and your family with many delicious dinners!

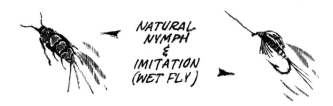

NATURAL
NYMPH
&
IMITATION
(WET FLY)

# Check the Skills

### Understanding the Selection

1. You have just read about three ways to catch fish. What are they? If you go fishing, which do you prefer—bait, lure, or fly fishing? If you haven't much fishing experience, which sounds best to you?

### Study and Research Skills Parts of a Book

2. If you want more information on lures, you might look in an index for the words *lure, plug, rubber worm,* and *fly*. Remember that the words in an index are listed in alphabetical order. Which word would be listed first, *plug* or *fly*?

3. Did the illustrations and labels help you understand certain lures better?

4. How do the pictures above help you understand how the imitation nymph compares to the natural one?

### Vocabulary Development Skills Context Clues

5. Use marginal notes to help you find the words *nymph* and *wary* in the selection. What is the definition context clue for *nymph*? What is a nymph? How could experience help you understand *wary* as it is used here?

# Selection 5

# Use the Skills

This selection contains many facts—and some figures—about the agave plant. The people of Mexico think this plant is very useful. Read the article to find out why.

A map with the selection gives you more facts. Remember to check the map carefully.

Remember to use context clues to figure out unknown words. Check for a definition of an unknown word in the sentences near the word. Or, use what you know about the subject to make a good guess at the meaning of the word.

There are no marginal notes with this article, so you are on your own. Try out the skills you have been learning.

# AGAVE

Bet Hennefrund

Everybody in Mexico knows the agave<sup>cg</sup> plants. For hundreds of years, they've been admired and used by the Mexican people. It's easy to see why.

Agaves are tough plants. They have to be to survive<sup>c</sup> the heat and wind of the desert. They look fierce. Swordlike leaves surround the center of each plant like a circle of armed guards. Sharp teeth line the leaf edges of many kinds of agave. On some agaves, the leaf tips end in long, two-inch spikes.

A thick, waxy outer layer shelters each leaf from the sun. The agave also has another way to keep from drying up. Tiny pores,<sup>c</sup> or openings in its leaves, close in the daytime heat. This keeps moisture in.

Most agave plants live for ten, twenty, or thirty years. A few live to be fifty. Some have been nicknamed century plants, since people thought they bloomed only once—after one hundred years. But agaves don't grow to be that old.

Nearly two hundred kinds grow in Mexico and in the southwest part of the United States. Some kinds flower each year. Others bloom once in a while. But most agaves bloom only once—at the end of their long, useful lives.

The agave blooms in the spring. From the plant's center, the flower stalk shoots up—ten to twenty feet tall. Short branches sprout at the top. The flowering branches on some agaves look like a row of candles. On other kinds, the branches are shorter, making the whole stalk look like a huge brush.

At the end of each branch, clusters of blossoms form. Then the plant smells like a perfume factory and looks like a burst of fireworks—with yellow, white, pink, or light green petals.

The sweet agave blossoms attract hummingbirds, bees, wasps, and bats. Wherever agaves grow wild in the hot desert, small animals find shade, shelter, and food. Doves, flickers, and other desert birds perch on the branches. Under the prickly leaves, kangaroo rats hide from coyotes, foxes, and hawks. Pack rats and pocket gophers chew tunnels through the base of the agave leaves.

People also have found many uses for agaves. They raise certain kinds, such as henequen[9] and sisal,[9] for the strong fibers,[c] or strings, that run through the leaves. Using sharp knives called machetes,[cg] people chop the leaves off the plants. Then the dry fibers from the leaves can be made into rope and into many other useful products.

At flowering time, the agaves' sap runs fast. That's when people collect sap from the maguey agave. Mexican people use it to make two popular kinds of drinks.

When the agaves have finished blooming, seed pods form on the plants. The long stalk turns pale and the circle of leaves turns brown. When the plant dies, its seeds are ready to grow into new agave plants. Soon there will be more fiber for people and more food and shelter for desert animals.

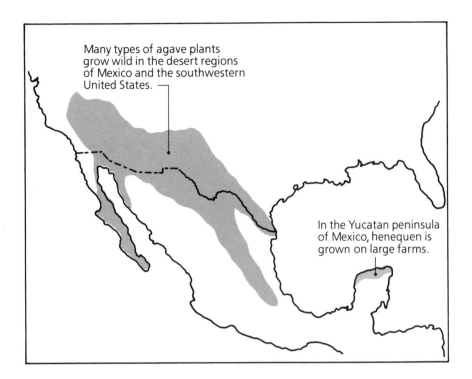

Many types of agave plants grow wild in the desert regions of Mexico and the southwestern United States.

In the Yucatan peninsula of Mexico, henequen is grown on large farms.

# Check the Skills

## Understanding the Selection

1.  How do animals use the agave plant? How do people use it? How long does it live?

## Study and Research Skills Parts of a Book

2.  What information does the map give? How did you figure it out?

## Vocabulary Development Skills Context Clues

3.  What is the definition context clue for *pores* in the following sentences from the selection?

    > Tiny pores, or openings in its leaves, close in the daytime heat. This keeps moisture in.

# Apply What You Learned in Unit 10

## The Theme

### Facts and Figures

1.  Facts and figures can be very useful. Think about the selections you have just read. You might use what you have learned about Japanese gardens to build a miniature garden of your own. The article on fishing may tempt you to try your luck with a colorful plug or fly. Remember, too, the articles on leaf pigments and the agave plant. These types of information might be useful in your science or social studies classes. And, of course, you can use the information on sports and TV in debates with your friends.

    These articles are examples of the wide variety of informational materials that are available to you. Newspapers, magazines, reference books, and textbooks are filled with facts and figures you may find interesting. Use them often.

**Study and Research Skills** Parts of a Book

2.	In this unit, you learned that a book may have several different parts. In addition to the text, there may be a table of contents and an index. These list the topics in the book and tell on what pages you can find information on these topics. Look over the table of contents and index before you read a book. They will help you decide if the book contains the information you need.

Various kinds of graphic aids may be used to illustrate a factual book. Maps, graphs, charts, tables, drawings, pictures, and diagrams are all graphic aids. They help you understand the information given in the text. Use them whenever they are included.

**Vocabulary Development Skills** Context Clues

3.	As you read, you will sometimes come across words that are unfamiliar to you. Before looking up such words in a glossary or dictionary, try using context clues to figure out their meanings. You may find definition context clues. These give the meaning of the word in the phrases or sentences around it. You can also use your own experience with the subject to make a good guess at what an unknown word means.

# Current Events

## Overview and Purposes for Reading

### The Theme

#### Current Events

1. Current events are things that are happening now or have happened recently. They may happen in your town or somewhere else in the United States or even in another part of the world. Why is it important to know about current events?

### The Skills

#### Study and Research Skills Reference Sources

2. What are some sources you can use to get information about current events?

3. What kinds of information does each source give?

#### Literary Appreciation Skills Style and Intent

4. What are some of the reasons authors have for writing? Why is it important to understand what the author's purpose was for writing the material you read?

# Learn About the Skills

## Study and Research Skills Reference Sources

You read history books to learn about the past. But how do you find out about current events, events that happened today, yesterday, or during the last several weeks? Most people use several sources to find out what they need to know about current events.

**Daily newspapers.** There are two main types of articles about current events in a newspaper.

> **Informational articles.** These articles present facts about current events. They tell you what happened.

> **Editorials or signed columns.** These articles give opinions about current events. They tell what the writer thinks about what happened. The writers of columns, whose names are given, are usually experts on the subjects they cover.

Newspapers provide information on a wide range of topics. They may give information about events in your town, in your state, in the United States, or in other parts of the world. The news may be about the birth of a baby in your town or about the start of a foreign war. Reading a daily newspaper is the best way to get an overall view of the major events that may affect you.

**Weekly newsmagazines.** Like newspapers, these magazines contain articles of fact and articles of opinion. But newsmagazines present few articles on local issues. These magazines concentrate on major events that involve a state, a country, or the entire world. If you want a detailed summary of the major events of recent weeks, you'll want to read a weekly newsmagazine.

**Radio and television news programs.** These may be daily newscasts or special programs. They may be national news broadcasts to the whole country by a network, or local programs seen only in your own community.

**Daily newscasts.** These programs are the best source for up-to-the-minute information on major events. Radio and TV reporters can cover events as they happen! Remember, though, that daily newscasts are usually too short to cover all the news events you need to be aware of. That's why it's a good idea to refer to a newspaper or newsmagazine for more complete information on current events.

**Special news programs.** These programs are shown weekly or when an important event occurs. They present detailed information on one, two, or several topics. They are good sources of information on the topics they cover.

Suppose you want to know if the people in your town have voted to build a new football field near your school. The local radio or television newscast might mention the vote, but the local newspaper would be the best source for more information. It would explain why people voted as they did and what will happen as a result.

Or, imagine you hear that an earthquake has just occurred in Mexico. The fastest way to find out if the report is true is to listen to a radio or television newscast. If an earthquake did occur, you would want to read newspaper and newsmagazine articles to find out more about it.

These are examples of how you can use several different sources to keep up with current events. You'll learn more about using the news media as you read this unit.

# Literary Appreciation Skills Style and Intent

You usually have a purpose for reading. Authors usually have a purpose for writing. To get the most from your reading, you should make sure the author's purpose and your purpose match.

Both of the following paragraphs are about beaches. However, each paragraph was written for a different purpose. What are those purposes?

> Did you know that waves make sand beaches? The waves wash over rocks again and again, breaking the rocks into smaller and smaller pieces. Finally, the waves grind the small rocks into sand. It can take thousands of years to make a sand beach.

> Our city has only one public beach. It is overcrowded. That is why concerned citizens should vote for the purchase of the beach on Seaside Avenue. The city can buy this beach at a very reasonable price. Our children need more beaches. Vote yes!

The author of the first paragraph wrote **to give information**. If your purpose was to find out how sand beaches are made, you'd want to read this paragraph.

The author of the second paragraph wrote **to persuade**, to convince readers to vote for city purchase of an additional beach. If your purpose was to find out people's opinions about buying a new public beach, this paragraph would interest you.

Think about your purpose and the author's purpose when you read. If you need facts, find authors who write facts. If you want opinions, look for experts who express—and support—their opinions. And, if you want to enjoy yourself, look for authors who write **to entertain.**

As you read the selections in this unit, see if you can recognize the authors' purposes.

# Use the Skills

### Understanding the Selection

The following selection is a newspaper article. It tells how a woman named Addie Cook helped make her town a safer place to live.

1.   Read the article to find out what Addie Cook did.

2.   Decide how the information given in the article might help people who keep up with current events by reading newspapers.

### Study and Research Skills  Reference Sources

3.   As you read this newspaper article, decide why Addie Cook's story probably would not be included in a newsmagazine or in a national television newscast. Marginal notes will help.

### Literary Appreciation Skills  Style and Intent

4.   Decide whether the author wrote this article to give you facts, to persuade you to share Addie Cook's opinions, or to entertain you.

# WORKING ON THE RAILROAD

William Michelmore

Addie Cook has been working on the railroad. Four years of persistent[9] phone calls, letters, and plain old nagging finally paid off.

"Now I can stop worrying every time my two young children cross the tracks in the school bus," said Mrs. Cook, of Crystal Lake, Illinois. For the last four years, she has been trying to get the railroad to install gates at a busy and dangerous crossing on East Crystal Lake Avenue. The crossing is in Crystal Lake, a town of 20,000 people northwest of Chicago. She finally called one of her state legislators and "he got right on it," she said.

The legislator wrote to the chairman of the Illinois Commerce Commission. An investigation led to a promise by the railroad to install[cg] the crossing gates at a cost of $80,000.

Not only that, the ICC[c] investigation will result in the installation of gates at the other four unguarded crossings on the railroad's northwest line.

The Crystal Lake crossing is currently protected only by flashing lights. The railroad right-of-way contains three sets of tracks. As many as 40 commuter[9] trains and 10 freight trains flash by the crossing at top speeds every day, said the chief railroad engineer of the Illinois Commerce Commission.

There have been no fatal accidents in recent years. "But we have had a problem with stalled cars on the crossing," the ICC engineer noted.

Mrs. Cook, her husband, David, and their two children, ages 6 and 9, moved to Crystal Lake five years ago. Almost immediately, she saw the danger of the crossing.

■ Here are more facts. There probably wouldn't be enough time to cover all these facts on a short TV newscast.

More than 400 school children cross the tracks daily in school buses. Employees<sup>cg</sup> of Oak Industries, the largest factory in the town, must cross the tracks to get to work. The road across the tracks is always heavily traveled because it is the main street through town.

"A thousand cars must cross there every day," said the vigilant<sup>g</sup> Mrs. Cook. She conducted her own traffic counts in her long and often frustrating<sup>cg</sup> attempt to get the gates installed.

"If there haven't been any fatal accidents, there have sure been a lot of close shaves," Mrs. Cook said. "A car stalled on the crossing and the driver got out just before a train smashed into it. Often there are lines of 20 cars or more crossing the tracks. The last car just gets across before a train comes roaring through.

"Railroad crossings are frightening things and this is one of the worst," Mrs. Cook said.

One of the main dangers, according to both Mrs. Cook and the I.C.C. is that at night commuter trains coming from the north stop just west of the crossing. Here they wait their turn "to hit their slot."<sup>c</sup> This is railroad talk for trains waiting for other trains to go by before they can get onto the main line.

Drivers approaching the crossing see the headlight of the stationary<sup>c</sup> train and believe that it is safe to drive across the tracks, not realizing that another train could zip by at any moment.

Many people in the area believe it is a miracle that no one has been killed at the crossing. They say that it is just a matter of time before a disaster<sup>cg</sup> occurs. The gates will not be installed for about a year, officials said.

Mrs. Cook said she waged a "one-woman battle" to achieve her goal.

"I made many calls to the train station and the railroad company, and I was told over and over that nothing could be done. I never got anywhere. It was always, 'We'll get back to you,' but no one ever did."

# Check the Skills

### Understanding the Selection

1.  Who did Addie Cook talk to about the dangerous crossing? Which of the people she talked to finally helped her?

2.  If your town had a dangerous crossing, what would you do to get help? How might this article help you think of someone who might listen?

### Study and Research Skills Reference Sources

3.  Why wouldn't Mrs. Cook's story probably be included in newsmagazines or national TV newscasts? Might a local TV station include it? Do you think such a newscast would have time to cover as many details as are included in this newspaper article? Why or why not?

### Literary Appreciation Skills Style and Intent

4.  What do you think the author's purpose for writing the article was? Why do you think as you do?

# Selection 2

# Use the Skills

### Understanding the Selection

Have you ever wondered what the United States Navy does with its old ships? The following article is from a national newsmagazine. It appeared in *Newsweek* in the issue of January 14, 1980. The article tells about an old ship named the *Nautilus*. It was America's first nuclear-powered submarine. Several groups want to put the *Nautilus* on display so that people can visit it.

1.  It takes much longer to publish a book than it does to put out a newspaper or a magazine. The current events mentioned in this unit, therefore, are no longer current as you read about them. You may need to call your local newspaper for information on what happened to the *Nautilus* and where it is now.

### Study and Research Skills Reference Sources

2.  Think about whether you expect a local newspaper to include similar information on the *Nautilus*.

### Literary Appreciation Skills Style and Intent

3.  Decide why you think the authors wrote this article—to inform, express opinions, or entertain.

# WHERE TO MOOR[9]
# THE *NAUTILUS?*

Eileen Keerdoja with Marc Frons

Ever since the Navy announced that it will formally retire the U.S.S. *Nautilus* later this year, the U.S. Naval Academy in Annapolis, MD, and the submarine base in Groton, CT, have vied[9] for the honor of keeping the world's first nuclear submarine on permanent display. In November, Secretary of the Navy Edward Hidalgo recommended that Congress choose a different site[cg] altogether: the Navy Yard in Washington, D.C. But supporters of both Groton and Annapolis vow that they have not yet begun to fight.

■ Chances are that the newspapers in these cities would include this news. But other papers might not be interested.

Launched[9] in Groton in 1954, the *Nautilus* could cruise around the world without rising to the surface, and one former skipper[9] insists that the ship can still "operate almost as well as the latest submarines." However, the *Nautilus* has become increasingly costly to maintain, and the Navy finally sent it to San Francisco for deactivation.[cg] In recommending that the government moor the retired vessel in Washington, Hidalgo said that the "national character" of the ship makes the Capital an ideal site. But Frank Scheetz, president of the Submarine Memorial Association in Groton, counters that "Washington has enough monuments."

■ These are opinions but they are not the authors' opinions.

The Navy estimates it will cost $7.6 million to build a suitable display at the Navy Yard, while the Groton supporters say that they could raise the funds themselves. They also point out that the channel[c] at Groton is deep enough for the ship and—unlike Washington's—would not require dredging.[9] The State of Connecticut has already pledged $500,000 to develop the display, which would be alongside another sub, the U.S.S. *Croaker* of World War II fame. "We got the *Croaker* to lay the groundwork for eventually getting the *Nautilus*," says Scheetz. "People will come here to see it, but nobody's going to go to Washington to see a submarine." Governor Ella Grasso has written letters to President Carter asking him to intervene.[cg]

Annapolis boosters are still pressing their case by circulating petitions and buttonholing[g] members of Congress. "Two internal Navy studies have recommended Annapolis," says James Brianas, head of the Maryland group. "It's obvious that this was strictly a political decision." Brianas claims that Groton is an unsuitable location because of tight security at the sub base, and as for Washington, "keeping the *Nautilus* there will enhance[g] the Navy Yard property,

but that's just a piece of ground. Let's enhance our future naval leaders by letting the *Nautilus* motivate[9] and inspire them here."

The decision now rests with Congress, which must appropriate[cg] the funds for the sub's final port. Though the lobbyists[9] for both Groton and Annapolis are fired up, they may be sailing against the wind. In such situations, Congress almost always follows whatever course the Secretary of the Navy recommends.

# Check the Skills

## Understanding the Selection

1. Why do people from Groton think the *Nautilus* belongs there? Why does the Annapolis group think it should get the *Nautilus*? Who will decide where the submarine goes? In your opinion, who should get the *Nautilus*? Why do you think as you do? You might want to try to find out what has happened since. The reference section of your local public library, or the one in the nearest large city, is probably the best source of current information.

## Study and Research Skills Reference Sources

2. Newspapers include information that affects the people who read it. Is your town affected by the argument over the *Nautilus*? Then would your local newspaper be interested in this news? Would the newspaper in a small town in Texas be likely to include this story? Why or why not?

## Literary Appreciation Skills Style and Intent

3. Do you agree that the author's purpose was to give information? Why do you think as you do?

# Use the Skills

### Understanding the Selection

The following selection is part of an article from a Chicago news-paper. The article describes a winter carnival in that city in 1980.

1.  Read the article to find what kind of information it gives.

### Study and Research Skills Reference Sources

2.  As you read, decide whether or not each of the following news sources might include information on Chicago's carni-val: newscasts on Chicago radio stations, newspapers in small California towns, or national television news broad-casts. Refer to pages 293 and 294 if you need help.

### Literary Appreciation Skills Style and Intent

3.  If you lived in Chicago and wanted to know where you could learn to cross-country ski, would the article interest you? Is the author writing to inform or to entertain?

# WINTER CARNIVAL

Howard Reich

Don't be surprised the next time you notice sleigh rides, ice shows, dogsled races, and ski clinics[9] under way in your neighborhood park. What you're seeing is Chicago's first Winter Carnival. This is a five-week, citywide snowfest designed to put the fun back into Chicago winters.

The carnival is created and sponsored[c9] by the Mayor's Office of Special Events. It originally was scheduled to get into full swing this weekend with a program of recreational activities and spectator[9] events. However, because of this season's unusual lack of snowfall, most of the activities won't begin until next weekend.

To keep tabs on the latest details, you can phone the WGN Winter Carnival Hotline. Most of the festivities will take place during the five weekends beginning January 12. Nearly all of the activities are free.

Because the Carnival will run during winter's cruelest months, the National Ski Patrol is advising Chicagoans to take great care in preparing for the fun. The Patrol explains that to best protect yourself you should dress in layers. This way you can peel away excess clothing as exercise raises your body temperature. Wear a hat to avoid loss of body heat. Bring along an extra pair of gloves or mittens. Always travel with a friend.

Once you've dressed for the occasion, you can enjoy free, one-hour cross country ski clinics. For more advanced skiers, free intermediate-level courses will be taught at 7 P.M. every Thursday in January. And for those who would rather practice skiing than study it, cross-country sport will be allowed at dozens of Chicago's parks throughout the winter.

If you'd rather take your winter sport sitting down, you'll like the horsedrawn sleigh rides available at Lincoln Park and at Grant Park.

■ WGN is a Chicago radio and television station. Do you think WGN would broadcast information about the Winter Carnival?

■ Here are facts about weather and clothing.

■ Here are some more facts about carnival events. Chicagoans who like to ice skate at high speeds will want to dash over to the Speed-Skating Championships at Waveland Avenue and the lakefront. Skaters of all ages are invited to compete for trophies and medals.

To give Chicago a peek at Arctic-style winters, the first Windy City Classic dogsled races will be held at Lincoln Park. Up to 90 teams from Alaska, Canada, and the Midwest will compete. Admission is free.

To reach any of the Winter Carnival events, you can save

yourself time and trouble by taking the CTA.<sup>cg</sup> Following is the basic information on how to travel to the carnival's major sites on public transportation.

■ Here are facts about public transportation to the carnival.

Grant Park: Take any rapid transit line downtown. Leave the train at Monroe or Adams streets. Walk three blocks east.

Jackson Park: Take the Jackson-Howard "B" train south to the end of the line. Walk about a block east.

Lincoln Park South Field: Take the Ravenswood "A" train to Armitage Avenue. Then take the No. 73 bus to the park.

# Check the Skills

### Understanding the Selection

1.  What kind of information is in this newspaper story? Do you think this was interesting information to people in Chicago in the winter of 1980 who wanted to keep informed of current events? Why do you think as you do?

### Study and Research Skills Reference Sources

2.  Did you decide which news sources listed on pages 293 and 294 would probably include information on Chicago's winter carnival? Chicago radio newscasts would certainly give carnival information because their listeners would be interested. But California newspaper readers and national television newscasts probably would not be interested in knowing the details of Chicago's carnival.

### Literary Appreciation Skills Style and Intent

3.  Did the article include information on cross-country skiing? Why do you think the author wrote this article?

# Selection 4

# Use the Skills

### Understanding the Selection

So far in this unit, you have read three factual news articles about current events. The following newspaper editorial gives an opinion about a current concern.

1.  Read the article to find out what the author's opinion is. Decide whether or not you agree.

### Study and Research Skills Reference Sources

2.  Both newspapers and newsmagazines contain editorials. These give opinions on current topics. These articles often are on a different page from the factual articles and are sometimes labeled with words like *editorials*, *opinions*, or *commentary*, so that you know you are reading opinion and not fact. As you read the following editorial, decide why it's helpful to know how people who write newspaper editorials feel about current events.

### Literary Appreciation Skills Style and Intent

3.  The author wrote this article to give an opinion. Look for words and phrases that tell you this is an article of opinion. Is this author's opinion helpful? Is that opinion supported by facts? Marginal notes will help.

# EDITORIAL

## WE NEED TO KNOW

Americans can buy almost any kind of food they want. Modern day science has found ways to make food taste better, look better, and last longer. Yet many of the substances that do these things are not good for us. Certain spices and food colorings make some people sick. Too much sugar or fat is not good for others.

■ Here the writer gives some factual reasons for the opinion that foods need better labeling.

It is very hard for shoppers to figure out just what is in the food they eat. We think this is wrong! Food producers should include more complete information on the labels of the food they produce.

■ The underlined words are clues to the author's opinion.

The U.S. Department of Agriculture and the Food and Drug Administration agree. These agencies have come up with stronger regulations on food labeling. These regulations need to be approved by the U.S. Congress. We urge Congress to take action. We need these regulations and we need them quickly!

## Check the Skills

### Understanding the Selection

1.  What is the author's opinion about this current concern? Do you agree or disagree?

### Study and Research Skills  Reference Sources

2.  People who write newspaper editorials give their opinions. But they try hard to make sure they know the facts first. Do you think this is one reason why knowing how they feel about current events can be helpful? Why do you think so?

### Literary Appreciation Skills  Style and Intent

3.  Words such as *should, think, urge, need* give you clues to the author's opinion. Did the reasons the author gives help to make the opinion convincing?

# Use the Skills

The following article is about jobs. It tells what kinds of workers will be most needed in the 1980s. As you read, think about kinds of work you might like to do when you finish school. In the last unit, you learned how tables and charts can be helpful sources of information. There is a table with this selection that you may want to refer to for the types of job you are interested in.

This article was taken from the January 21, 1980, issue of the newsmagazine *U.S. News & World Report.* Decide why this information probably wouldn't be included on a TV newscast. Think, too, about the author's purpose for writing. Was it to present facts or opinions?

# TOMORROW'S NEW JOBS

A boom[9] in white-collar[cg] work awaits job seekers in the 1980s.

A new forecast by the Labor Department projects that more than half of the estimated 66.4 million job openings available between 1978 and 1990 will be in white-collar occupations. These are professional, technical, managerial, sales, and clerical fields.

Nearly 20 million of those openings will be newly created jobs. The rest are existing jobs that will become vacant through retirement, resignation,[9] and death. Over all, approximately 55 percent of the openings will be white-collar, 24 percent will be blue-collar, 18 percent service jobs, and 2 percent farm jobs.

Although job opportunities may grow faster than the labor force, unemployment won't necessarily decline during the 1980s. The reason is that many new workers will not be properly trained for the available jobs. Officials are particularly concerned about hundreds of thousands of economically disadvantaged young people. Many of them are not literate[9] enough to qualify for entry-level white-collar jobs.

Meanwhile, many new workers will be overqualified for the jobs that are open to them. Government analysts say that 1 in 4 future college graduates will be unable to find a job that requires a degree. Many of them will be slow to settle for less.

Computer technology[9] will create some new white-collar jobs and eliminate[9] others over the next 10 years. Openings for clerks and office-machine operators, for example, will drop as computers take over more billing and payroll duties. But the need for computer experts will grow. Secretaries and typists will be in high demand.

Despite labor-saving advancements such as computerized checkout, employment is expected to rise in the retail-sales industry. New stores and longer hours will require more workers.

More scientists, engineers, and technicians will be needed as the nation invests more in energy production, mass transportation, and environmental protection. With health services expanding, there will be greater demand for nurses, doctors, orderlies,[cg] and nursing aides.

Cooks, cosmetologists, and other personal-service workers also will be needed as a result of rising family income.

| | Latest Employment (1978 estimate) | Average Annual Openings to 1990 |
|---|---|---|
| **All Occupations** | 94,373,000 | 5,533,000 |
| **Administration** | | |
| Accountants | 985,000 | 61,000 |
| Bank officers, managers | 333,000 | 28,000 |
| Health Administrators | 180,000 | 18,000 |
| Public-relations workers | 131,000 | 7,500 |
| Purchasing agents | 185,000 | 13,400 |
| Urban planners | 17,000 | 800 |
| **Computer Specialists** | | |
| Computer operators | 666,000 | 12,500 |
| Computer repairers | 63,000 | 5,400 |
| Programmers | 247,000 | 9,200 |
| Systems analysts | 182,000 | 7,900 |
| **Engineers** | | |
| Aerospace | 60,000 | 1,800 |
| Electrical | 300,000 | 10,500 |
| Industrial | 185,000 | 8,000 |
| Mechanical | 200,000 | 7,500 |
| Petroleum | 17,000 | 900 |
| **Teachers** | | |
| College | 673,000 | 11,000 |
| Kindergarten, elementary school | 1,322,000 | 86,000 |
| School counselors | 45,000 | 1,700 |
| Secondary school | 1,087,000 | 7,200 |
| **Mathematics** | | |
| Actuaries | 9,000 | 500 |
| Mathematicians | 33,500 | 1,000 |
| Statisticians | 23,000 | 1,500 |
| **Scientists** | | |
| Astronomers | 2,000 | 40 |
| Chemists | 143,000 | 6,100 |
| Geophysicists | 11,000 | 600 |
| Life scientists | 215,000 | 11,200 |
| Meteorologists | 7,300 | 300 |
| Oceanographers | 3,600 | 150 |
| Physicists | 44,000 | 1,000 |
| **Health Services** | | |
| Dental assistants | 150,000 | 11,000 |
| Dentists | 120,000 | 5,500 |
| Dietitians | 35,000 | 3,300 |
| Licensed practical nurses | 518,000 | 60,000 |
| Nurses' aides, orderlies | 1,037,000 | 94,000 |
| Operating-room technicians | 35,000 | 2,600 |
| Pharmacists | 135,000 | 7,800 |
| Physical therapists, aides | 42,500 | 3,100 |
| Physicians, osteopaths | 405,000 | 19,000 |
| Registered nurses | 1,060,000 | 85,000 |
| Veterinarians | 33,500 | 1,700 |
| **Social Sciences** | | |
| Economists | 130,000 | 7,800 |
| Geographers | 10,000 | 500 |
| Historians | 23,000 | 700 |
| Psychologists | 130,000 | 6,700 |
| Sociologists | 19,000 | 600 |

| | Latest Employment (1978 estimate) | Average Annual Openings to 1990 |
|---|---|---|
| **Technicians** | | |
| Drafters | 296,000 | 11,000 |
| Engineering, science technicians | 600,000 | 23,400 |
| Food technologists | 15,000 | 500 |
| Forestry technicians | 13,700 | 700 |
| Soil conservationists | 9,300 | 450 |
| **Other Professions** | | |
| Actors | 13,400 | 850 |
| Airplane pilots | 76,000 | 3,800 |
| Architects | 54,000 | 4,000 |
| Dancers | 8,000 | 550 |
| Foresters | 31,200 | 1,400 |
| Interior designers | 79,000 | 3,600 |
| Lawyers | 487,000 | 37,000 |
| Librarians | 142,000 | 8,000 |
| Musicians | 127,000 | 8,900 |
| Newspaper reporters | 45,000 | 2,400 |
| Personnel, labor relations | 405,000 | 17,000 |
| Photographers | 93,000 | 3,800 |
| Radio, TV announcers | 27,000 | 850 |
| Singers | 22,000 | 1,600 |
| Social workers | 385,000 | 22,000 |
| **Services** | | |
| Airline flight attendants | 48,000 | 4,800 |
| Barbers | 121,000 | 9,700 |
| Building custodians | 2,251,000 | 176,000 |
| Cooks, chefs | 1,186,000 | 86,000 |
| Firefighters | 220,000 | 7,500 |
| Gasoline station attendants | 340,000 | 5,200 |
| Guards | 550,000 | 70,000 |
| Motion-picture projectionists | 11,000 | 750 |
| Police officers | 450,000 | 16,500 |
| **Building Trades** | | |
| Bricklayers | 205,000 | 6,200 |
| Carpenters | 1,253,000 | 58,000 |
| Construction electricians | 290,000 | 12,900 |
| Construction laborers | 860,000 | 49,000 |
| Ironworkers | 78,000 | 4,100 |
| Painters | 484,000 | 26,000 |
| Plumbers and pipe fitters | 428,000 | 20,000 |
| Roofers | 114,000 | 4,500 |
| Sheet-metal workers | 70,000 | 3,500 |
| **Mechanics and Repairers** | | |
| Air-conditioning, heating mechanics | 210,000 | 8,200 |
| Aircraft mechanics | 132,000 | 3,500 |
| Appliance repairers | 145,000 | 6,900 |
| Auto mechanics | 860,000 | 37,000 |
| Industrial—machinery repairers | 655,000 | 58,000 |
| Office machine repairers | 63,000 | 4,200 |
| TV, radio service technicians | 131,000 | 6,100 |
| **Driving Occupations** | | |
| Local truck drivers | 1,720,000 | 64,000 |
| Long-distance truck drivers | 584,000 | 21,500 |
| Taxi drivers, chauffeurs | 94,000 | 4,300 |

| | Latest Employment (1978 estimate) | Average Annual Openings to 1990 | | Latest Employment (1978 estimate) | Average Annual Openings to 1990 |
|---|---|---|---|---|---|
| **Machine Occupations** | | | **Other Crafts** | | |
| Machine-tool operators | 542,000 | 19,600 | Boilermakers | 37,000 | 3,100 |
| Machinists | 484,000 | 21,000 | Furniture upholsterers | 29,000 | 1,100 |
| Metal molders | 21,000 | 500 | Locomotive engineers | 34,000 | 2,000 |
| Tool-and-die makers | 170,000 | 10,400 | Maintenance electricians | 300,000 | 15,500 |
| | | | Railroad conductors | 37,000 | 1,700 |
| **Printing** | | | | | |
| Bookbinders | 69,000 | 2,600 | | | |
| Composing room occupations | 181,000 | 3,900 | **Other Operatives** | | |
| Lithographers | 28,000 | 2,300 | Assemblers | 1,164,000 | 77,000 |
| Printing pressmen | 167,000 | 5,000 | Automobile painters | 42,000 | 2,000 |
| | | | Factory inspectors | 771,000 | 35,000 |
| **Telephone Industry** | | | Meatcutters | 204,000 | 5,200 |
| Central office craft workers | 135,000 | 1,000 | Railroad shopworkers | 76,000 | 2,100 |
| Installers, repairers | 115,000 | 3,000 | Welders, arc cutters | 679,000 | 35,000 |
| Operators | 311,000 | 9,900 | Farm Workers | 2,798,000 | 108,000 |

# Check the Skills

### Understanding the Selection

1. According to this selection and chart, what kinds of jobs will have the most openings in the 1980s? What kinds of work might you like to do? Have you chosen some kinds of work for which many jobs will be available? Why is this kind of current event information very important to people, especially those your age?

### Study and Research Skills Reference Sources

2. Would there be time on a national TV newscast to present all the information given in this newsmagazine article?

3. Your local newspaper might not include the information in this article, but it does list the jobs available in your town. Take time to look through the section of your paper that advertises job openings. See if there are jobs available that you would like to do.

### Literary Appreciation Skills Style and Intent

4. What do you think was the author's purpose for writing this article?

# Apply What You Learned in Unit 11

## The Theme

### Current Events

1.  People need information about current events. The people of Crystal Lake needed to know that a dangerous railroad crossing in their community would soon be fixed. The people of Chicago wanted to know that their city was sponsoring a winter carnival. And everyone should be interested in learning about food labeling and jobs in the 1980s.

    Take time to read about current events. Try to read a newspaper daily and look through a newsmagazine whenever possible. Keeping up with current events will make it easier to understand and live in the day-to-day world. It will also make you a well-informed person and good citizen!

# The Skills

## Study and Research Skills Reference Sources

2.    There are three major news sources: the news-
      paper, the newsmagazine, and radio and TV news
      programs. To be a well informed person on current
      events, use all of these news sources. Read news-
      papers and newsmagazines, and keep up with
      radio and television news programs.

3.    You have seen that there is some difference in the
      kinds of current events covered in these different
      news sources.

## Literary Appreciation Skills Style and Intent

4.    Remember that a newswriter has a purpose for
      writing. It may be to inform, to persuade, or to
      entertain. Figure out why the author wrote the
      material you read. Be especially careful to sepa-
      rate fact from opinion. Be sure you are getting the
      kind of information you need and want.

# Unit 12

# Making Choices

## Overview and Purposes for Reading

### The Theme

#### Making Choices

1.   People make choices every day. They pick out foods to eat, clothes to wear, and friends to enjoy. What are some other choices people make? Why do they make the choices they do? How can you learn to make good choices?

### The Skills

#### Study and Research Skills Reading Techniques

2.   How can you learn to improve your reading of factual material?

3.   What is the SQ3R reading technique? How can you use it to become a better reader?

#### Comprehension Skills Literal Meaning

4.   How can you learn to remember the important details in what you read?

## Study and Research Skills Reading Techniques

It isn't easy to read textbooks and other informational articles. They are often filled with new facts that are hard to understand. But there is a way you can read faster and understand more. It is a five-step plan called SQ3R. Here is how it works.

**SQ3R**

| | |
|---|---|
| **S**urvey | Look over the material first to see what it is about. |
| **Q**uestion | Decide what questions you should be able to answer when you finish reading. |
| **R**ead | Read the selection to answer those questions. |
| **R**ecite | After reading the selection, try to tell yourself the answers to all the questions. |
| **R**eview | If there are questions you can't answer, review the material to find the answers. |

The first step is S or *survey*. To do this, look quickly over the material. Look at the title, other headings, any words emphasized by being in *italics* or **boldface**, and illustrations for clues to what the material is about. Don't read the text at this time. Just try to get an idea of what you are going to read.

The second step is Q or *question*. Think about your purpose for reading and put that purpose into question form. Sometimes your teacher will help. Suppose your teacher said, "Read this article to find out how Navajo rugs are made." The question you would ask is "How are Navajo rugs made?"

After you set your main purpose for reading in this way, you need to develop more specific questions in order to do SQ3R. The information you found when you surveyed the material can help. If there are headings or illustrations, use them to make up questions. Sometimes your survey will show you that there are questions at the end of a chapter or an article. Use these as SQ3R questions. They usually cover the main ideas in the material.

After you have come up with your questions, move on to the first R in SQ3R. This R is *read*. Read the material to answer the questions you have asked. Do not read every word. Read only to find the answers to the questions.

The next is *recite*. Look over your questions. Tell yourself the answers you found in your reading. Be sure you have an answer for each question.

If you can't answer a question, use the last R in SQ3R. This R is *review*. Go back over the material, looking for the answer to your question. Again, do not read it all. Look only for the information you need.

It may take a little time to become a good SQ3R reader. But it's worth the effort. You'll read faster and remember more of the material you have to read and study. Use SQ3R as you read the following selections.

# Comprehension Skills Literal Meaning

Do you remember everything you read? Most people don't. But you often need to make a special effort to remember, especially when you are reading something for school. The main secret is to know before you read what you need to remember. This is like the Q in SQ3R. Ask yourself first what questions you need to find answers for. Perhaps you want to find out what a glacier is. Read the following paragraph.

> Glaciers are large fields of ice that are slowly moving. Here is how glaciers are made. High in the mountains or in very cold areas, snow falls and does not melt. After many years, the layers of snow become ice. If the ice becomes very heavy, or the temperature becomes warmer, the ice starts to move.

A few days later, suppose you come across the following paragraph in a newspaper article. If you can recall the definition of a glacier that you read earlier, the newspaper article will be easier to understand.

> John Cramer, President of ABC Energy, says that his company can make heat from glaciers. He wants to melt the glaciers and use the water for steam heat.

Help yourself remember better what you read by thinking back over other experiences or reading that included similar ideas. Think how the ideas fit together.

You will see how to use this skill as you read this unit.

# Use the Skills

## Understanding the Selection

1. Do you know what a snow survey is? Find out in the next selection, which tells what it is and why it's important.

2. What are some of the choices people make as a result of these surveys?

## Study and Research Skills Reading Techniques

3. Use SQ3R. First, *survey* the article to find out what it is about. Look for words in boldface. Ask yourself *questions* about these words. Look at the questions in the Check the Skills section at the end of the selection. Next *read* the article. Then *recite* answers to the questions you asked. If necessary, *review* the article to find answers to your questions. The notes in the margin will help you.

## Comprehension Skills Literal Meaning

4. You may want to use the first two questions above, and the additional ones you decided upon for SQ3R, to decide exactly what you will want to recall about this article.

# SNOW SURVEYS

R. H. Windbigler

Rainfall is scarce in our western states. Much of the water used for drinking, cooking, bathing, watering crops, and producing electricity comes from mountain snow. Water from the snow in the mountains is called **snowmelt.**[c] Snow melting in the mountains runs down in rivers and streams during the spring and summer. Too much snowmelt can mean terrible flooding. Too little means that plants, animals, and even people may die of thirst.

■ Here is a word in boldface. Use it to form the question "What is snowmelt?" Skim the rest of the selection for other words in boldface type. Make up questions about those, too.

People aren't able to change the amount of snowmelt. But if they know ahead of time how much snowmelt there will be, they can make plans to deal with it. Heavy snows or a very warm spring may cause lots of snow to melt at once. People and things can sometimes be moved out of the way of floods. Or temporary[g] dams can be put up to keep the waters in safe areas. If there have been light snows, people can save or conserve[cg] water to use when there is not enough to go around.

In 1935, the U.S. Department of Agriculture began trying to find out how much snow fell in the mountains each winter. Measuring snow and finding the amount of water in it is called **snow surveying.**

Snow surveyors use a scientific technique[g] known as **sampling.**[c] Sampling means taking measurements in many places and then predicting[g] the whole amount. This is much easier than measuring everything and is almost as accurate.

Snow surveyors go into the mountains from January to May. They measure the depth and weight of the snow in over two thousand snow courses.[c] A snow course is a place chosen for sampling. Snow courses are generally small meadows high in the mountains. Small meadows are chosen because they give a good idea of average snow conditions in an area. Trees have not caught some of the snow, and there are not likely to be large, unusual snowdrifts.

A typical snow course is 300 meters long. Usually ten measurements are taken, one every 15 to 30 meters along the course. This gives enough information to figure out roughly how much water will come down the mountainside during the spring and summer months.

Here is how the snow is measured. The snow surveyor puts together as many pieces of aluminum tubing as it will take to reach the bottom of the snow. The tube's tip has a jagged steel cutting blade which must be driven through all the layers of ice and hard-packed snow.

Once ground is reached, the tube and its snow core are brought up to the surface. The length of the core is then measured. Following this, the core is weighed. Two cores of the same length often have different weights because the heavier one is more tightly packed and therefore contains more water.

Recent inventions may make it possible to use radio waves to do future snow surveying. This means that soon surveyors will not have to climb high into the mountains to measure snow. They will simply stay inside radio stations and keep track of the information sent back by radio waves from special measuring instruments.

■ After you finish reading, recite the answers to the questions you asked yourself. Include the answers to the questions in the Check the Skills section below. Review the selection if you need to.

# Check the Skills

### Understanding the Selection

1.  What are snow surveys? Why is it important that snow surveys be made?

2.  What choices must people make as a result of the information a snow survey gives them?

### Study and Research Skills Reading Techniques

3.  Here are the questions you should have asked as you surveyed the article for words in boldface type.

    What is snowmelt?
    What is snow surveying?
    What is sampling?

    What are the answers to these questions? What should you do if you can't answer the questions?

### Comprehension Skills Literal Meaning

4.  What did you decide would be important to remember in order to answer the questions? Did knowing what answers you were looking for help you remember them better?

# Selection 2

# Use the Skills

### Understanding the Selection

This is an article about the effects of television on young people.

1.  As you read the article, think about the television programs you watch. Why do you make the choices you do?

### Study and Research Skills Reading Techniques

2.  SQ3R will help you understand the article. *Survey* before you read. Look for the questions in **boldface** type. Use these as SQ3R *questions*. There is a chart at the end of the selection. Form one or two questions by looking at the chart before you read. Also, read the Check the Skills section on page 329. Then *read* the article to answer these questions. *Recite* the answers and *review* if necessary.

### Comprehension Skills Literal Meaning

3.  See what information you think you need to recall. Your own experience with watching TV should help you.

# THE BIG FUSS

Marilyn Burns

## Who is arguing about what is shown on television?

Many people disagree about how TV should be for kids.

These disagreements have grown into big arguments. The people who argue are those who make the TV shows, the people who pay to have the shows made, the people who are upset about much of what kids see on TV, the advertisers[c] who hope you'll spend your money on their products, and the people in government who make the laws about TV.

■ This paragraph answers the questions in boldface above.

There are different kinds of people who make the TV shows. There are the people you see on TV. There are the people who make the cartoons. Others write scripts for shows. Then there are those who do all the technical[g] work.

Next, there are the people who pay to have the shows made for you. They are the television broadcasters.[c] They decide what programs you'll get to see. They're the ones who run the TV stations and put the programs on the air.

Then there are the people who are upset about much of kids' TV. One important group is called Action for Children's Television. They're busily working all over the country. Other groups have gotten in on the arguments. There are local committees on children's television in many cities, PTA groups, and groups of pediatricians[g] and eye doctors. There are organizations that send out information about what shows kids should and shouldn't be allowed to watch.

Another group is the advertisers. They've got some information they want you to have. They want you to think about it enough that you'll be inspired[cg] to spend your money.

The government is also involved. The Federal Communications Commission (FCC) licenses and regulates all TV channels in the United States. The commission is made up of seven people. They are appointed by the President for seven years. They have to follow a law that says that all TV stations have to show programs that are "in the public interest, convenience and necessity." That means that it's the people who watch TV who are to be served by the programs. In 1971, the FCC set up a Children's Bureau.

### What are the arguments about violence<sup>c</sup> on television?

Violence is a big part of television. It causes a big part of the hassle<sup>c</sup> about what kids see on television.

What's meant by TV violence? That's when there is either some threat of physical harm or actual physical harm shown.

Think of the cartoons on Saturday morning TV. Those characters have incredible<sup>cg</sup> experiences. Their heads get blown off by cannons. They fall off cliffs. They get run over by trucks. Flattened by cars. Dropped from hooks in the sky. Bopped on their heads. Crushed by rocks. Rolled

over by boulders. Sometimes all in less than five minutes.

Think of the evening shows. People get shot. People get beaten up. People get strangled. Sometimes they're troublemakers, lawbreakers, general "bad guys." But often they're heroes. Check out who uses violence when you watch TV.

You learn something from everything you see. What do you learn from seeing violence? That's what's troubling many people.

The argument goes like this. You do learn from TV. And you do imitate[9] what you see on TV. Did you ever hear people singing advertising jingles? Why, some people ask, would anyone want to fill kids' eyes full of violent acts?"

■ The next three paragraphs give the answer to the question in boldface type on page 326.

The U.S. Surgeon General has reported that violence on television does have an effect on children. The viewing of violence on television encourages[cg] violent behavior in kids. Because television shows that violence is a way to solve problems, many kids think that is true in life, too.

Nonsense, say the people who produce the violent TV shows. Kids can see the difference between TV and the real world. Just because you see some kung fu on TV doesn't mean you're going to kick your brother next time you're having a disagreement.

■ You may want to recall this information when you choose which TV shows to watch.

Besides, violence is exciting. And an exciting program means a bigger audience. And a bigger audience makes advertisers happier. And the happier they are, the more money the broadcasters make. That's called a chain reaction.

How much is your weekly violence intake? Make a form like the one below. Keep it near the TV so it will be handy to use. Every time there's a situation that fits one of the categories,[cg] make a check mark. Then decide what *you* think about violence on TV.

■ You should look at this chart *before* reading the selection.

**A Week of Violence**

| | Monday | Tuesday | Wednesday | Thursday | Friday | Saturday | Sunday |
|---|---|---|---|---|---|---|---|
| Murders | | | | | | | |
| Gunfights | | | | | | | |
| Fistfights | | | | | | | |
| Violence used to solve a problem | | | | | | | |
| Talking used to solve a problem | | | | | | | |

# Check the
# Skills

### Understanding the Selection

1.  What television programs do you watch? Why do you choose these programs? Will your choice of programs change as a result of reading this article? Why or why not?

### Study and Research Skills Reading Techniques

2.  You should be able to *recite* the answers to the following questions in your own words. *Review* the selection if you need to. Marginal notes and underlines will help.

    a. Who is arguing about what is shown on television?
    b. What are the arguments about violence on television?
    c. What should you use the chart for?

### Comprehension Skills Literal Meaning

3.  What information in the selection do you want to remember? Why?

# Use the Skills

### Understanding the Selection

1.  This selection gives facts about space. Read the article and decide if you would choose to travel out into space as the astronauts have. The picture above shows a view of Earth as seen from its moon, 100,000 miles away.

### Study and Research Skills Reading Techniques

2.  Follow each step in SQ3R with this article. Review the steps listed on page 317 if you need to. Marginal notes will help.

### Comprehension Skills Literal Meaning

3.  You will recall the information in the selection better if you decide now what you will need to remember. Read the questions on page 335 before you read the selection. Then you'll know what to pay attention to.

# ABOUT SPACE

Ruth A. Sonneborn

Here are some of the questions people most often ask about space. Perhaps the answers will clear up some things that have been puzzling you, too.

## What Is Space?

Space is the vast and limitless expanse[9] that is all around us. Our earth is traveling in space, and so are the sun, the moon, the planets, and the stars. There are many millions of heavenly bodies in space. Some are little particles like specks of dust. Others are so big that, compared to them, the earth would seem very tiny.

■ The author has used questions as headings in this article. Reading them should be part of the *Survey* step of SQ3R. They can also be part of the *Question* step.

## Where Does Space Begin?

Our earth is a whirling body in space. And because you live on the earth, you are living in space. But when we talk about *out* into space we mean traveling far, far away from earth into what is sometimes called outer space.

Scientists do not agree on how many miles away from earth outer space begins. Some say it begins fifty miles away. Some say eight hundred. But scientists agree that to reach outer space we must go beyond our atmosphere.[cg]

■ This tells you that there is no known answer for the question above.

## What Is the Earth's Atmosphere?

Wrapped around most planets is a mass made up of bits of dust and gases called the planet's atmosphere. It swirls around with the planet. The earth's atmosphere is made of dust, gases, and water. It is called air. One of the gases in air is oxygen. We need oxygen to breathe. Without oxygen we cannot live.

Close to earth the air is thick. It has lots of oxygen in it. We breathe easily. But the farther away from earth we go, the thinner the air becomes.

Have you ever been on top of a high mountain? It is harder to breathe there because the air has much less oxygen in it. And so when people leave earth for the higher stretches of the atmosphere and for space, they have to take their own supply of oxygen with them—their own supply of air.

## Can You See Space?

In the daytime, when you look away from earth, you see clouds, blue sky, bright sunshine. You do not see space. But you can see some objects in space, such as the moon, on certain clear days. Between you and space there is a bright curtain of light that makes it hard for you to see beyond it.

The sun's rays stream through the atmosphere. They strike against particles and bits of dust. The rays light up these particles, and the particles scatter the light all around the atmosphere. Some of it looks blue to us. That is the sky. This scattered light keeps you from seeing faraway space.

But on a clear night when the sun has gone, you look up. You see stars, planets, perhaps the moon. You see blackness all around them. You see space.

## Where Does Space End?

■ Here's another question for which there is no answer yet.

Nobody knows. We know that our solar system takes up only a very small part of space. Through our most powerful telescopes we can see stars that look tiny because they are billions and billions and billions of miles away from earth.

But what lies beyond? We cannot see. We do not know. Perhaps there is no end to space at all.

## Does an Astronaut See a Blue Sky?

Astronauts in space look *away* from earth. They do not see sky. The sky is part of the earth's atmosphere and the astronauts are far, far beyond the atmosphere.

The sky looks blue to us on earth when the blue-green-violet colors of the sunlight strike the tiny dust particles in the atmosphere. The other colors of sunlight stream

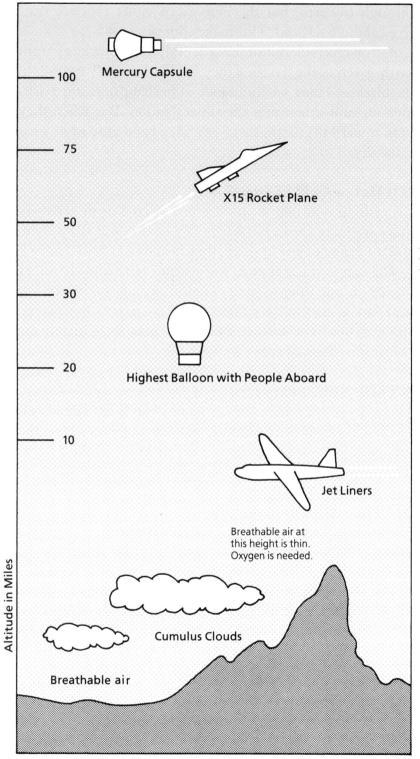

100

75

50

■ Remember to form questions from this chart, too.

Mercury Capsule

X15 Rocket Plane

30

20

Highest Balloon with People Aboard

10

Jet Liners

Breathable air at this height is thin. Oxygen is needed.

Cumulus Clouds

Breathable air

Altitude in Miles

through to earth, but the blue-green-violet rays are scattered about overhead. This makes our sky look blue.

Astronauts look out of the spaceship windows *away* from earth. Even in the daytime they see blackness all around. In the blackness they see thousands of brilliant stars, the flashing sun, and sometimes the silvery moon. But when they look toward the earth, they see a blue band around it. That is the sky.

### Is It Hot or Cold in Space?
Everything whirling in space is hot or cold or in between. Stars are huge furnaces. When rays stream out from them and reach any object in space, they heat it.

The sun is the star that warms our earth and the other planets in our solar system. These heavenly bodies reflect heat just as they reflect light. Near a star or a hot planet, space is hot. The farther away one gets from them, the colder it is. Most of space is very cold.

### Is There Noise in Space?
There is no noise that human beings can hear. Sounds on earth make waves in the air and these waves carry the sounds to our ears. But there is no air in space. And so, to the human ear, space is absolutely quiet.

### Are There Clouds in Space?
There are no clouds in space. There is no water. Clouds are made up of water and bits of dust. Without water, clouds cannot form.

The photographs of clouds that satellites[9] take show part of the earth's atmosphere. These photographs have been taken from many, many miles beyond these clouds.

These pictures of six of the planets in our solar system and of the Earth's moon were taken at separate times from National Aeronautics and Space Administration spacecraft. The combination photograph shows, in the foreground, Earth rising over the moon's surface with a sun flare on the edge of the Earth. The first planet above the moon is Venus. At the top, from left to right, are the planets Jupiter, Mercury, Mars, and Saturn.

# Check the Skills

### Understanding the Selection

1. Would you choose to go into space if you could? Why or why not?

### Study and Research Skills Reading Techniques

2. It was easy to *survey* the article and find the *questions* in boldface. Can you *recite* the answers to the questions? What should you do if you can't answer a question?

### Comprehension Skills Literal Meaning

3. There are two questions in this article that could not be answered. They are examples of the things we don't yet know about space. Can you recall what they are? If not, review the marginal notes on pages 331 and 332.

# Selection 4

## Use the Skills

### Understanding the Selection

1. This selection is about a number. Decide if you think you would choose to use the same examples that the author did. Above, you can see some of the million bottle caps Ralph Rivera of Chicago has collected.

### Study and Research Skills Reading Techniques

2. *Survey* the article to find out what number the author is writing about. What *question* should you *read* to answer?

### Comprehension Skills Literal Meaning

3. Think about whether you should try to recall all the details in this selection.

# HOW MUCH IS A MILLION?

Ellen H. Goins

■ Your *survey* should include reading the title. In this case, the title also tells you the *question* you should read to answer.

*Million* is such a big number that it is hard to imagine how much it really is. Here is how much it would take to make a million (1,000,000) pounds.

| | |
|---|---:|
| 10 children weighing 70 pounds each | 700 |
| 4 pigs weighing 300 pounds each | 1,200 |
| 3 deer weighing 200 pounds each | 600 |
| 1 moose weighing 1,000 pounds | 1,000 |
| 1 lion weighing 500 pounds | 500 |
| 2 oxen weighing 2,000 pounds each | 4,000 |
| 1 horse weighing 2,000 pounds | 2,000 |
| 10 hippos weighing 8,000 pounds each | 80,000 |
| 8 bears weighing 1,500 pounds each | 12,000 |
| 10 rhinos weighing 8,000 pounds each | 80,000 |
| 6 gorillas weighing 500 pounds each | 3,000 |
| 9 walrus weighing 2,000 pounds each | 18,000 |
| 16 elephants weighing 12,000 pounds each | 192,000 |
| 8 buffalo weighing 2,000 pounds each | 16,000 |
| 2 sperm whales weighing 147,500 pounds each | 295,000 |
| 1 blue whale weighing 294,000 pounds | 294,000 |
| | 1,000,000 |

■ You don't need to remember all these details.

## Check the Skills

### Understanding the Selection

1. Would you choose something besides the weights of children and animals to show a million? If so, what would you choose?

### Study and Research Skills Reading Techniques

2. Did you use the title as the *question* in SQ3R? You may not be able to give the exact answer to the question. But chances are you have a clearer idea about the answer than you did before you read the selection.

### Comprehension Skills Literal Meaning

3. Why do you think it is not important for you to recall all the details of the list?

# Selection 5

## Use the Skills

The following article gives a short history of some eating utensils, especially the fork. Follow the steps in SQ3R. There are no boldface headings or questions to help in your *Survey*. Look through the selection to see what else you can use. Review the steps on page 317 if you need to. Be sure you know what questions you want to answer as you read the article. Think about how the information in this article can help you understand facts you already know.

There are no notes in the margins of this selection, so you are on your own. Good luck!

# FINGERS WERE MADE BEFORE FORKS

Althea Jackson

When primitive[g] people were thirsty, they cupped their hands to hold the water they wanted to drink. When they were hungry, they broke up food with their hands and ate with their fingers. They used a sharpened stick to spear chunks of meat. They used a forked stick to remove the food from the fire. Food that could not be torn apart was cut up with sharp stones or shells. Soup or stew that was too hot to be touched with bare hands was scooped up with a shell or gourd.[g]

Stone[g] Age people made their knives of slate,[g] flint,[g] or bone. They used the knives to kill animals, to prepare the animal skins for clothing, and to cut up the meat for food. But the spoon was the first tool made just for eating.

Archaeologists[g] have dug up clay spoons that were made at least seven thousand years ago. The ancient Egyptians made spoons of ivory, wood, and slate. The Greeks and the Romans made spoons and knives of metal. They used bronze, iron, copper, and silver.

For thousands of years people in the Orient have used pairs of sticks for eating. The people of Japan, China, and other oriental countries still eat with these sticks today. We call them chopsticks. The word *chop*[c] means "quick." Usually made of bamboo[g] or ivory, chopsticks are about eight inches long, with the upper half squared and the lower half rounded.

Traditionally,[g] Oriental people never eat with utensils[cg] that someone else has used. They have personal sets of chopsticks that they carry with them everywhere. Once a Chinese gentleman, dining in England, was offered a fork by his host. He refused it, saying, "This fork may have been in hundreds of mouths before mine, and among them possibly that of my enemy. This idea is repulsive[cg] to me."

In Western civilization, knives and spoons have been used for at least seven thousand years. But forks did not appear until about 1,500 years ago. Then a man in Byzantium—now called Istanbul—decided that he should be able to eat preserved fruits without getting his fingers sticky. So he invented a two-pronged fork. He never dreamed that his invention would change the eating habits of the Western world.

In those days people had little opportunity to travel and see how other people lived. New customs[9] were adopted very slowly. People seemed shocked by the extravagance[9] of carrying food to the mouth with something other than their fingers. So it was centuries before the fork became popular outside Byzantium.

In Western Europe, during the Middle Ages, people still ate with a knife and spoon just as their ancestors[9] had. A typical family rose at dawn and had a bit of bread and something to drink. By nine o'clock everyone was hungry and hurried to the dining hall.

All people sat in pairs. A man and a woman shared a single plate and cup, but each had a knife for cutting meat, and a spoon for scooping up vegetables. They had no napkins, so they wiped their soiled fingers on the tablecloth.

Slowly the use of the fork was passed from Byzantium on to Italy. Around 1500, the common tableware[c] in Italy included forks. Elsewhere in Europe, first the nobility[9] and then the common people began to add forks to their knives, spoons, plates, and metal drinking cups.

Britain was slow to follow. In 1600, when Queen Elizabeth I of England tried to introduce forks, the clergy[9] preached against the use of these vulgar[9] foreign objects. You should not throw food into the mouth as you would toss hay into a barn with a pitchfork, they insisted. One angry clergyman made it clear that "Fingers were made before forks," and this meant that people should use fingers instead of forks.

Fingers were still used instead of forks when the Pilgrims and Puritans left England for America in 1620 and 1630. Good table manners in the Colonies called for knives and spoons, fingers and napkins. Forks or "tines"[c9] were used only for cooking and for holding the meat while it was being carved.

As in the Middle Ages, each couple shared one plate or trencher.[c] A trencher was made of wood or of pewter.[9] It was a foot square and three or four inches deep, with the center hollowed out to hold the food. Only the host and the hostess had chairs. They sat side by side at the end of the table. The other grown-ups sat on long benches on each side of the table. Children stood behind their parents, who handed them food.

During the seventeenth century the fork was finally accepted in England and in America—1,300 years after the Byzantine inventor had first thought of it.

## Study Questions

1. What was the first tool made just for eating?
2. Why was the two-pronged fork invented? How long ago was it invented?
3. How did people in Western Europe eat before they began to use forks?
4. When did the people of England and America begin to use forks?

# Check the Skills

## Understanding the Selection

1.  Why did people choose not to use forks at first?

## Study and Research Skills Reading Techniques

2.  When you *surveyed* the article, you found Study Questions to use as SQ3R *questions*. Did you *recite* the answers to these questions? Did you need to *review*? What are the answers to the questions?

## Comprehension Skills Literal Meaning

3.  Suppose you read an article about everyday life in Japan. What could you recall from this selection about eating utensils that would be related to that?

# Apply What You Learned in Unit 12

## The Theme

### Making Choices

1. In this unit, you were asked to think about making choices. You read about how mountain snows sometimes force people to make choices about how they use water. You learned that some people choose to use eating tools different from your own. And you thought about making choices about TV programming and exploring space.

   But how do you learn to make good choices? The best way is to get all the information you can on a subject and then make your decision. Some day you will vote for the person you think will be the best President of the United States. You will need to do some research to make a good choice. Reading some history can help. Current newspaper and magazine articles might help, too. After using these sources, you should have the information you need to make an intelligent choice. Informed people usually make the best choices.

# The Skills

### Study and Research Skills Reading Techniques

2.    SQ3R is a five-step plan to help you understand the informational materials you read. It can help you improve your reading.

3.    The first two steps of SQ3R are *survey* and *question*. They will help you get and idea what the material is about and set up purposes for reading. The 3Rs, *read, recite,* and *review*, complete the plan. *Read* the article to answer your questions. Then *recite* the answers you have found. If there are questions you can't answer, *review* the article.

Use SQ3R whenever you read informational materials. Use it in your reading inside and outside school.

### Comprehension Skills Literal Meaning

4.    Use your memory to help you understand what you read. As you read, try to recall other materials you have read on similar topics. Think about how the materials fit together. You may be surprised how many of the materials you read are related.

## Apply the Skills As You Do Your Schoolwork

Use the study and research skills you have learned in this section as you work through your school assignments. They will make your studies easier and more understandable. The following selection is from a newspaper article that you might be asked to read in a social studies class. It uses a diagram to help explain the article. Read both the diagram and the article carefully.

The questions below will show you how these study and research skills can help you to better understand both the diagram and the article. First, read the questions. Think about them as you go on to the next page. When you've finished the article, answer the questions.

1.  **Making a study plan.** Suppose you are making a study plan for a report on the eruption of the Mt. St. Helens volcano in 1980. You are to include in your report as many facts about this disaster as you can find. This article would give you some of the facts you need. But you'll have to check other sources as well. What sources might you use? How long do you think it would take you to locate all the information, take notes, and write the report?

2.  **Diagrams.** Study the diagram. It gives you further information about the Mt. St. Helens volcano. What, exactly, does it tell you?

3.  **News media.** How would you compare the Mt. St. Helens report on the next page with a television news report on the same disaster? How would they be alike? How would they be different?

4.  **SQ3R.** Skim the article and write down one or two questions to answer as you read. After you finish reading the article, answer the questions.

# President Visits Disaster Area

KELSO, Wash.—President Carter toured the Mt. St. Helens area by helicopter today. He flew within two miles of the volcano, which erupted last Sunday leaving at least 14 people dead and 75 missing. An area of 150 square miles is still covered with mud and volcanic ash. "There was nothing left except piles of mud and what used to be mountains," said the President.

After landing, the President visited the elementary school at Kelso, where some of the thousands left homeless are now being housed. Talking with them, he promised federal aid in rebuilding the area. "It will take years," he said.

When someone compared the area around the volcano to the desolate landscape on the moon, Carter disagreed. "From what I know from pictures," he said, "the moon looks like a golf course compared to this." He was referring to the miles of destroyed forests and the damage done to roads and towns by the mud and the ash.

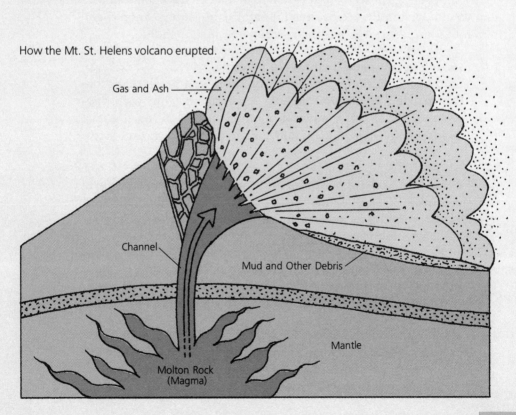

How the Mt. St. Helens volcano erupted.

Gas and Ash

Channel

Mud and Other Debris

Mantle

Molton Rock
(Magma)

## Apply the Skills As You Deal with the World

These study and research skills can help you understand the materials you read outside of school, too. The following newspaper article is about the scientific study of daydreams. Read the article to find out why daydreaming is good for you. Again, the questions below show how the study and research skills you have learned can help you understand what you read. Read the questions. Keep them in mind as you read. Answer them when you finish reading.

1.  **Making a study plan.** If you were planning to write a two-page report on daydreams, what information would you take from this article? Would you include examples of your own daydreams? What other sources might you use to learn about daydreams? How long would it take to research and write the report?

2.  **Index.** The table of contents and the index are the two parts of a book that tell you what information is in the book. What words would you look up in an index if you were doing research on daydreams? Why?

3.  **News media.** Would you expect to find information on daydreams on a daily television newscast? in a newspaper editorial? in a newsmagazine? Why do you think as you do?

4.  **SQ3R.** Write down one or two questions you have about daydreams. When you finish reading the article, decide if it answers your questions. If not, decide where you might look to find the answers to your questions.

# DAYDREAMING? GOOD FOR YOU!

Ronald Kotulak

Research in the last 10 years has destroyed the myth that daydreams are bad for you. Not only are they healthy and normal, but they are one of the brain's important and previously unrecognized ways of solving problems.

Anyone who offers you a penny for your thoughts is short-changing you, according to Dr. Eric Klinger, a University of Minnesota psychologist who has done pioneering research in daydreams.

Many famous people have had productive daydreams. Mozart would often have melodies come to him while daydreaming and Robert Louis Stevenson essentially wrote up his dreams.

Daydreams usually are defined as involuntary thoughts, something that pops into your mind while you are doing something else. Often they are characterized as fanciful.

Average people spend about 50 percent of their waking hours daydreaming. The typical daydream is fleeting, lasting only 14 seconds. Half of them take 5 seconds or less, while some may last a minute or more.

The shorter daydreams are brief thoughts that scamper through the brain with such messages as "I've got to sharpen my pencil." The longer ones tend to be full-blown fantasies that momentarily lift the daydreamer to the heights of "stardom."

Daydreams appear to be good for the brain, like healthy exercise, Klinger said. Daydreams both relax and stimulate the brain.

Researchers have discovered that daydreams, far from being a waste of time, serve an important role in helping a person solve problems.

"Daydreams are often about goals people have that they haven't yet achieved but haven't given up on," said Klinger.

Their function is to thrash over ongoing concerns at a time when a person is not directly working on those concerns.

"It is important to know that is is OK to have wild ideas. Daydreams are a resource that people can harness by paying more attention to the products of their thoughts," he said.

# Section 4　Literary Appreciation Skills

# Escape

## Overview and Purposes for Reading

### The Theme

#### Escape

1.     Do you sometimes want to escape from your everyday life? What are some ways to do so? Are there helpful short escapes, as well as permanent ones? Have you ever had an exciting escape from some real danger? What kinds of things can you think of that people may want or need to escape from?

### The Skills

#### Literary Appreciation Skills Types of Literature

2.     You know that fiction is a type of writing based on imagination more than on fact. Do you know what historical fiction is?

3.     How is historical fiction different from other realistic fiction?

#### Study and Research Skills Reference Sources

4.     How do you use a card catalog? Why is it important to know?

# Learn About the Skills

## Literary Appreciation Skills  Types of Literature

A work of fiction is a product of a writer's imagination. The author makes up a story about imaginary people, events, and places. Some facts about real people, events, and places may be included. But the main purpose of fiction is not to give facts.

You have already read many different types of fiction. Chances are that you have read stories or books of **realistic fiction.** This type of fiction is a favorite of many people. In it the people, places, and events seem lifelike and real. In fact, they may seem so real that you can't judge for sure whether you're reading fiction unless you are told.

Some authors of realistic fiction would say that their characters are based on real people. Some of the events in their stories may have been suggested by real happenings. But such authors don't write about what really happened to real people. That wouldn't be fiction. They tell stories they've made up. Using some traits of real people and some parts of real events only helps to make the story seem realistic, or believable.

One kind of realistic fiction is **historical fiction.** You can guess that this kind of fiction gets its name from the word *history*. Historical fiction is about some time in the past, a time you read about in history books.

History books tell facts, not stories. Writers of historical fiction use some of those facts in the stories they make up. Some of what happens in such stories really did happen. For example, in a historical novel about the American Revolution, some of the imaginary characters may take part in the Boston Tea Party, which was a real event.

The conversations, the specific details, and at least some of the characters and events in historical fiction are imaginary. Writers of historical fiction usually do a great deal of research, though. You can get a true sense of what it was like to live in a historical place and time from reading historical fiction. The writer tries to make life in another time seem real. He or she tries to make up a good story about some events that *could* have happened way back then—and about some that really did happen.

Realistic fiction deals with imaginary people and events—and can take place at any time. Historical fiction is realistic fiction that takes place in the past.

You'll see some examples in this unit.

# Study and Research Skills   Reference Sources

The card catalog in a library includes cards for every book in that library. You can find a book of fiction by looking for a card with the title of the book at the top. Another card lists the same book with the author's name at the top. The cards are all in alphabetical order. Remember that authors are alphabetized by their last names. Also keep in mind that, if the title begins with the word *a*, *an*, or *the*, it is usually alphabetized by the second word in the title. This is done because so many titles begin with these words.

| Author Card | Title Card |
|---|---|
| Y629.44  Bergaust, Erik<br><br>    Colonizing space.--Putnam's, c1978<br><br>    62 p.    ill. | Y629.44    Colonizing space<br><br>    Bergaust, Erik<br><br>    Colonizing space.--Putnam's, c1978<br><br>    62 p.    ill. |

   Books of nonfiction can be found by author or title, too. There usually is a third card in the catalog as well. This is a subject card. You can find out the titles of all the nonfiction books the library has on a subject by looking for the subject itself in the card catalog.

Subject Card

```
Y629.44       SPACE STATIONS

    Bergaust, Erik

        Colonizing space.--Putnam's, c1978

        62p.    ill.
```

   You will find out more about how to use a card catalog as you read this unit.

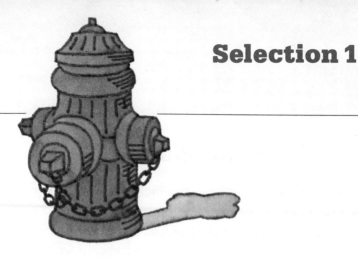

# Selection 1

# Use the Skills

### Understanding the Selection

1.  In the next selection, a man tries a small escape from the ordinary. He tries to do something nice for himself and his neighborhood and gets in trouble with the law. He thinks he's right, but the law tells him he's wrong! He comes up with a clever solution that satisfies him and the law. See how early in the story you can guess what the solution will be.

### Literary Appreciation Skills  Types of Literature

2.  This story is fiction. As you read, think whether it is realistic. Watch for clues that tell you whether it could happen today or whether it takes place in a historical time.

### Study and Research Skills  Reference Sources

3.  This is one story in a book that includes several stories. Think how you could use the card catalog to find out if the book is in the library.

# THE PURPLE PLUG

Benjamin M. Ashcom, Morton A. Maimon,
and William W. Reynolds

When Mr. Snagg went into the paint store Saturday morning, he didn't have any idea how hard it was to buy a gallon of paint. In the old days you just went in and asked for a bucket of red paint or brown paint or green paint. Or maybe, if you liked it, you asked for a bucket of blue paint. No problem.

■ You could look in the card catalog for the names of the authors of this story. If the library has a copy of the book of stories they wrote, you would find a card about it there.

"I'd like two gallons of purple paint, please," he told the clerk.

"Yes sir," the clerk said politely. "What kind of purple did you have in mind?"

That stumped Mr. Snagg. Purple was purple. He was a bit uneasy about the clerk asking strange questions. Was there something funny about the man?

"Purple purple, I guess." Mr. Snagg was a plain man, but he knew what he liked.

The clerk smiled very pleasantly. "Come over and look at our color wheel. Show me exactly what you want."

They went over to a huge wheel that had about a million squares of different colors pasted on it. The wheel kept turning dizzily, which confused Mr. Snagg. He pointed at a little square that was coming his way.

"Something like that," he told the clerk.

The clerk looked at the number on the square and looked it up in a chart.

"Yes sir, that's Hawaiian Orchid."

Mr. Snagg went home with two gallons of purple paint.

All day Sunday, Mr. Snagg painted the woodwork of his small row house. He started at the top and worked down, saving the easiest part for last. High up by the eaves[9] on a swaying ladder he splashed purple over the dingy[9] wood. The window frames came next. The front of his house began to look new. The houses on either side began to look old.

The lady next door came out to watch Mr. Snagg work.

"That's a funny color to paint a house, Mr. Snagg," she said. "Whoever heard of a purple house? And it doesn't go with the bricks. And it doesn't go with my house or Mrs. Penny's house on the other side."

Mr. Snagg kept painting. "I like it," he called down from the ladder. "It's a free country. You paint your house whatever you want. I'll paint mine. And it's not purple, anyway. It's Hawaiian Orchid."

She seemed to like the name. "Oh, that's different," she said and went back into her house.

Finally Mr. Snagg was down to the front door. He painted the door very carefully because everybody who came to the house would see it close up. By late afternoon he was done.

After dinner, Mr. Snagg came outdoors and walked across the street to get a good view of what he had worked so hard on all day. It certainly looked different. He had the newest-looking house on the street. And it was bright and cheerful. None of that drab<sup>cg</sup> brown or dark green! Hawaiian Orchid.

Something caught Mr. Snagg's eye. Something didn't fit the picture. No, it wasn't that the color didn't go with the bricks. It went fine. He thought it even went fine with the houses on either side. Then he saw what was spoiling the picture. On the sidewalk in front of Mr. Snagg's front door was a fireplug. And it was orange.

"Orange sure doesn't go with Hawaiian Orchid," Mr. Snagg said to himself. "It spoils the whole picture."

So Mr. Snagg went back home. He got his paint and brush. And in the late-evening light he painted the fireplug Hawaiian Orchid.

■ By now you can tell that this story is *not* historical fiction. Paint stores, clerks, and fireplugs are part of modern life.

"There! That's the prettiest fireplug in the city! And it goes with my front door. It's perfect."

The next morning when Mr. Snagg was on his way to work, the lady next door was standing in her doorway waiting for him.

"Hey, Mr. Snagg. I saw what you did. You're going to get into a lot of trouble. That fireplug's city property. You can't get away with that. You're asking for trouble."

Mr. Snagg hadn't thought of that. He stopped to think.

"Well now," he said to the lady next door. "If that's city property, it belongs to you and me as well as everybody else. Right?"

"I guess so."

"Well, I bet you like Hawaiian Orchid better than orange."

"I guess so."

"It sure goes better with my front door. So the city's

a little prettier since I painted that fireplug. We'll call it 'urban[9] renewal' and I won't even send them a bill."

The lady laughed. "I guess you're right, Mr. Snagg."

Mr. Snagg felt better now that he had thought it through.

Three days later Mr. Snagg came home from work and saw the fireplug. It was freshly painted shiny, violent orange. A sign hung on it saying "Fresh Paint." It was signed "Fire Department."

The lady next door came out.

"I tried to stop them, Mr. Snagg. But they said all fire-plugs have to be orange so they'll be easy to see. It's against the law to paint them yourself. You'd better not fool around with that plug. That's what they said. And I think you'd better do as they say."

"It sure doesn't go with my Hawaiian Orchid front door."

"Maybe not," she said. "But you won't even see your front door if they put you in jail."

Mr. Snagg went in to watch television. But he couldn't keep his mind on the program. He kept thinking of what the lady next door had said. Sure, there was a good reason for the city to paint fireplugs orange. Maybe it wasn't a good idea to let everybody in the city paint fireplugs any old color. But he still thought it was very important for things to go together, for things in the city to be pretty and match each other. Like his door and the fireplug.

He thought and thought. He worried and worried. He didn't want to break the law about fireplugs. But he knew there were other "laws." Laws about beauty and about things matching and colors going together. And finally, just before he went to bed, he figured out what he could do to obey both kinds of laws.

The next afternoon, Mr. Snagg hurried home from work carrying a package. He left it on the doorstep while he went in to change into his painting clothes. He came out with a big clean paint brush and took a fresh can of paint from the package he had left out front.

He painted all afternoon and far into the evening. And he

hummed to himself as he painted. He had solved his problem and he was happy.

When the lady next door came out, she could see in the evening light that Mr. Snagg had repainted his front door and window frame. And there he was high up on a ladder putting fresh paint on the eaves. Bright orange paint. Paint that matched the fireplug.

"That's a mighty pretty front door, Mr. Snagg. That's the prettiest orange door I ever saw. And it goes just fine with the fireplug."

"I like it," he called down from the ladder. "Now I have the only house in the city with a matching fireplug!"

"You're right, Mr. Snagg. But I'm not sure orange goes with the color of my house."

"It's a free country. You paint your house whatever you want. I'll paint mine. And it's not orange anyway. It's Tropical Sunshine."

# Check the Skills

## Understanding the Selection

1. Did you guess what Mr. Snagg's solution would be? Was he able to carry out his small escape from drabness?

## Literary Appreciation Skills  Types of Literature

2. Do you think this story is realistic? Could it really happen? Why do you think as you do? How did you know it takes place in modern times?

## Study and Research Skills  Reference Sources

3. This story is from a book whose title is *Stories of the Inner City*. Could you find it listed in the card catalog by its title? If you looked for an author card, you would look first in the *A*'s for Ashcom, Benjamin M. Why?

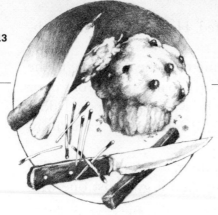

# Use the Skills

### Understanding the Selection

This exciting story tells of a young man's escape from the danger he met while he was "spelunking," or exploring a cave.

1.   Read to find out why he had to escape. Discover how he got into this serious situation.

### Literary Appreciation Skills   Types of Literature

2.   As you read, look for clues to help you decide whether this is historical fiction. You may not be able to decide until you finish reading.

### Study and Research Skills   Reference Sources

3.   How could you use a card catalog to find books about caves or spelunking?

# DANGERS UNDERGROUND

Mary Zettelmier

It was still early in the morning when the lanky[9] sixteen-year-old adjusted the burlap bag on his shoulder. He glanced quickly around the Virginia countryside. Then he dropped into the hole at his feet that was almost concealed[cg] by a mass of low bushes. He and his brother had found the hole the day before. He knew that it opened into a large passageway[cg] that looked as if it wound its way for miles underground.

He had wanted to explore the cave yesterday, but they hadn't had the right equipment with them for spelunking.[cg] Now he had returned alone with the things he needed. He had two large candles and plenty of matches, several blueberry muffins, some beef jerky,[9] and a piece of charcoal. His wool jacket and thick boots would keep him warm and dry underground. He felt ready for adventure.

The only thing he hadn't done, in fact, was tell anyone where he was headed. His brother had said they would explore the cave together sometime next week, but the boy couldn't see waiting that long. He knew he was breaking the most important rules for spelunkers. The first rule is never go underground alone. The second rule is to let someone on the surface know of your plans for entering a cave. But it was too nice a day to worry. He'd be back before anyone missed him.

He lit the first candle and started groping[cg] his way down the narrow path. Away from the daylight at the entrance, the cave was pitch black. He could see no farther than the flicker his candle threw out. More than once he hit his head sharply on rock ledges hanging out over the path.

When the path turned, he marked a large X on the gray-white cave wall with his charcoal. That was the method he had chosen to find his way out when he was

■ Here is some information about exploring caves. You could look in the card catalog for subject cards on *spelunking* or on *caves* to see if the library has any books about these subjects.

ready to go home. As he slowly moved forward, he thought about what his brother had told him. "Caves are living things, always changing and growing. Dripping water makes beautiful rock formations. Sometimes rivers or streams rush through the underground rooms. Wind blows in through the entrance hole or any other surface openings, and together the wind and the water change the cave throughout the years. Many creatures live in caves. Watch for them."

■ Do you have any reason, so far, to believe that this is historical fiction? No historical events or people have been mentioned. It does seem to be realistic fiction.

Crouching<sup>cg</sup> under an overhanging ledge, the boy heard a noise in the still, lonesome blackness. It was a sound he knew—the trickle of water. He rounded the next turn of the hallway and lowered his candle to see a small stream. He made another X at the turn. Then, very carefully, he wedged his candle between a rock and the wall. He slid his hand along the slippery wall and into the stream. The water felt only a little cooler than the air. He remembered that caves, protected as they are by thick layers of earth and rock, stay about the same temperature all year round.

He picked up his candle and began to make his way along the edge of the stream. He wanted to find out what lay beyond this hallway before his candle went out. Sometimes the trail narrowed so that he had to step into the stream, getting his boots wet. No matter how carefully he felt for ledges jutting<sup>cg</sup> out over the path, he occasionally found one with his head instead of his hand.

Finally, the hallway opened into a huge room. By moving his candle around, he saw an enormously high ceiling. Slowly he circled around the edge of the room, marveling<sup>c</sup> at the beauty of the grotto.<sup>cg</sup> Limestone formations<sup>g</sup> seemed to flow like rippling<sup>c</sup> waterfalls down the cavern<sup>cg</sup> walls, and others hung, ropelike, from the ceiling.

As he started to move on, something slithered<sup>g</sup> across his feet, startling him. At the same moment, his candle stub gave a last flicker and burned out completely, and he was left in total darkness.

"Hold on there. Don't get scared," he muttered to himself, groping<sup>cg</sup> in his bag for his last candle and a match to light it with. When the light once more flickered in the room, he leaned against the wall. He felt suddenly tired and hungry. Inside the cave he had lost all track of time. It was another world altogether from that above ground.

He chewed on a little beef jerky and ate a muffin while he rested. He knew he must start back soon. If one candle had brought him to this strangely beautiful room, it would surely take one more to return him to the entrance.

It was easy enough to find the hallway through which he had entered the grotto. But when he came to an intersection° where two paths met, he became confused. There was no charcoal X on the wall. Apparently he had not noticed the second path before. He decided to try the right-hand way. Now it occurred to him that he had not seen any of his charcoal markings on the walls for a long time. Why hadn't he been more careful about placing them regularly? More important, why hadn't he told his brother or a friend that he was exploring the cave? He wondered what time it was.

He knew that the dangers of spelunking included poisonous gases, sudden flooding from storms on the surface, diseases carried by bats and other cave animals, and, worst of all, the danger of losing your way. And now he had let himself get lost!

This could not be the right passage, he was sure of that. Where were the large rocks that he had so often bumped his head on when he was coming in? He must backtrack° and try the other way.

The candle was burning down more quickly, it seemed, than the first one. He reached the intersection where he had taken the wrong turn and hurried up the left-hand path, casting his light about for his X markings. Nothing.

Suddenly, he thought he saw something familiar on the wall far ahead. His candle didn't shine brightly enough to be sure, but it looked like one of his big charcoal Xs. With a sigh of relief, he hurried along even faster. He didn't dare think what he would do if his candle burned out.

He hadn't gone far when all of a sudden he heard a deafening noise. His heart pounding, he pressed against the wall as thousands of large brown bats filled the passageway. The candle flickered, then went out in the draft created by their wings. He could feel the bats swarming around him and over him as they passed through the hall. It must be sunset time, he realized suddenly. His brother had told him that early every evening the bats swarmed out of their caves to find food.

Then he had another, happier thought. If the bats were on their way out, then he must be headed in the right direction, too! Encouraged,[cg] he reached in his knapsack for a match and relit his candle. The bats had all flown past him by now.

He followed them along the quiet passageway. A large X stood out on the wall ahead. When the passage turned to the right, he could see a small speck of daylight far in the distance. He breathed a sigh of relief. He wasn't lost after all—but he had come uncomfortably close to it. Next time, he would tell his brother where he was going or, better yet, bring him along. Now he only wanted to leave as quickly as possible, but there was one last thing he had to do. Taking his knife from his pocket, he carved his name and the date of his exploration on the wall just inside the cave entrance: G. Washington—1748.

■ This story has a surprise ending. Until now, the writer has given you no clue that the boy is someone famous or that the story took place long ago. Do you think it really could have happened?

# Check the Skills

## Understanding the Selection

1. Why was this spelunking trip especially dangerous for George Washington? Why did he have to escape from the cave? How did he manage? How did he get himself into such danger?

## Literary Appreciation Skills  Types of Literature

2. Until you came to the very last line and learned that the boy in the story was young George Washington, you might have thought the story took place in modern times. Even though the author has pretended this escape happened to George Washington, it didn't. It's not a historical event, but just a good story with a surprise twist at the end to make it more fun to read. Do you think the story is realistic fiction? Why or why not?

## Study and Research Skills  Reference Sources

3. If you wanted to read a book about caves or spelunking, you could check the card catalog for subject cards. How could you use a card catalog to find other books written by the author of this selection?

# Use the Skills

### Understanding the Selection

Julie is a thirteen-year-old Eskimo girl. Her mother has died, and her father is believed to be dead also. As her father had arranged, she is sent from her home on Nunivak Island in the south of Alaska, to Barrow, far north in the Arctic Circle. In Barrow, for many months in the winter, the sun does not rise at all. Julie is terribly unhappy in her situation, and the dark days do not help her mood.

1. As you read, try to decide what Julie, her friend Pearl, and the other residents of Barrow are escaping from on this great day.

### Literary Appreciation Skills  Types of Literature

2. Can you tell whether this selection is historical fiction?

### Study and Research Skills  Reference Sources

3. *Julie of the Wolves* is a novel. This selection is just a small part of it. Do you think you could find the book in the library if you wanted to read it? Where and how would you look?

# JULIE OF THE WOLVES

Jean Craighead George

January twenty-fourth was a day of celebration. Beginning about the twenty-first, the top of the world began to glow like an eclipse[9] as the sun circled just below the horizon.[9] The Americans began to smile, and the Eskimos put away their winter games of yo-yo and darts. Excitement mounted higher and higher each day.

The morning of the twenty-fourth, Julie and Pearl ran all the way to school, for this was the most beautiful day of the year, the day of the sunrise.

Just before noon, Julie and her classmates put on their parkas[9] and mittens and skipped out the school door in awesome[9] silence. The gussak[9] principal was already outside watching the southeastern sky anxiously. His face seemed to say he really did not believe the miracle would happen.

"There it is!" a little boy shouted as a brilliant light, first green then red, exploded on the horizon. Slowly the life-giving star arose until it was round and burning red in the sky. The Eskimos lifted their arms and turned their palms to the source of all life. Slowly, without any self-consciousness, every gussak raised his arms, too. Not one person snickered[9] at the old Eskimo tradition.

For an hour and a half the sun moved above the horizon, reminding the Eskimos that the birds and mammals would come back, that the snow would melt, and that the great ice pack that pressed against the shore would begin to retreat and set them free to hunt and fish.

■ Up in the Arctic Circle, daylight and dark are very different from what you are probably used to. There are months in summer when it is never dark, as well as months in winter when there is no daylight. If you want to know why this happens, a book on the seasons might help you.

Even on Nunivak there was no such wonderful day, for the sun appeared for a little while every day of the year.

"Bright sun, I missed you so," Julie whispered, and her palms felt vibrant[9] with life.

■ This story is a work of the author's imagination. There are no historical characters or events. It is not about a real historical time.

# Check the Skills

### Understanding the Selection

1. Why is this January day so important to the people of Barrow, Alaska? What do they feel they are escaping from?

### Literary Appreciation Skills Types of Literature

2. This selection is fiction. Do you think it is realistic? Why or why not?

### Study and Research Skills Reference Sources

3. You should be able to find the book *Julie of the Wolves* by Jean Craighead George in the library. It is about another kind of escape, and a very exciting one. If you can find a card for it in the card catalog, then your library has the book. It will be listed both under the name of the book and under the name of the author.

# Selection 4

# Use the Skills

### Understanding the Selection

The next selection is an excerpt from a well-known book about a boy in Boston during the American Revolution. The book is *Johnny Tremain* by Esther Forbes.

1. The most important escape in the American Revolution, of course, was the escape of the Americans from British rule. In this selection there is a much less important and much more humorous escape described. See what it is.

### Literary Appreciation Skills   Types of Literature

2. *Johnny Tremain* is a fine example of historical fiction. It is considered by many people to be a classic. As you read this excerpt, find out if you get some idea of what life was like on this day.

### Study and Research Skills   Reference Sources

3. Think how you could use a card catalog to find books about the leaders of the Revolution. Also decide how you could find out if your library has the book *Johnny Tremain*.

# JOHNNY TREMAIN

Esther Forbes

This day, this unreal day, in which Boston waited hour upon hour for news—any news, good or bad—was well begun. Suddenly, people were saying, "Have you heard? At sunrise this morning over in Lexington the British fired on us." No one seemed to know where this rumor had started, but it was everywhere.

Although half of Gage's[9] forces had left town for the battlefield, there were more officers than usual hanging about the streets and taverns. Their faces were bland.[9] They reassured the people glibly[9] that not a shot had been fired and not a person killed. They begged all and sundry[9] smoothly to keep calm and go to their shops or their homes. All this made Johnny confident that the British as well as the inhabitants had heard now that the war had begun.

By noon little bands of soldiers appeared on the streets going quickly from house to house. Too late General Gage had given orders that the leaders of the opposition[cg] should be arrested. But the leaders were all gone. The angry, frustrated soldiers might scare Sam Adams's housekeeper out of her wits. They could break John Hancock's fence. But these gentlemen had quietly left Boston a month before. The soldiers stormed into Joseph Warren's house. He was gone. And so was Paul Revere. Not one of the principal[cg] leaders was left. And seemingly no rebel[cg] printers. Isaiah Thomas's shop was empty. He and his press had left the night before. At Edes and Gill's, where the *Boston Gazette* was published, they did grab young Peter Edes. His father and press had been smuggled[9] out to Watertown.

Robert Newman, suspected of having hung the lanterns in Christ's Church the night before, was thrown into jail. John Pulling, merely suspected of having helped, was forced to hide. Paul Revere's cousin was in jail. And every minute the temper of the soldiers was growing shorter and

■ How could you locate books about these leaders in a card catalog?

a queer feeling of jubilation[9] was apparent among the people. You couldn't see, you couldn't guess, why they began feeling so confident. Confidence was in the air.

As soon as Johnny heard that arresting parties were on the streets, he sent a message to Uncle Lorne. Uncle had best make himself scarce.[9] Soon after, having stood about the jail and noted exactly who was put in it, he himself headed for Salt Lane. There was not a person in the street, but at every window he saw a face. The lane itself had changed. He glanced about him and saw what was wrong. There was no little man in a blue coat observing Boston through a spyglass. The familiar sign had been torn down, stamped to kindling. The door of the shop was shattered. He went in. The presses were broken. The type pied.[cg] Upstairs his bed had been ripped open by bayonets. Frightened, he ran across the street.

Aunt Jenifer sat in her kitchen. Half in her lap and half on the floor was an enormous feather bed. She was peacefully sticking on it a new ticking. The only unusual thing was the great number of feathers this deft[cg] housewife had carelessly spilled over her kitchen floor.

Rabbit, enchanted with these new toys, was constantly picking up a feather, putting it in his hair, and saying "Yankee-do."

"They've been here?" asked Johnny.

"Yes. Are they gone?"

"Not one in sight."

"We got your message just as they were turning down Salt Lane."

The feather bed began to heave on the floor.

"You can come out now," Aunt Jenifer whispered to it.

Out of the bottom rolled Uncle Lorne, choked with feathers and looking more bird than human. Rabbit shrieked, "Da, Da." He evidently[cg] thought his father much improved. Still trembling, for Uncle Lorne was a timid[cg] man, he kissed his wife and hugged his child.

"It was all I could think of," Aunt Jenifer said to Johnny. "Mr. Lorne just stood there and said he wasn't afraid to die.

We could hear the men marching down the street…it was terrible. So I just popped him in and went on sewing."

"Were the soldiers rough?"

"Rough? They were furious."

"Good," said Johnny grimly. "That means they are really scared. Something pretty awful has happened to all those men Gage has sent out. Some of the officers may know already. But the men have guessed it. They are running about with uniforms unbuttoned yelling, 'If they want a war, we'll give it to 'em. And they won't pay taxes? We'll collect in blood.'"

"You don't say! Are you sure the fight's going for us?"

"Pretty sure. I was down by the ferry⁹ slip and saw a British major coming over from Charlestown. Well, he had a civilian coat over his uniform—sort of disguised—and he tore off the boat and ran for the Province House. He'd come to tell Gage that Colonel Smith's and Percy's men are getting licked."

"Boy, you're jumping at conclusions."

"Not I. I saw his face. It was just done in and tied up with disgust. His uniform was a mess. His feelings had been hurt. People who have been winning battles don't go around with faces like that. But British officers who have been beaten by 'peasants' and 'yokels' do."

"Oh, Johnny, I do like to hear you talk like that. But I'm not counting much on one man's face. Where you off to?"

"Beacon Hill. I've an idea that major got back to Gage to tell him one thing. The British are going to try to get to Charlestown, just the way he did, and under protection of the *Somerset's* guns. They won't back-track the way they came. Too dangerous. If I've guessed right, before long from Beacon Hill we'll be able to see them—running, and our men after them."

"Johnny, here's half a mince pie for you. You're a real smart boy."

Uncle Lorne came back from the bedroom where he, with Rabbit's help, had been picking off feathers. "Even if they hang me," he said in a proud tremolo, "I will feel I have not lived in vain." He was still pretty scared.

Out on the street, Johnny met officers yelling at their men, trying to get them back into their barracks, striking at them even with the flat of their swords. You couldn't say the British regulars[c9] lacked fight. All they could talk about was how many cowards and rebels they were going to kill. In one day all was changed in Boston.

On both sides the gloves were off and the hands underneath were bloody. War had begun.

■ Johnny was only sixteen when all this was happening, but he took an active part in the Revolution. Do you get a feeling of what this day must have been like for him?

# Check the Skills

### Understanding the Selection

1.  How did Johnny's Uncle Lorne escape from the British soldiers?

### Literary Appreciation Skills Types of Literature

2.  a. Did you get a sense of what life was like in Boston on that day? Why or why not?

    b. Do you think this is a good example of historical fiction? Why or why not?

### Study and Research Skills Reference Sources

3.  You might find books about the leaders of the Revolution by looking up their names in a card catalog. Can you think of another subject card you could check, too? If you looked for the title *Johnny Tremain,* you would look in the *J*'s. This is because it is a *title*, not a subject or an author. A title is alphabetized by its first word even if the title is a person's name.

# Selection 5

## Use the Skills

Sometimes people want something so much they will do just about anything to get it. The boy in this story goes about getting what he wants in the wrong way. See if you think this story could really happen. What kinds of escape are involved?

Look for clues that tell you what kind of fiction this is. This time there are no notes in the margin.

# THE QUARTER

Piri Thomas

A child wants to have a few cents at least, some money to be able to go to the movies, to be able to buy a hot dog or a *bacalaito*.[9] You know, things that other people that have wealth can enjoy. To have some money in your pocket, that's a joy indeed.

My father worked very hard on a construction gang. When he left for work in the morning he would give my mother money to buy food, always leaving something extra on top of the table to make sure that we'd also have dessert. On this day, he put one quarter, some dimes, and a nickel, maybe forty-five or fifty cents, a whole lot. I really wanted to go to that movie. I looked at the money and said, "Well, they would not miss it, you know." So I took the quarter and put it into my socks, pushing it all the way down until it was underneath—inside my sneaker.

As my father started to walk out the door to go to his job, he said to my mother, "I left some change." And my mother said, "Bring it to me." My father came back for the money, and he looked and he quietly said, "There is a quarter missing." Oh, if he had only gone, I thought, then Mama would not have known a quarter was missing.

I immediately began to look all over the floor and under the beds and over everything. And my father just stood there, looking at me. I, who always complained about going down to the grocery store or even washing behind my ears, I, who always was the last to volunteer, was all of a sudden so willing to look for the missing quarter.

My father said to my sister, "Have you seen the quarter?" My sister said, "No." My father said to me, "Have you seen it?" And I said, "No, Poppa, can't you see I'm trying hard to find it?" I was really wishing I had never taken that old quarter. I was not born a criminal, I just wanted a chance to see what it was like to have a quarter.

My father looked at me, and I knew that he knew that the quarter was somewhere on me. Not to make me feel completely guilty, he said, "I'll frisk everybody." He left me there sweating to the last—till finally, it was my turn. He emptied my pockets, and while he was doing all this frisking I was loudly proclaiming[9] my innocence.[cg]

"Poppa, how could you even think this? Poppa, have you ever known me to take anything that didn't belong to me?"

Poppa said, "Take off your sneakers." I took my smelly sneakers off. Poppa beat them awfully hard against each other. He said, "Your socks." I took one sock off. The sock with the quarter was the last to go. I slipped it off, holding the coin inside with my thumb and forefinger, hoping that the quarter would stay in the sock, which it did not. *Plink-ling-ling* the quarter came tumbling out. My face said, "How did that get there?"

I wondered if Poppa would believe that quarter had just rolled off the table and without me feeling a thing had slipped into my sock and

wormed its way under my foot.

My father came after me like Superman, faster than a speeding bullet, more powerful than a locomotive, able to leap backyard fences in a single bound. He was a natural-born athlete who had played for the Cuban Stars, the Black Stars, the Puerto Rican Stars—*Olé, Olé.* And then—I was caught. I tried to smile as I waited for the blows that were to come, but my father just looked at me and said, "Son, why didn't you ask for it? I would have given it to you. Did you have to steal it?" I just looked at Poppa and began to cry. My sorry tears ran down my cheeks. I just stood there feeling like a chump. What can a guy say at a time like that?

# Check the Skills

### Understanding the Selection

1. What is the boy trying to escape from? Does he succeed? What is wrong about the way in which he goes about it? After the father finds that the quarter is missing, what is the boy trying to escape from? Do you think he ever escaped his regrets for what he had done?

### Literary Appreciation Skills Types of Literature

2. How did you decide that this is realistic fiction?

### Study and Research Skills Reference Sources

3. This is one story from a book. The title of the book is *Stories from El Barrio.* Its author is Piri Thomas. How could you use a card catalog to see if your library has the book?

# Apply What You Learned in Unit 13

## The Theme

### Escape

1. Almost everyone wants, at times, to escape. It may be from a real danger, like being lost in a cave. Or you may need to escape from poverty or sickness or pain. Perhaps you just need to escape from the sameness of everyday life. Escapes can be lasting or just temporary. But even a brief escape, such as reading a good book or listening to music or going for a walk, can sometimes be very helpful.

• Think of some of the escapes you have just read about. With the return of the sun, the people at Barrow, Alaska, escape each year from winter darkness. The people in Johnny Tremain's time wanted escape from British rule. You will probably read other books that deal with escape. Watch for this theme, too, in movies and TV programs you see. Do you think escapes are always a good idea?

# The Skills

## Literary Appreciation Skills Types of Literature

2.    Reading realistic and historical fiction can provide you with a kind of temporary escape. Reading historical fiction can give you not only a good story, but also a picture of what life was like in another time. It can also give you some information about important events and people of that time.

3.    Fiction is the work of the author's imagination, it is true. But because it is realistic, and therefore believable, it can give you good ideas about how people live and act and solve the problems in their lives. "Julie of the Wolves" and "The Quarter" are examples of realistic fiction.

## Study and Research Skills Reference Sources

4.    Remember that the easiest way to find out if your library has a certain book is to use the card catalog. It is important that you know how to do this because it will save you time. You also will be better at doing research for reports for school.

# Trouble

## Overview and Purposes for Reading

### The Theme

### Trouble

1. How do people react when trouble enters their lives? What effect does trouble have on the kind of people we are?

### The Skills

### Literary Appreciation Skills Story Elements

2. What is the plot of a story? What is the climax?

3. Why is it helpful to recognize the plot and the climax in what you are reading?

### Vocabulary Development Skills Word Meaning

4. When you come across a word that has more than one meaning, how do you figure out which meaning the author has in mind?

## Literary Appreciation Skills Story Elements

A story contains three major elements—characters, setting, and plot. This unit focuses on plot and on climax. The climax is a part of the plot.

The **plot** is the plan or development of the story. It includes the important events and situations. The high point of interest or excitement in the plot is called the **climax.**

Read the following very short story. Think about what happens. This is the plot of the story. Think about the high point. This is the climax.

> Jill closed the door of her apartment and started up the hall. If she didn't hurry, she would be late for school. But something made her pause. She sniffed and realized that she smelled smoke. Looking around, she saw a trace of smoke coming from under the door of an apartment up the hall. "Someone must have burned the toast," she thought, smiling.
>
> As she was about to pass the door with the mysterious smoke, Jill paused again. What if it was a real fire? She knocked on the door. There was no answer, and she wondered what to do next. Then she heard it—a cry like that of a baby. Trying the door, she found it unlocked and opened it.
>
> The room was so filled with smoke that she could just make out a crib in the far corner. The cry she had heard before was repeated. Without a second thought, Jill ran to the crib and grabbed the tiny baby, now gasping for breath. Dashing back into the hall, Jill called out "Fire!" The door of a nearby apartment opened, and a young woman rushed out to take the baby from Jill's arms.
>
> Jill was late for school that morning. But when she explained why, no one seemed to mind.

What is the plot of this little story? It's simply that Jill, leaving for school, notices smoke and then a baby's cry. She rescues the baby and gives it to its mother. Then she goes to school.

The high point of interest and excitement, the climax, occurs when Jill goes into the smoke-filled room and brings the baby out. Did you notice how the story line built up to the climax? It started with the everyday happening of a girl leaving for school. Then the smoke and the baby in danger changed the whole picture. Jill's rescuing the baby provided the excitement and the climax.

**Try the Skill.** Read this even shorter story.

> Barry and Joe had passed the old haunted house on Maple Street many times. Tonight, however, was to be different. They had decided to go inside. It was a dark and windy night, just the night for a haunted house.
>
> The front door creaked open, and the boys stood staring into a large and empty room, with stairs leading up. "Let's leave the door open, just in case," Barry suggested, as they stepped inside. Joe nodded, and then grabbed Barry's arm. "Look!" he whispered, pointing to the stairs. A white and shadowy figure was slowly floating down. The boys bolted through the open door and out into the street.

The plot, again, is simple. What is it? Two boys decide to enter an old house that is supposed to be haunted. They do so, and see a ghostly figure on the dark stairs. They depart hastily. What is the point of most excitement? This, the climax, is when they see the "ghost."

You'll learn more about plot and climax as you read this unit.

# Vocabulary Development Skills Word Meaning

Read the following sentences.

> Jack will train hard for the big race.
> Her train is due at six o'clock tonight.
> The settlers were saddened by a train of misfortunes.

The underlined word in each sentence is the same. But in each sentence it has a different meaning. You can decide what this meaning is by the way the word is used.

You know that a train is a connected line of railroad cars. You know that *train* can also mean "to get in shape through diet and exercise." You know that it can also mean a series. Reread the sentences. Choose which of these meanings fit each one.

*Light* is another word that has many meanings. You will probably find thirty or forty definitions of *light* in a dictionary. When you come across such a word, note what is being talked about in the rest of the sentence. Then decide which of the word's many meanings makes sense in that sentence. Read these sentences. Decide what *light* means in each one.

> The next speaker put the matter in a different light.
> Animals active at night prefer the dark to the light.
> Let's light the candles for Maria's birthday cake.

Remember to use the meaning of the rest of the sentence to help you decide. Use a dictionary or glossary only if you must.

You'll get more practice in choosing the correct meanings for words as you read the selections in this unit.

# Use the Skills

### Understanding the Selection

1.  This selection is an old tale from Hungary. In this story, an honest man finds trouble in the form of a greedy innkeeper. Notice how he reacts until help comes from an unexpected direction.

### Literary Appreciation Skills Story Elements

2.  The story starts well for the honest man, who is able to pay all his debts. Then, both bad things and good things happen. This is the plot. Watch how it unfolds.

3.  A marginal note will help you identify the climax.

### Vocabulary Development Skills Word Meaning

4.  Use the notes in the margins for help with several words that have more than one meaning.

# HARD-BOILED EGGS

retold by Tom R. Kovach

Once upon a time, in the kingdom of Hungary, there lived a man named Janos Kadar. After many years of hard work, he was able to pay off all his debts⁹ and still have enough money left to live comfortably for the rest of his life. So on a bright and sunny morning Janos set out happily to repay the inn-keeper⁹ who had helped him when he was poor and hungry.

This innkeeper was very surprised to see Janos. "A good day to you," said Janos. "Ten years ago you gave me two boiled eggs when I was hungry and had no money. Today I want to reward your kindness by paying for those eggs a hundredfold!"⁹

But the ten years had changed the innkeeper from a generousᶜ man to a greedyᶜ one. He began figuring what would have happened if the two eggs had hatched little chickens, and if those chickens had grown up and hatched more chickens, and so on. He finally concludedᶜ that Janos must give him everything he had, even his savings.

Now Janos was very surprised and upset that his kind gesture⁹ should be met with such greedy demands. The news of his predicament⁹ spread throughout the land. Finally the King of Hungary himself heard the story and agreed to sit in judgment of what should be done.

As the time drew near for Janos and the innkeeper to present their cases before the King, poor Janos became more and more unhappy. His hard-earned savings would be lost, for the King was sure to decide in favor of the crafty⁹ inn-keeper.

One day, as he sat thinking about his misfortune,ᶜ a wandering gypsy came by. "Why so sad, my good man?" he asked Janos cheerfully. When Janos explained about the eggs, the gypsy laughed. "Why, you needn't worry. Let me

■ The plot begins to unfold when Janos decides to pay the innkeeper.

■ Case has several meanings. Here *cases* means "matters for a court of law to settle."

■ The appearance of the gypsy brings an unexpected turn to the plot.

present your case to the King, and you'll surely win." Now Janos had heard that gypsies were clever people. So, although he had little hope that anyone could help him, he agreed to let the gypsy try. What else was there to do?

The day of the trial arrived, but when Janos reached the King's chamber, the gypsy was nowhere to be found. Everybody sat waiting and waiting, until finally the King grew impatient. "Janos Kadar," he said, "if the man representing you does not arrive in one minute, you shall have to pay the innkeeper all he asks for."

■ The meaning of *bursting* here is "coming in suddenly."

Just at that moment the gypsy came bursting through the door. "I am sorry for being late, Your Majesty," he said breathlessly, "but I was at home boiling corn, trying to turn it into more corn!"

At this, everyone in the King's chamber laughed. "You silly man," said the King, "how can you make more corn from boiled corn?"

The gypsy smiled. "Well then, Your Majesty, how can you hatch chicks from boiled eggs?"

■ The climax is the gypsy's clever solution to the problem.

The King rubbed his chin thoughtfully. "You are right," he said finally. "If the eggs were boiled, it would be impossible to hatch chicks from them. Janos, you have only to pay for the two eggs you ate."

So Janos thanked the King and the gypsy traveler, paid the innkeeper, and went home content. As for the innkeeper, well, because of his greed he only got paid for the two eggs, instead of getting the reward that Janos had first offered him.

# Check the Skills

### Understanding the Selection

1.  How did Janos react to trouble? What saved him? Do you think this was a reasonable solution? Why or why not?

### Literary Appreciation Skills Story Elements

2.  The plot seems to take a new turn every time a new character appears in the story. Do you agree? Why or why not?

3.  The gypsy's solution represents the climax of the story because it is the high point of interest in what is happening. Do you agree? Why or why not?

### Vocabulary Development Skills Word Meaning

4.  How could the meaning of the sentences that included the words case and bursting help you decide what those words meant in this story? Notes in the margin can help you locate the words again if you need to.

# Selection 2

# Use the Skills

### Understanding the Selection

Trouble sometimes creeps up on us, and we can see it coming. At other times, it's with us in an instant, with no time to prepare.

1.  In this brief selection you will see how a Russian boy, who later became a famous poet, reacted to the second kind of trouble.

### Literary Appreciation Skills Story Elements

2.  This selection is part of an autobiography. The author has written the story of his own life. This is not fiction, but it still has a plot—and a definite climax. Note how the plot builds up to the moment of excitement.

### Vocabulary Development Skills Word Meaning

3.  You'll find a few words with more than one meaning, but the author's intent should be clear.

# SUDDEN TROUBLE

Yevgeny Yevtushenko

I quarreled with Mother and ran away to join my father. I traveled on the roof of a train all the way to Kazakhstan.

I was fifteen.

I wanted to become a man and stand on my own feet. At that time my father was working as chief of a geological[g] expedition[g].

When I arrived, ragged and skinny, he looked me over and said, "So you want to stand on your own feet. Well, if you really do, no one here must know you're my son. Otherwise you'll be favored whether you want it or not, and that isn't going to make a man of you."

I joined the expedition as a laborer.[cg]

I learned to break the ground with a pick, to split off samples of rock as flat as my hand with a mallet[g], to use a razor blade to make three matches out of the only one we had left, and to light a fire in driving rain.

I couldn't swim. And I lived in fear of being found out and disgraced.[cg]

One day I was walking with a geologist[c] along a narrow mountain path above a noisy stream. We both carried knapsacks[c] filled with specimens[g] of rock. Suddenly the geologist took a false step and the ground gave way under his feet. He tried to catch hold of a bush, missed it, and fell headlong from the steep bank, down into the river. Within seconds I saw him thrashing[c] about in the foaming water, struggling to keep afloat, but his knapsack was dragging him down.

I flung mine off my shoulders, whipped my knife from inside my belt, and jumped in.

It was not till I had swum up to the geologist, cut the straps of his knapsack, and we had both scrambled ashore, that I remembered I didn't know how to swim.

■ The plot begins to unfold immediately, as Yevgeny runs away from home.

■ Four of the last six words in this sentence carry more than one meaning. But the sense of the sentence makes it easy to figure out what the author intended them to mean.

■ The high point of excitement is here. This is the climax.

And from that day on I have known that the best way of learning something is to take a leap into the unknown without looking back. That way, you either learn or perish.[cg]

# Check the Skills

### Understanding the Selection

1.  How did the suddenness of the trouble influence Yevgeny's reaction to it? What effect did the incident have on the boy's character? Reread the last paragraph if you're not sure.

### Literary Appreciation Skills Story Elements

2.  This selection is nonfiction. It is an autobiography. But the author tells of his own life as if he were telling a story, so it reads like a story. We don't usually think of plots and climaxes in such nonfiction works. But this story certainly has a plot and a climax. What is the climax?

### Vocabulary Development Skills Word Meaning

3.  How did you know that the word *driving* in the sentence on page 391 had nothing to do with operating a car? The marginal note can help you find it if you want to read the sentence again.

# Use the Skills

### Understanding the Selection

1. In this story, Patricia and Dorothy have trouble with a friend. Read to see what steps they take to deal with their problem. Decide whether their plan helps or not.

### Literary Appreciation Skills Story Elements

2. This is a chapter from the novel *Next Door to Xanadu*. The plot centers on Patricia's relationship with her classmate, Bill. In this chapter, Patricia's friend Dorothy helps her take some action which, the girls hope, will put Bill in his place. As you read, note how the plot unfolds.

3. The climax in this story may not be as evident as were the climaxes in the two selections you have just read. See if you agree with the marginal note on page 397.

### Vocabulary Development Skills Word Meaning

4. Use your skill with choosing appropriate word meanings. A marginal note points out one word that has more than one meaning.

# SWEET REVENGE

Doris Orgel

Thursday was the day! We'd be able to start at last. The coast was clear, Dorothy said.

We went straight to Dorothy's kitchen. The first thing we did was get down a box of confectioners'⁹ sugar because in all this time the idea had ripened into a sweet, sweet revenge<sup>c</sup> plot.

■ And we go straight to the plot.

We took an empty coffee can and filled it up to the top with the sugar. We didn't put a lid on, of course. We just wrapped it up neat and tight in a big piece of aluminum foil.⁹ Then we turned it upside down.

We were concentrating<sup>c</sup> so hard we didn't even talk. Finally Dorothy said, "Do you think we should make up some sort of spell<sup>c</sup> to go with it?"

■ *Foil* has more than one meaning. The general meaning of this sentence helps you know which one fits here. Check the glossary if you're not sure.

That was funny because when I had told her about Halloween, I hadn't mentioned the spell I'd cast outside the Wexlers' door. I said, "Cats and sevens all over again!"

"What are you talking about?" she asked.

"Well, your mentioning spells, it's as if you knew—"

"Knew what?"

"About the one I made up on Halloween after what Bill did."

"How did it go?"

"Well, it didn't work, exactly."

"Tell it to me anyway," said Dorothy.

So I told her the spell:

WEXLERS, WEXLERS, MOVE AWAY
FROM APARTMENT TWO-OO-A!

"No wonder it didn't work," she said. "It doesn't scan."⁹

I wasn't sure what "scan" was. "How doesn't it?" I asked.

"Well, listen. 'Wexlers, Wexlers, move away,' that scans all right. But 'From Apartment Two A' doesn't. It's one syllable<sup>c</sup> short. That's why you had to put that 'oo' in between 'two' and 'A.'"

"Oh. If it had scanned, would they have moved, do you think?"

"We'll never know. But let's make one up now."

I said, "Okay," and I thought of one. "How about 'Powdered sugar, pour and spill—'"

I stopped to check if it scanned, and Dorothy beat me to the ending. "'Out all over awful Bill!' That scans fine. It's got to work!"

Then we moved our hands back and forth in mystic motions[c] over the wrapped-up can and said the spell together.

"Now we need a ribbon," said Dorothy as she looked at the green headband I had on.

It was a new one, and I liked it. Still, I took it off and tied it around the can. Then we took our shoes off. Dorothy whispered, "Okay, let's go!"

We didn't make a sound, crossing the hall. I put the gift package down on the Wexlers' doormat. Dorothy gave the bell a quick jab. Both of us dashed back into 2C. Then we waited with our ears pressed to the door.

Soon we heard their door open and Bill's voice. "Hey, a package! It's a present for me!" Then we heard the door shut again.

"Now he's ripping the wrapping off," I said, "and now—"

"Wrapping's off! Now, sugar, spill! And pour all over awful Bill!" Dorothy commanded via[c] remote[9] control.

We got the giggles.

But we had to stop. Our faces had to look as though nothing had happened. We put our shoes back on. "Let's go over there now," I said.

"Wait!" Dorothy went into the kitchen and came back with a measuring cup.

"What's that for?" I asked.

"You'll see. Come on."

We rang the Wexlers' bell again, only this time we didn't run. Mrs. Wexler came to the door. She was holding part of a vacuum cleaner, and she looked annoyed. "Well? What do you want?" she asked.

Behind her stood Bill. I wish I'd had a camera with me to take his picture! But even without one, I doubt I'll ever forget what he looked like: a giant Christmas cookie that somebody very messy had tried to put frosting on, with great big sloppy patches of white all over him. He was still in a daze. He just stood there holding the empty can. Under his feet the carpet was snow-white, not green like the rest of the Wexlers' foyer.[9]

■ This paragraph seems to be the climax, as the girls dare to return to the "scene of the crime."

Dorothy held out the measuring cup. She managed to keep a perfectly straight face as she said, "We were wondering if we could borrow a cup of sugar."

Bill said, "Sugar!" I thought he'd haul off and hit us. I got behind his mother just in case. But then he started to laugh, and he said, "Sure, all the sugar you want!" And he shook his arm to make some sugar fall into the cup Dorothy was holding out. Then his brothers Sherman and Marshall came crawling and toddling over to see what was going on. Sherman stuck his tongue out and licked some sugar off Bill's shoe. That got Bill laughing so hard and shaking some more so that sugar blew off him like snow in a storm. And we all started laughing, even Mrs. Wexler.

Finally Dorothy said, "We were just kidding; we don't really need to borrow any sugar. But we'll help clean up the mess if you want us to, Mrs. Wexler."

We picked up the torn pieces of aluminum foil from the rug, and I took back the green headband we'd used as a ribbon. Then Mrs. Wexler handed me the vacuum cleaner hose. "Go ahead and vacuumͨ Bill," she said. "He needs it more than the rug." Bill ducked. But I wasn't going to anyway. I vacuumed the rug and an armchair that some sugar had spilled on.

"Now, will somebody please tell me what in the world's going on here?" Mrs. Wexler asked. She looked from Bill to Dorothy to me.

Dorothy said, "Well, um—"

I said, "Er—"

It was very hard to explain.

"Oh, nothing, Mom," said Bill. "Just sort of a joke between me and"—he pointed to me. I wondered what name was coming. "Between me and...um...Patricia here and Dorothy Rappaport," said Bill.

Dorothy and I looked at each other, meaning we won!

"'Among,' not 'between,'" said Bill's mother. She didn't like his grammar.ͨ

We liked the way he had explained everything. We even thought that perhaps he might be decent͡ to us from now on.

# Check the Skills

## Understanding the Selection

1. The troubles seem to have been settled by the end of "Sweet Revenge." What does this fact tell you about Patricia, Dorothy, and Bill? Do you think the girls' method of dealing with Bill was a good one? Why or why not?

## Literary Appreciation Skills Story Elements

2. The plot moved toward the climax, then ended on a hopeful, "upbeat" note. How might it have moved differently? What influence did the characters, and the kind of people they were, have on the plot?

3. Do you agree with the marginal note regarding the climax? Why or why not?

## Vocabulary Development Skills Word Meaning

4. How did you decide which definition of *foil* was meant on page 395?

# Selection 4

# Use the Skills

### Understanding the Selection

1.    Both the rabbit and the monkey, in this African folk tale, find themselves in a bit of trouble. Read to find how they use their wits to get out of it.

### Literary Appreciation Skills Story Elements

2.    Think of the plot as you read. It's a simple one, as is the plot of most folk tales. Where does the climax occur?

### Vocabulary Development Skills Word Meaning

3.    You'll find words such as *engaged* and *provide* used in special ways. Watch for them.

# NATURE CANNOT
# BE CHANGED

One day, a rabbit and a monkey were engaged[cg] in conversation. However, while talking, each of them constantly[c] indulged[9] in his own bad habit. The monkey, of course, kept scratching himself with his paw. The rabbit, constantly fearing to be attacked by an enemy, kept turning his head about in all directions. The two animals were unable to keep still.

■ What does *engaged* mean here?

"It's really amazing,"[c] said the rabbit to the monkey, "that you cannot stop scratching yourself even for a moment."

"It's not more amazing than to see you turn your head constantly for no good reason," replied the monkey.

"Oh, I could easily stop doing that," said the rabbit, "if I only wanted to."

■ Here the plot really gets under way.

"Very well! Let's see if you can. Let's both try, you and I, to keep still. The one who moves first will lose the bet."

The rabbit agreed. And so they both watched to see if the other moved.

Soon the situation[c] became unbearable[c] for both of them. The monkey itched all over. Never in his life had he itched so badly. The rabbit, on the other hand, was sure that some enemy was going to jump on him from behind.

Finally when he could stand it no longer, the rabbit said, "Our bet did not provide[9] that we could not tell each other stories to pass the time, did it?" "It did not," answered the monkey, foreseeing[c] some ruse[9] on the part of the rabbit but intending to use the same trickery[c] himself. "All right then, I'll start," said the rabbit. "Imagine, one day when I was in an open field, I was in terrible danger…" "Curiously enough the same thing happened to me one day," interrupted the monkey. "Oh really?" continued the rabbit. "I saw dogs jumping through the field in all directions. They came from the left, from the right, from the front, from behind. I turned my head

■ What meaning of *provide* fits here?

this way, that way,…you see? Like this…" And as if to illustrate[c] his point the rabbit turned his head in all the directions he had indicated[c] in this story.

Of course the monkey too had a story to tell. "That day," he said, "I was tormented[c] by a group of children who kept throwing stones at me. They threw one here, and another there…." And with each place he mentioned in the story, he gave himself a good thump with his paw to stop the itching.

The rabbit, who well understood the subterfuge,[9] burst out laughing, and said to his companion, "Let us be frank. As much as we would like to, we cannot change our natures. This proves it. Neither of us has won the bet, nor has lost it."

■ Is this the climax of the story?

# Check the Skills

### Understanding the Selection

1. How did the two animals get out of their troublesome situation? How did their trickery lead to a better understanding of themselves?

### Literary Appreciation Skills Story Elements

2. Skim the story and outline the plot in your mind. Remember that the plot is made up of the events and situations that keep the story moving. Would you agree that the climax comes when both animals practice the same sort of trickery on each other? Why or why not?

### Vocabulary Development Skills Word Meaning

3. What do the words *engaged* and *provide* mean in this selection? Marginal notes can help you find the words again if you need to.

## Use the Skills

The next selection is a fable about someone in trouble. Like all fables, this one has a clear plot and climax, even though it is very short.

Watch for the moral of the story stated at the end.

# THE ARTIST

Isabelle C. Chang

There was once a king who loved the graceful curves of the rooster. He asked the court artist to paint a picture of a rooster for him. For one year he waited and still this order was not fulfilled.[cg] In a rage, he stomped into the studio and demanded to see the artist.

Quickly the artist brought out paper, paint, and brush. In five minutes a perfect picture of a rooster emerged[cg] from his skillful[cg] brush. The king turned purple with anger, saying, "If you can paint a perfect picture of a rooster in five minutes, why did you keep me waiting for over a year?"

"Come with me," begged the artist. He led the king to his storage room. Paper was piled from the floor to the ceiling. On every sheet was a painting of a rooster.

"Your Majesty," explained the artist, "it took me more than one year to learn how to paint a perfect rooster in five minutes."

*Life is short, art is long.*

## Check the Skills

### Understanding the Selection

1. Why is the artist in trouble in this fable?

### Literary Appreciation Skills Story Elements

2. The climax—or point of highest interest—seems to be the second paragraph. Do you agree? Why or why not?

### Vocabulary Development Skills Word Meaning

3. In the second sentence, how did you know that *court* did not mean "a place marked off so a game can be played"?

# Apply What You Learned in Unit 14

## The Theme

### Trouble

1.　　Reactions to trouble come in many shapes and sizes. Yevgeny Yevtushenko was in real trouble. He couldn't swim and his companion was drowning. His reaction was instinctive, without thinking. Janos, in "Hard-Boiled Eggs," seemed to give up, until the gypsy came along. Patricia and Dorothy, in "Sweet Revenge," decided to take definite action. The rabbit and the monkey resorted to trickery.

•　　How do you react to trouble? Is this the best way for you or might there be a better way? Think it over.

•　　Do you agree that dealing with trouble helps to build and broaden a person's character? Why or why not?

# The Skills

## Literary Appreciation Skills Story Elements

2.   The plot is one of the three main elements of a story. (The other two are the characters and the setting.) *Plot* is another word for the plan of a story. The important events and situations make up the plot. A novel has a plot which carries through the entire book. More often than not, each chapter in a novel has its own plot, which is part of the main plot.

     In any good story, the plot reaches a high point of interest or excitement. We call this part of the story the *climax*. The climax is usually near the end of the story.

3.   Being aware of the plots and climaxes in what you read will give you a better understanding of the stories. Look for these story parts in all the reading you do.

## Vocabulary Development Skills Word Meaning

4.   When you come upon a word that has more than one meaning, you can usually decide which fits by the way it is used in the sentence. The meaning that makes more sense is the suitable one.

# Rural Living

## Overview and Purposes for Reading

### The Theme

**Rural Living**

1. Rural living means living out in the country, away from cities, towns, and suburbs. What are some kinds of experiences people face in everyday rural living?

### The Skills

**Literary Appreciation Skills** Style and Intent

2. How does description make your reading more interesting?

**Comprehension Skills** Critical Reading

3. What is empathy? How can this feeling help you understand better what you read?

## Literary Appreciation Skills Style and Intent

Most authors of fiction try to make their writing as interesting to you as possible. They want you to get to know their characters and to become familiar with the different settings and situations. In other words, they want you to feel a part of what you're reading. One way they do this is by using descriptive writing.

One type of description is **sensory imagery**. Sensory imagery appeals to one or more of your senses: sight, hearing, smell, taste, and touch. The following example is written without any form of sensory imagery. Trying to stay interested in it may make you more aware of the importance of this type of imagery.

> Thanksgiving Day arrived. We all got up early. We had breakfast. Then Mom peeled the sweet potatoes and got them ready for the oven. Dad stuffed the turkey. I started the cranberries. Joe set the table. Then he started a fire. As we all sat there, it began to snow.

Not very interesting, was it? That's because the writer didn't use sensory imagery to help you become involved in the situation. Only the bare facts were presented. Now read the same story with sensory imagery included. It is on the next page. See if the situation "comes alive" this time.

Thanksgiving Day arrived. The angry buzz of the alarm cut through my dreams. I hopped out of bed, eager for the day to begin. It was the one day of the year when my family spent the whole day together—working, eating, and playing. I knocked on Joe's door as I flew down the hall. He was already up and struggling into his bathrobe.

Mom and Dad were up, too. Dad was singing his favorite silly song about the duck as he cracked eggs into a bowl. The fresh smell of bacon sizzling in the pan drifted out of the kitchen. Fluffy golden brown pancakes, dripping with butter and syrup, were stacked on the warming tray. Sweet, juicy pink grapefruits were cut and ready. I could hardly wait to sit down at the table.

After breakfast Mom began fixing the sweet potatoes. She sliced them, put them in the pan, and crumbled brown sugar on top. Afterwards, Joe drizzled melted butter over them. Dad made the stuffing with crisp red apples and celery mixed with freshly made oven-browned croutons. Meanwhile I started cooking my favorite—ruby red cranberries. Soon they were bubbling away. Joe was in charge of setting the table.

After Mom and Dad and I had finished in the kitchen, we went into the family room. Joe had a fire started. The flames flickered blue and orange, creating dancing shadows on the walls. The logs crackled and sizzled, and the smell of pine filled the air. As we sat there feeling warm and snuggly, new snow began to fall. It sparkled like tiny diamonds as it drifted by the window and clung to the trees and bushes.

Were you more aware of sights, sounds, and smells in this second example? As you read this unit, you'll see more examples of sensory imagery.

# Comprehension Skills Critical Reading

To make your reading more fun, you must get involved in what you read. One way to do this is to use **empathy**. This means that you look for something familiar in what you are reading. You try to share the feelings of the characters.

The following questions will help you do this.

---

### Using Empathy

1. Have you ever had the same feelings as the main character? Have you ever done the same things?

2. Do any of the characters remind you of people you know?

3. Have you ever been to any places like the ones in the selection? What thoughts do you have about these places?

---

Ask yourself questions like these. You will get more involved in what you read and will find that you enjoy your reading more. You may find that you understand yourself better when you look for familiar thoughts, feelings, and ideas.

As you read the selections in this unit, remember these questions. Get more involved with the characters and situations. Look for something that is familiar to you.

# Selection 1

# Use the Skills

### Understanding the Selection

Agba is an Arabian boy. He has lived on a farm all his life. He is very familiar with daily chores. In this selection he is in the stable waiting for a special foal—a newborn horse—to be born.

1. Find out how a foal spends the first few hours of its life.

### Literary Appreciation Skills Style and Intent

2. Watch for examples of sensory imagery. Think about which of your senses is being appealed to. See if this descriptive writing helps you understand better what is happening.

### Comprehension Skills Critical Reading

3. Use empathy as you read. Think about whether you have ever felt the same way Agba does. You don't have to have shared the same experience to share the feeling.

# A FOAL IS BORN

Marguerite Henry

The boy's dreams spun themselves out until there was nothing left of them. He slept a deep sleep. The candle in the lantern sputtered and died. The new moon rode higher and higher. Bats and nighthawks were flying noiselessly in the velvet night. They went about their business, swooping insects out of the air. With the gray light of morning they vanished, giving way to the jangling chorus of the crows.

*■ You should be able to hear the candle and the crows and imagine what the sky looks like at night and in the morning.*

Agba woke. The stable walls had closed in again. And there was the mare lying on her side as before. But her head was raised now, and she was drying off a new-born foal!ᶜ Her tongue-strokes filled the silence of the stall, licking, licking, licking.

The boy watched in fear that if he took his eyes away the whole scene might vanish into the mist of the morning. Oh, how tiny the foal was! And so wet there was no telling what its color would be. But its eyes were open. And they were full of curiosity.

*■ Think about a time you were so excited about seeing something for the first time, you couldn't believe it was really happening.*

Agba's body quivered with the wonder of the little fellow's birth. He had seen newborn foals before, but none so small and finely made. In the distance he could hear the softly paddingᶜ feet of the grooms.ᵍ He could hear the wild boarᵍ grunting and coughing in his hole behind the stables. He wondered if the boar really did keep evil spirits from entering into the horses.

Afraid to move, he watched the mare clumsilyᵍ get to her feet. He watched her nudgeᶜᵍ the young thing with her nose.

The foal tried to get up. He thrust out his forefeet, but they splayed.ᶜᵍ He seemed to get all tangled up with himself. He tried again and again. For one breathless instant he was on his feet. Then his legs buckled and he fell in a little heap. Agba reached a hand toward him, but the mare came between. She pushed the little one with her nose. She pushed him with her tongue. She nickeredᵍ to him. He was trying

*■ Sensory imagery helps you imagine how difficult it was for the foal to stand.*

again. He was standing up. How spindly[9] he was! And his ribs showed. And he had hollows above his eyes.

"I could carry him in my arms," thought Agba. "He is not much bigger than a goat, and he has long whiskers like a goat. Long and silky. And his tail is curly. And he is all of one color. Except—except..." Suddenly the boy's heart missed a beat. On the off hind heel there was a white spot. It was no bigger than an almond, but it was there! The white spot—the emblem[9] of swiftness!

■ Think about a time when you felt so excited about something that happened that you wanted to let everyone know.

Agba leaped to his feet. He wanted to climb the tower of the mosque.[9] He wanted to blow on the trumpet. He wanted to cry to the four winds of heaven. "A foal is born. And he will be swift as the wind of the desert, for on his hind heel is a white spot. A white spot. A white..."

■ Here you should be able to see exactly what the author wants you to see.

Just then a shaft of early sunlight pierced the window of the stable and found the colt. It flamed his coat into red gold. It made a sun halo around his head.

Agba was full of fear. He opened his mouth but no sound escaped. Maybe this was all a dream. Maybe the foal was not real. The golden coat. The crown of sun rays. Maybe he was a golden horse belonging to the chariot of the sun!

"I'll capture him with a name," the boy thought quickly. And he named the young thing Sham, which is the Arabic word for sun.

No sooner had Agba fastened a name on him than the little creature seemed to take on a new strength. He took a few steps. He found his mother's milk. He began to nurse.

Agba knew he should be reporting to Signor Achmet. He knew he should be standing in line for his measure of corn. But he could not bear to break the spell. He listened to the colt suckling, to the mare munching the dried grasses. He smelled their warm bodies. A stable was a *good* place to be born.

# Check the Skills

### Understanding the Selection

1. What did you find out about horses that you didn't know before? Do you think Agba's day-to-day life is very different from your own? Why or why not?

### Literary Appreciation Skills Style and Intent

2. Look back at the second marginal note on page 414. Do you think that paragraph would have been as effective if it had been written this way?

> The sunlight shone through the window. It made the foal's coat look very shiny.

This example shows you how descriptive writing can really help you understand your reading better.

### Comprehension Skills Critical Reading

3. Although you may never have seen a newborn foal, were you still able to understand Agba's excitement? Why or why not?

# Use the Skills

### Understanding the Selection

1.  The following short selection is about a New Hampshire sheep farm. Find out what a typical spring day is like.

### Literary Appreciation Skills Style and Intent

2.  Remember as you read that sensory imagery is meant to appeal to your senses: sight, hearing, smell, taste, and touch. In this selection look for examples of sight and sound.

### Comprehension Skills Critical Reading

3.  Think about what spring is like for you and how you feel about it. How is it the same as this description? How is it different?

# MOUNTAIN BORN

Elizabeth Yates

It was a wild March day and the sky was full of tattered clouds, like a flock of heavy-wooled sheep. The wind was at their heels every moment. Never once were they allowed to rest or change their course. On the far side of the mountains there was a pasture that the wind was heading them toward.

■ You can probably "see" the clouds and "hear" the banging doors, flapping clothes, and sounds of the sheep.

The wind was everywhere. It was banging doors in the house and flapping clothes on the line. It was whirling dried leaves into the air and searching out winter in all its hiding places and preparing the way for spring. But not all the gustiness of the wind could rise louder than the baaings of sheep in the barn. Their sounds were deep and tender or high and imperative.

## Check the Skills

### Understanding the Selection

1. Do you think the spring day described in the selection is only typical on a New Hampshire sheep farm? Why or why not?

### Literary Appreciation Skills Style and Intent

2. Did sensory imagery help to make this scene seem real to you? Why or why not?

### Comprehension Skills Critical Reading

3. Are your impressions of spring at all like those described in the selection? How do your experiences of spring compare?

# Selection 3

# Use the Skills

### Understanding the Selection

Mary is spending the summer with her aunt and her grandfather at the seashore. She cares a great deal for her grandfather. But Mary can't seem to get along with Aunt Alice. Here Mary becomes angry because her aunt wants her to wear a woolen undershirt.

1. Decide for yourself whether or not Mary likes life at the seashore.

### Literary Appreciation Skills Style and Intent

2. Remember what you learned about sensory imagery and watch for examples that appeal to one or more of your senses.

### Comprehension Skills Critical Reading

3. Think about times you have felt the same way Mary does. Decide whether or not she should have been so angry.

# THE RUNAWAY SUMMER

Nina Bawden

This morning Aunt Alice wanted Mary to wear her woolen vest.⁹ It was such a lovely July day. The wind was blowing and the small clouds scudding.⁹ So Mary had been in a better mood than usual when she came down to breakfast. She had even eaten her porridge. She knew her grandfather believed it was good for her. When he saw her empty plate, he had beamed over his newspaper. He said, "Well, it looks as if our good sea air is giving you an appetite at last." He seemed so pleased, as if in eating a plateful of porridge Mary had done something quite remarkably good and clever. So she wondered what else she could do. She thought she might say, "I think I'll go down to the sea and skim stones after breakfast." She knew this would please her grandfather too. He worried when she did what he called "moping indoors."

And now Aunt Alice had spoiled everything by asking Mary if she had put on her woolen vest!

"That jersey's not thick enough for this treacherous weather," she said. She looked nervously at the window as if the weather were a dangerous dog that might suddenly jump through it and bite her.

Mary scowled and felt her face go solid and lumpy like a badly made pudding. "It's not cold," she said. "And I'm hot *now*. If I put my vest on, I'll be boiling to *death*."

■ Can you see what Mary's face looked like?

"There's quite a wind out. It's blowing up cold. I know I'm wearing *my* vest! Just between you and me and the gatepost!"

Mary looked carefully round the room. "I don't see any gatepost," she said.

Aunt Alice laughed in her high, silly way. It was not as if she were amused, but as if she were trying to apologize for something.

"It's just an expression, dear. Haven't you heard it before?"

■ Have you ever had to wear something you hated? Think about how you felt.

"I've *heard* it all right, but I think it sounds dotty,[cg]" Mary said. "And I just *hate* those horrible old vests. They've got sleeves! Sleeves and *buttons*! I expect you knew I'd hate them; that's why you bought them for me!"

She stabbed her spoon into her boiled egg, and some of the yolk spattered out.

■ What senses is the author appealing to here?

"Oh, Mary," Aunt Alice said in a sad, fading voice. Pale eyes bulging, nose twitching, she looked like a frightened rabbit.

Mary knew her aunt was frightened of her. And this made her more bad-tempered than ever. It was so ridiculous for an old woman to be frightened of an eleven-year-old girl.

She said bitterly, "No one else in the *whole world* wears vests with sleeves and buttons."

Aunt Alice said, "Oh, Mary," again. She sounded as if she were trying not to cry. Grandfather put down his newspaper and looked at her. Then he smiled at Mary.

"My dear child, someone must wear them or the shops wouldn't stock them, would they? It's a case of supply and demand. No demand, no supply."

■ From this paragraph you should have a good idea of what grandfather looks like.

For a second, Mary almost smiled back at him. It was indeed quite difficult *not* to smile at her grandfather. He looked, with his round rosy face and round blue eyes, rather like a cheerful, if elderly, baby. He was bald as a baby, too—balder than most, in fact. The top of his head was smooth and shiny as if Aunt Alice polished it every day when she polished the dining-room table. Usually, just to look at her grandfather made Mary feel nicer—a bit less cross, certainly. But now after that first second she felt worse, not better. She saw that his blue eyes were puzzled. And he was playing with his right ear, folding the top over with his finger and stroking the back with his thumb. This was something he did only when he was thinking hard or worried about something. Mary knew he was upset because she had been rude to Aunt Alice. Although this made her ashamed and miserable underneath, it made her angry on top.

She said, "But children don't buy their own clothes, do they? They just have to wear what grown-ups buy for them. They don't have any say, they just have to do what they're *told.*"

A lump came into her throat at this dreadful thought. She swallowed hard and glared at Aunt Alice.

"Children don't have any say in anything. They have to wear what they're told and eat what they're given and... and... live where they're *put.* It's not *fair.*"

The lump seemed to have gone from her throat and settled in her chest, like a stone.

Aunt Alice made a funny noise, midway between a gasp

and a sigh.

Grandfather said, "Mary, you don't seem to want any more to eat. Perhaps you'd like to leave the table and go upstairs for a while."

He spoke gently and reasonably, as he always did, whatever Mary had said or done. Sometimes she wished he would shout at her instead. His being so nice made her feel nastier, somehow.

She got down from her chair and left the room without another word, but as soon as she had closed the door she stopped to listen. She knew that people always talked about you, once you had gone.

# Check the Skills

### Understanding the Selection

1.  Do you think Mary likes her life at the seashore? Why or why not?

### Literary Appreciation Skills Style and Intent

2.  Look back at the second marginal note on page 420. What senses is the author appealing to here? Do you have a better understanding of what Aunt Alice is like because of the description? Why or why not?

### Comprehension Skills Critical Reading

3.  Have you ever been as angry at someone as Mary is? Can you understand why she is so angry? Do you think she said some things she really didn't mean? Why do you think as you do?

# Selection 4

# Use the Skills

### Understanding the Selection

1.   Think about whether the things mentioned in the poem can be related only to life in the country.

### Literary Appreciation Skills Style and Intent

2.   This poem is filled with sensory imagery. See how it appeals to your senses.

### Comprehension Skills Critical Reading

3.   Think about how you react to the different things mentioned in the poem. Do they remind you of any special thoughts, feelings, or ideas?

# WHAT MAKES A POEM?

Eve Merriam

What makes a poem?
Whatever you feel:
The secrets of rain
On a window pane,
The smell of a rose
Or of cowboy clothes,
The sound of a flute
Or a foghorn hoot,
The taste of cake
Or a fresh water lake,
The touch of grass
Or an icy glass,
The shout of noon
Or the silent moon,
A standstill leaf
Or a rolling wheel,
Laughter and grief:
Whatever you feel.

■ What senses is the poet trying to stimulate with the different images?

## Check the Skills

### Understanding the Selection

1. Can the things mentioned in the poem be experienced only in the country? Why do you think as you do?

### Literary Appreciation Skills Style and Intent

2. What senses is the poet trying to appeal to? Can you find an example for each? What are they?

### Comprehension Skills Critical Reading

3. Does using empathy give you a better idea of what the poem is really about? Why do you think as you do?

# Selection 5

## Use the Skills

Tobias and his father, Old Tobias, had moved away from their home of many years. They left behind them their snug cabin and their corn crop. Now they had to build a crude cabin before winter set in and figure out some way to get food. They and some friends are trying to start a new town. As you read the selection, try to decide whether the story takes place many years ago or if the same events could occur today.

Be alert for the author's use of sensory imagery. Decide for yourself if it helps to make the story come alive.

You may never have been in a situation like Tobias's. But try to imagine how he felt at different times within the selection. Think about times when you have had the same feelings.

There are no marginal notes this time to help you. By now you shouldn't need them.

# THE VALLEY OF
# THE SHADOW

Janet Hickman

For many days, Tobias felt only two things: the weariness[9] in his bones and the pinch in his stomach. There was little time for talking to his friend Thomas, no time for exploring the small height upon which the town was being built, no time for idle[9] hunting. There was time only to swing the ax, drag the logs, mix the chinking.[9] Despite[9] their work, the houses they built were crude ones. They were nothing like the snug cabins of Salem and Gnadenhutten.

Already it was the midst of the harvest month. Crinkles of ice sometimes formed in the wet cattle tracks at night. All must have houses before snow fell. So Tobias worked with his father to build their own cabin of round logs. The floor was of earth. There was no time to split logs for flooring. Neither was there time to gather stone and build a fireplace. They left a smoke hole in the roof and dug a fire pit beneath it. When that much was finished, they moved on to help others who needed bigger shelters for large families.

Tobias did not complain of the hard work. But he thought more and more often of Salem and of the other towns behind them. He remembered the familiar river of home, and the hills. He could close his eyes and see the slopes where the thick forests grew, sheltering the deer and the bear and the wild turkey. Soon there would be good hunting for elk.

Once he was dreaming of the slow sizzle of venison[9] upon a spit, the drip of the fat and the rich good smoke. He grew careless with his ax and slit the side of his moccasin.[9] He was thankful that his foot was only bruised, the skin still whole. He told himself that he would keep his mind no longer on the things which were behind. Yet each time his stomach drew itself up to protest[cg] its emptiness, he was reminded of the corn left standing in the home plantations,[9] ripe now for harvest. He had never been hungrier than now. The harder he worked, the more his body cried for food. And each day he worked, there was less food to be had. The idea that greater hunger was to come did not enter his mind. To himself he would not admit that such a thing could be.

There came a morning when Tobias mixed the last of their warrior's bread, the ground parched[9] corn mixed with water. It swelled to many times its size and satisfied the stomach. Justine would share from her stores, he was sure. He had tended her plantation and garden plot on many a hot afternoon. But even as he assured[c9] himself, he wondered if she too had scraped out the last bit of her supply.

Old Tobias looked into their empty corn jar. His mouth was a thin straight line that told his son nothing. But later, when Tobias took up his ax to start the morning's work, the old man shook his head.

"Go bring our horses," he directed. He fumbled with morning-stiff hands to loosen the knot on the packet of valuables which he always kept close. When he had opened it, he drew out some coins, counted them from one hand to another. He tipped them into the pocket of his shirt. "Today we must find a town where we can buy corn," he said.

Tobias' heart leaped. A day with no chopping and lifting and stretching one's muscles, and a day to bring food, besides! He hurried out to find the horses. They roamed with all the others, free but not

far. He gloried[cg] in the sparkle of sun on the frosted grass and the glow of the trees in their full autumn colors. They were the colors of fire and of sunsets, of ripe fruits and harvest. He longed suddenly for his lost journal.[cg] He wanted to sit on the first log in front of him and write all that he saw and felt so that it would not be forgotten. Then he heard his father calling. He realized that he was no longer seeking the horses but standing still. Dreaming, his father would say. He hurried once more.

Old Tobias had spread word of their going, and they did not go alone. Isaac Glikkikan rode with them and John Martin with Anthony, and several other men and boys. Many families were in need of corn.

There were several small Wyandot villages, as well as Captain Pipe's town, down the Sandusky. Each who wanted corn agreed to go to a different town in hopes of getting more alone than in company. Tobias and his father went to Pipe's Town. Pipe was, after all, a Delaware kinsman.[9] Tobias fell to wishing he had brought two great baskets instead of one as they neared the cluster of houses and huts. Dogs yelped and children stared solemnly out of doorways.

# Check the Skills

### Understanding the Selection

1.  Do you think that some people still live as Tobias and old Tobias did, or do you think this story took place a long time ago? Why do you think so?

### Literary Appreciation Skills Style and Intent

2.  Did sensory imagery help to make the story and its characters come alive for you? What senses was the author trying to appeal to? See if you can find some examples.

### Comprehension Skills Critical Reading

3.  Have you ever had to do something you really didn't want to do but knew you must? Did you have empathy with Tobias' acceptance of the hard work and the hunger? What kind of person was Tobias? Why do you think as you do?

# Apply What You Learned in Unit 15

## The Theme

### Rural Living

In this unit you learned some things about rural life that you may not have known if you've always lived in towns or cities. You read about the behavior of a newborn foal and found out something about how log cabins are constructed. But you also read about spring and getting angry—which you probably do know something about. Do you think that there are some things that are the same no matter where a person lives? What are some of these things? Why do you think as you do?

1.     What are some benefits of rural living? of city living?

•      Do you think it would be more pleasant to live on a farm or in a high rise apartment building in a city? Why do you think as you do?

# The Skills

## Literary Appreciation Skills Style and Intent

2.    You learned that authors use sensory imagery to make your reading more interesting. They do this by using descriptions that appeal to one or more of your senses: sight, hearing, smell, taste, and touch. Be alert for examples of sensory imagery in whatever you read and try to understand the author's message. Try using sensory imagery yourself in your writing assignments. You'll find that what you write will be more interesting to you as well as to those who read it.

## Comprehension Skills Critical Reading

3.    Whenever you are reading fiction, you will find that you will enjoy it more if you get involved in what you read. Use empathy to get to know the characters. Look for thoughts, feelings, actions, and experiences that are familiar to you. Imagine how you would react if you were in a situation similar to the characters' situation. Not only will you get to know the characters but you will probably get to know yourself better as well.

# Rituals

## Overview and Purposes for Reading

### The Theme

### Rituals

1.   Many organizations and groups have rituals or special ceremonies that must be conducted in a certain way. Individuals establish rituals, too, when they do certain things in the same way time after time. What are some of these kinds of rituals?

### The Skills

### Literary Appreciation Skills Figurative Language

2.   What is exaggeration? Why should you be aware of exaggerations when you read?

### Vocabulary Development Dictionary

3.   When you look up a word in the dictionary, how can you decide which definition fits what you are reading ?

# Learn About
# the Skills

## Literary Appreciation Skills Figurative Language

Have you ever said, "I'm so stuffed, I don't think I'll ever eat again"? Does this mean that you are really stuffed like a turkey? And do you really believe that you won't ever want to eat again? Of course not. What it really means is that you ate more than you usually do or more than you think you should have. You were just using exaggeration. Almost everyone, the world over, uses exaggeration at one time or another.

**Exaggeration** describes something as much more than it probably could be. You could never eat so much that you would be "stuffed." Nor could you be "walking on air" or be "tired enough to sleep for a week." But using these exaggerations helps you let people know how you feel.

You will come across exaggeration in your reading, too. Most often it will be in fiction. But it may appear in non-fiction as well. Any selection that contains conversation or information about people's behavior will probably have an exaggeration or two. Some you may not have heard before. If you aren't sure what the exaggeration means, look at the surrounding sentences. Think about the sense of the paragraph and what you know about the character and situation. Look for the key word or words in the exaggeration. You should be able to figure out most exaggerations.

**Try the Skill.** How does the writer use exaggeration in these sentences?

> Jim was up in his room listening to his stereo. His favorite song was playing. So he turned up the volume. "Turn that thing down," yelled Dad. "I can't hear myself think!"

You're right if you chose "can't hear myself think" as the exaggeration. Of course you can never "hear" yourself think. What Dad meant was that the loud music was bothering him. The key words "can't hear" and the other sentences should help you figure out the meaning.

Look at another example:

> "I don't think I can carry this box of books upstairs," said John. "It weighs a ton."

Did you pick out "weighs a ton" as the exaggeration? The books didn't really weigh a ton. However, if you read the same phrase in this sentence, it is *not* exaggeration.

> The pick-up truck weighs a ton.

Here it is really true that the truck weighs a ton.

So if you ever hear someone say that the school library is "a mile away" and that it takes "hours to get there," you will know that is probably exaggeration. You will see more examples of exaggeration as you read the selections in this unit.

# Vocabulary Development Skills Dictionary

What do you do when you are reading and you come across a word you don't know? Of course the first thing you do is look for context clues. But sometimes the context clues don't seem to help. Or they may give you only an idea of the meaning, but you want to be more definite.

That's when you look the word up in a dictionary. Using the guide words at the top of the page, locate the word. Then find the definition. Read the following sentences taken from the first selection in this unit.

> For lack of something more exciting to do, he directed his steps toward Market Street. The goods, displayed there on the open stalls, offered nothing of unusual interest. It was not until he had turned into one of the larger business thoroughfares that evil fortune gripped him.

Do you know the meaning of *thoroughfare*? If so, good for you! If not, you may want to look in a dictionary. You might see an entry that looks something like this. Read it and decide which meaning fits here.

> **thor ough fare** (thėr′ə fãr), n. 1. a main road or public highway. 2. any place of passage from one location to another. 3. right to such passage. 4. a heavily traveled passage, such as a waterway, strait, or channel.

If you decided that the first meaning is the one that fits best in the paragraph above, you're right. As you read this unit, you will find out more about using the dictionary to choose the appropriate meaning.

Unit 16

# Selection 1

# Use the Skills

### Understanding the Selection

Young Fu lives with his mother Fu Be Be and works for a man named Tang. Although both Young Fu and Fu Be Be work very hard, they are very poor. They can afford only the necessities of life. But a clever shopkeeper convinces Young Fu that he can afford a little luxury.

1.  Learn about the ritual the shopkeeper Hsui uses to persuade possible customers to buy his merchandise.

### Literary Appreciation Skills Figurative Language

2.  Find out how exaggeration plays a part in Hsui's sales pitch.

### Vocabulary Development Skills Dictionary

3.  Decide whether context clues will help you figure out the meaning of *acumen, beckon,* and *paltry.* Or will you have to use a dictionary? Marginal notes will help.

# YOUNG FU

Elizabeth Foreman Lewis

One evening, as Young Fu returned early from the last errand of the day, Tang dismissed him with the suggestion that he go play a little. Surprise at this unexpected freedom held the apprentice[9] motionless for a moment. Then he folded his leather apron, laid it away, and passed into the street. For lack of something more exciting to do, he directed his steps toward Market Street. The goods, displayed there on the open stalls, offered nothing of unusual interest. It was not until he had turned into one of the larger business thoroughfares that evil fortune gripped him.

There, in a jeweler's shop, hung a shining nickel watch. It was large and round and, strange to say, black of face. Young Fu had seen several watches in his lifetime, but never one with a dark face. He stopped and studied it. Then, following his fate, he crossed the sill and asked the shopkeeper to tell him the reason for such a color.

Hsui, the jeweler, was stout and prosperous[9] and knew all of the tricks of the trade. "I do not recognize you," he began, "but you are a young man of a very great acumen. That valuable treasure has been hanging there on display for three days. You are the first with sufficient intellect to note its extraordinary[9] appearance."

■ Context will not help here. The dictionary tells you that this means "accuracy of judgment."

Open-mouthed, he stared into Hsui's face, charmed by this sudden acceptance of his own feelings about himself. In a daze[c] he watched Hsui take down the watch and then beckon him to a dark corner of the shop. Right there, Young Fu was given one of the greatest shocks of his life. Held in the darkness, the watch glowed into a live thing. The figures upon its face turned into so many tiny snakes of fire. He felt cold all over. But now that another person thought so highly of him, he concealed his trembling. He mumbled only in a shaky voice, "*Shi chi deh hun* (extremely odd)!"

■ The definition is "to call by nodding or waving." The sense of the sentence will help to make the meaning clear.

Hsui, fully aware of his victim's state of mind, pursued the game. "And only you, of all the people in Chungking, knew what to expect of this gift for an emperor. You must, indeed, be a much traveled man and a learned one. This is the first time that anything of this sort has been shown in this great city.

Young Fu was almost overcome with delight. The hypnotizing voice droned on. "Let me press this gift upon you. I can sleep without dreams if I know that it is in your possession. A sacrifice for me, yes, a great one. But then to meet with one of your intelligence is a rare privilege. I am willing to pay for the experience!"

"Do you mean to give me this precious gift?" asked Young Fu.

"Just that!" insisted Hsui. "You may take the watch with you now. I ask only one small favor: that you sign this bit of

■ Hsui uses exaggeration to make a sale. He suggests that no one is as smart as Young Fu.

paper. My neighbor, Liu, will witness. Sometime when fortune is yours, send me the <u>paltry</u> sum of five dollars."

The neighbor appeared as if by magic. Before the youth could catch his breath, he found himself on his way home. The watch was in his hand.

His pleasure in the newly acquired treasure soon faded. To begin with, Fu Be Be was horrified at the debt of five dollars. "We shall have to beg on the streets, or starve!" she wailed. "I shall have no coffin for a decent burial!" At this last thought, tears took the place of words. For the ruling desire of her life was to save enough from their income to purchase her coffin. Now all of her hopes lay about her. Her son earned nothing, and she very little. A debt of five dollars was something not to be faced and all because this stupid boy had shown no more sense than to buy this "foreign devil's" machine.

■ The meaning is given as "very small, unimportant." You should see that this fits with the sense of the paragraph. It is exaggeration here, though.

# Check the Skills

### Understanding the Selection

1.  Do you think that Hsui uses the same ritual sales pitch with other people? What makes you think so?

### Literary Appreciation Skills Figurative Language

2.  Look back at the marginal note above the picture on page 438. How do you know that Hsui is using exaggeration here? What is he trying to do with his exaggerations?

### Vocabulary Development Skills Dictionary

3.  Look back at the marginal notes if you need to. Do you think you would have been able to figure out the meaning of *acumen* without using a dictionary? *beckon*? *paltry*? Why or why not?

# Selection 2

## Use the Skills

### Understanding the Selection

1. In the next selection, a poem, you will find out about the ritual Peggy Ann McKay uses to avoid going to school.

### Literary Appreciation Skills Figurative Language

2. Think about how Peggy Ann uses exaggeration to make her family believe she is sick. Remember that exaggeration describes something as much more than it probably could be. Decide, too, if you think the whole poem is an exaggeration. Would anyone *really* behave this way?

### Vocabulary Development Skills Dictionary

3. You will come across the word *wrenched* in the poem. You may have to use a dictionary to find out its meaning.

# SICK

Shel Silverstein

"I cannot go to school today,"
Said little Peggy Ann McKay.
"I have the measles and the mumps,
A gash, a rash and purple bumps.
My mouth is wet, my throat is dry,
I'm going blind in my right eye.
My tonsils are as big as rocks,
I've counted sixteen chicken pox
And there's one more—that's seventeen,
And don't you think my face looks green?
My leg is cut, my eyes are blue—
It might be instamatic flu.
I cough and sneeze and gasp and choke,
I'm sure that my left leg is broke—
My hip hurts when I move my chin,
My belly button's caving in,

■ You will probably realize after the first four lines that the basis is exaggeration. Think about whether anyone could have all these things.

My back is wrenched$^g$, my ankle's sprained,
My 'pendix pains each time it rains.
My nose is cold, my toes are numb,
I have a sliver in my thumb.
My neck is stiff, my spine is weak,
I hardly whisper when I speak.
My tongue is filling up my mouth,
I think my hair is falling out.
My elbow's bent, my spine ain't straight,
My temperature is one-o-eight.
My brain is shrunk, I cannot hear,
There is a hole inside my ear.
I have a hangnail, and my heart is—what?
What's that? What's that you say?
You say today is...Saturday?
G-bye, I'm going out to play!"

# Check the Skills

### Understanding the Selection

1.  Remember that a ritual is a method of doing something in the same way, time after time. Do you agree that Peggy Ann's method of avoiding going to school is a ritual? Why or why not?

### Literary Appreciation Skills Figurative Language

2.  Give some examples of the exaggerations that Peggy Ann uses. How do you know that they are exaggerations? Do you think the whole poem is an exaggeration? Why or why not?

### Vocabulary Development Skills Dictionary

3.  Were you able to figure out, using context clues, what *wrenched* means? Or did you have to use the glossary?

# Use the Skills

## Understanding the Selection

Espie Sanchez is an explorer scout. She and the other girls in her troop have gone through a training program at the police academy. Now they can answer incoming calls at the police station and handle problems that are not too serious.

1.     Decide whether Mrs. Caldwell, one of Espie's callers, is practicing a form of ritual with her calls.

## Literary Appreciation Skills Figurative Language

2.     Think about how Espie's second caller uses exaggeration to try to get action from the police department.

## Vocabulary Development Skills Dictionary

3.     Only a couple of words in the selection are in the glossary. See if you can figure out their meanings from context. Check a dictionary or the glossary if you need to.

# THIS IS ESPIE SANCHEZ

Terry Dunnahoo

Espie answered the phone on the first ring. "Northeast Division, Explorer Sanchez speaking. May I help you, please?"

A woman said, "I don't want an Explorer. I want a police officer."

Espie glanced at Sergeant Ernie Jackson who was checking reports with the eraser of his pencil pointed at every word. She said, "Ma'am, if you tell me what you want, maybe I can help you."

"I have a lion in my living room. Can you get rid of it?" the woman asked angrily.

"You have a lion in your living room?"

Sergeant Jackson frowned. "Mrs. Caldwell," he said to Espie, and picked up the receiver on his phone. "Good evening, Mrs. Caldwell. This is Sergeant Jackson."

"Why do you waste my time by letting those children answer the phone?" the woman asked. Espie stiffened.

Sergeant Jackson said, "The Explorer Scouts take a lot of work off our backs. I think you should give them a chance."

The woman's voice rose. "Well, I have a lion locked up in my living room and that child can't get it out, can she?"

"Mrs. Caldwell, we don't have lions in Los Angeles."

"Maybe one escaped from the zoo."

"There's no lion missing from the zoo," Sergeant Jackson said. Espie wondered how he could be so patient.<sup>cg</sup>

"Are you sure?"

"We'd be the first to know."

"Then where did the lion in my living room come from?"

Sergeant Jackson smiled. "Mrs. Caldwell, is your television on?"

"Of course it's not on. I turned it off when I went to bed. The lion woke me up."

"Maybe you only *think* you turned off your television."

"You telling me I'm crazy?"

Sergeant Jackson sighed. "Mrs. Caldwell, the door to the living room is closed. Right?"

"You think I'd leave it open with a lion snarling at me?"

"I want you to go to the door and listen. Then come tell me what you hear. Okay?"

■ Can you get an idea what this means from context clues? Or do you need to check the glossary?

The woman hesitated,[g] then said, "All right, but don't hang up on me."

Espie heard Mrs. Caldwell put down her receiver. The sergeant said to Espie, "She calls a couple of times a month. Lonely, I guess. Sometimes we send somebody out to talk to her and check her story. She comes up with wild ones."

Mrs. Caldwell picked up her telephone. "Why, it's just an old movie, Sergeant. How do you suppose I forgot to turn off the television?"

"We all forget things, Mrs. Caldwell. Good night." Sergeant Jackson put down his phone and Espie slammed hers into place.

The policeman said, "Hey, you're not going to let her get to you, are you?"

Espie straightened the navy-blue skirt of her uniform. "I trained eight Saturdays at the police academy and I couldn't even handle my first call," she said.

Sergeant Jackson chuckled. "I went three months, five days a week. Now after fifteen years on the force, I'm still not always sure how to answer a call." The sergeant picked up his pencil. "You'll handle it okay next time," he said.

Espie stared at the telephone and dared it to give her another chance. When it rang, she picked it up immediately. "Northeast Division, Explorer Sanchez speaking. May I help you, please?" she said in her best Academy manner.

A man said, "Yeah, you can help me. Make that police helicopter stop circling my house. I can't hear my television."

Espie heard the roar of the helicopter. "If a chopper is circling your area, the men are answering a call for help from one of our ground units."

"They're disturbing my peace."

Espie glanced at Sergeant Jackson. He was watching her.

"Sir, the officers are doing their job." The noise from the other end of the line grew quieter. "They seem to be moving away," she said.

"Yeah, they are. Okay, I'll let them get away with it this time. But next time they come around here I'm going to have them arrested for disturbing the peace."

■ Do you think this statement is true? Or is it a form of exaggeration?

"It's your right, sir," Espie said, and put down the telephone.

Ernie Jackson said, "Sounds like you handled that one okay."

"A citizen complaining about our chopper."

■ If you can't figure out the meaning, you will have to check the glossary.

Sergeant Jackson smiled. "You talk like a veteran$^{cg}$ police officer," he said.

# Check the Skills

## Understanding the Selection

1. Do you think Mrs. Caldwell's two calls a month to the police station could be considered a ritual? Why or why not?

## Literary Appreciation Skills Figurative Language

2. Look at the first marginal note on this page. Do you think this man really means what he says? Or is he using exaggeration? Why do you think as you do?

## Vocabulary Development Skills Dictionary

3. Did you need to use the glossary to find the suitable definitions for *hesitated* and *veteran*? What do those words mean as they are used in the selection? Marginal notes can help you locate the words again if you need to.

# Selection 4

# Use the Skills

### Understanding the Selection

1.   Like Hsui in the first selection of this unit, the Liar depends on ritual to sell his merchandise. Find out what this ritual is.

### Literary Appreciation Skills Figurative Language

2.   Notice how the Liar uses exaggeration to make his merchandise more desirable.

### Vocabulary Development Skills Dictionary

3.   Use context clues first to figure out the words you don't know. If that doesn't work, you will have to check the glossary or a dictionary. Think about the sense of the sentence to find the appropriate meaning.

# HARD BARGAIN

Nick Engler

*At a crossroads near the top of Mount Nebo in Athens County, Ohio, there used to be a sign that welcomed you to Liar's Corner. The Liar of Liar's Corner was a dealer in junk and a teller of outrageous*[cg] *fibs. He could make up a story about any piece of junk you wanted to buy, and the only way you could get a good deal was to listen to his tale.*

It was Tuesday, and the Liar had said he wouldn't be home. So that's where Gordon found him.

"Howdy," said Gordon, hoisting[cg] himself up the stoop. "I came to see if you had anything new for sale."

The Liar just kept staring over the Ohio ridgetops.[g] After a moment he said, "I thought I told you if I ever saw your horsetrading face around here again, I'd feed you to Big Red."

■ Does context help with this word?

"I guess I forgot," Gordon apologized.

The Liar turned to the hound. "Get'im, Red," he commanded. Red rolled over so Gordon could scratch his belly.

"You're mighty lucky," said the Liar. "Red ate a couple of salesmen earlier this morning, and he's all filled up."

■ Is this really true or an exaggeration?

"Mighty lucky," Gordon agreed. He gave the dog an affectionate[cg] rub, then began threading his way through the odds and ends on the porch. He stopped at a pile of used hand tools. "You've got some new items here," he observed.

The Liar did not reply, but watched Gordon's round face carefully to see what he thought of each tool and how much he was willing to pay. Gordon, mindful that he was being watched, did not raise an eyebrow or bat an eye.

After a time, Gordon picked up a scythe[c] from the pile. He ran his thumb along the long, curved blade and found it freshly sharpened. The hickory handle was smooth and brown from years of use, but the wood showed no cracks. "What will you take for this one?" he asked the Liar.

"It's not for sale," the Liar informed him. "It's going to be a hard winter, and I'm going to need that scythe."

Gordon almost smiled. A scythe is a warm weather tool used for cutting grass and grain, and has no use in the winter. Gordon asked the question the Liar wanted him to ask. "What would you need a scythe for in the wintertime?"

"What for?" The Liar looked as if he had never expected the question. He acted as if the answer should be plain to anyone. "Why, for a good many things, too many to tell you about if you can't figure them out for yourself. But I'll tell you what I did with a scythe in the winter of 1937.

"It was a hard winter in 1937, like I said," the Liar began. "And going into it, I was worried. I knew it was going to be a hard winter, and I didn't have enough money to see me through it.

"Well, I had an idea. I knew of a restaurant up in Chicago that was paying a dollar apiece for frogs' legs. And I also knew where there was a pond that had five, maybe six hundred frogs. Now six hundred frogs meant twelve hundred frogs' legs, which I could sell for twelve hundred dollars, if you follow my arithmetic.

■ Could this be true?

"There was just one problem. These weren't ordinary frogs. They were smarter, lots smarter. There wasn't anybody who could boast of ever having caught one. When one of these frogs saw you coming, he'd let out a croak to warn all the others. Then they'd jump—all six hundred of them—for the pond. As soon as they hit the water, they'd dive for the bottom and bury themselves in the mud. They wouldn't come up again till you went away.

"It was a problem all right, but I solved it. The first thing I did was to get hold of the U.S. Weather Service.

"'Your honors,' I said to them, 'I need to know the exact second when winter is going to hit this year.'

"So they consulted for a bit, added up some big numbers, and flipped a coin. They finally told me that winter would hit Athens County on the eleventh month of the year, on the eleventh day of that month, the eleventh hour of that

■ Is this possible?

day, the eleventh minute of that hour, and the eleventh second of that minute.

"I thanked them all very much, went back to my business, and waited for winter to arrive.

"Come the eleventh day of November, I got up bright and early. I took my shotgun and my scythe—a scythe just about like the one you were admiring. And I went down to that frog pond.

"Those frogs, of course, saw me coming. One let out a croak, and they all jumped for the pond and buried themselves in the mud. But I wasn't worried. I had expected it. Besides, it wasn't the eleventh hour yet, if you can begin to see what I'm driving at. I walked up to that pond, loaded a double charge[cg] in both barrels of my shotgun, sharpened up my scythe, and sat down to wait for winter. I sat there as still as a statue, shotgun in one hand, scythe in the other.

■ Context clues may help you here. If not, you will have to check the glossary.

"Now, the trouble with smartness is that it makes you nosy. Soon, two frogs came up to have a look at me, then four, then eight. Finally the whole six hundred came up. There were twelve hundred frog eyes watching me just sitting there, shotgun in one hand, scythe in the other.

"After a while, all the frogs came to the conclusion that I was crazy, or dead, or both, and they lost interest in me. They all crawled up on the bank and went back to doing whatever frogs do to pass the time. I just sat there, scarcely breathing, waiting for the eleventh hour.

"On the eleventh minute of the eleventh hour, I pointed the shotgun in the air and pulled both hammers back. I had those frogs' undivided attention now.

"Then, on the ninth second, I pulled both triggers. The gun let out a tremendous KABLAM! The explosion scared those frogs silly. On the tenth second they all jumped for the pond. They hit the surface of the pond on the eleventh second of the eleventh minute of the eleventh hour of the eleventh day of the eleventh month of the year. It was the very same second the U.S. Weather Service had predicted winter would hit. And for once, they were right.

"The pond froze over that very second. Six hundred frogs stuck headfirst in the ice, kicking twelve hundred frog legs in the air. And that is when I needed the scythe."

The Liar paused and looked at his audience. Gordon was keeping the straightest of faces, trying hard not to smile. But the Liar guessed Gordon was laughing inside and settled back in his couch with a look of smug<sup>cg</sup> satisfaction.

"It's going to be a cold winter," he reminded Gordon, as he surveyed<sup>cg</sup> the advancing autumn marching across the Ohio ridgetops. "I'm going to need a scythe."

Gordon stretched, yawned, and rose to go. "Well," he said, "I've got to be getting on."

"I wouldn't part with that tool for the world," the Liar assured him.

Gordon took his time descending the stoop.

"Not for a million bucks in gold," the Liar went on.

Gordon reached the bottom step.

"I might even take it with me when I die," said the Liar to his back.

Gordon stopped and turned around. "I'll pay you three dollars for that scythe," he offered.

"Sold!" said the Liar.

# Check the Skills

### Understanding the Selection

1.  What ritual does the Liar follow before he sells anything? Why do you think he does this? How are the Liar's and Hsui's sales pitches alike? How are they different?

### Literary Appreciation Skills Figurative Language

2.  Look back at the second marginal note on page 449. Could this be true or is it a form of exaggeration? How do you know?

### Vocabulary Development Skills Dictionary

3.  What is the meaning of *ridgetops* on page 449? Of *charge* on page 451? Were you able to figure out their meanings, using context clues?

# Use the Skills

Bushmen are small in size. They live in the south of Africa in a barren district stretching across the Kalahari desert. They are a peace-loving people. They will accept outsiders as friends so long as the proper greeting ritual is followed. Find out how exaggeration plays a part in this ritual. Use your dictionary skills if you have to. But most of all, enjoy the article about an unusual group of people.

# THE BUSHMEN

Robert Martin

His clothing is a leather breechcloth[9] and a leather shoulder bag bulging with a water-filled ostrich egg. He holds a small bow in his hand as if it were a natural extension[9] of his arm. A short spear juts from his belt and a handful of arrows bristle from the quiver slung at his hip. Perhaps he also has an arrow sticking from the band around his head so it will be instantly available.

He is closer than he seems, for he is small and perfectly proportioned. And if you are quick of wit and polite in the way of the Bushmen, you will descend[c] from your jeep. And you will say quietly, "*Tshjamm*"[c]—"Good day, I saw you from afar." And he will know that you have come as a friend. You have, in the way of the Bushmen, told him that he is as big as any man.

He will place his bow and arrows carefully in the sand. It is impolite to greet someone with a weapon in hand. And he will walk to you. And you will sit with him in the desert. You will hunch your shoulders so your eyes are level with his. He will say, "Good day. I have been dead. But now that you have come, I live again." And you will reply, "It is well that I found you, for I am dying of thirst." Your jeep may be bulging with water cans. Your canteen may gurgle at your side. It does not matter. You will drink from the ostrich egg he offers. You will tell him, "Now I am safe."

And if it should be decided that you are indeed a friend, then you may be ushered[cg] to his camp. There the life of the hunter is as it was ten thousand years ago.

His camp is called a *werf*. It is on the sandy floor of a dried-up watercourse. It is nestled among the sparse thorn trees where there is a bit of shade. Except for the smoking fires and the people—who in polite Bushman fashion try not to stare at strangers—you could probably walk right through the camp without realizing it was there. It's as if the Bushmen had merely sat down in some thicket to rest awhile and soon would be gone.

It is a dry camp, like most Bushman camps. The nearest water hole is a half mile or more away. This makes extra work for the women who carry water. But it cannot be otherwise. If they lived closer, the timid antelope would not come to drink. Game would soon abandon the area. Then, with their main food supply gone, the Bushmen too would have to leave.

The usual band of Bushmen numbers about twenty people, divided into four or five family groups. But the number changes frequently as families come and go on hunting expeditions or to visit friends and relatives. It matters not to the Bushman if he belongs to one band today and another one tomorrow. The important thing to him is that his immediate family ties remain strong. If he follows a headman, it is because the headman has good judgment and offers sound advice.

The home of the Bushman, called a *skerm*, is a cone of sticks covered with grass and leaves. It is small. Sometimes the whole werf is pitched within the speckled shade of a single tree.

The skerm is not intended to shed rain. It serves more as a windbreak. Sometimes the Bushman doesn't even bother to build one. He merely plunges a stick into the sand to mark his homesite. Around this the family members arrange their possessions and build their fire. At night they scoop hollows in the sand and line them with grass, like nests.

The possessions that go with this home are as simple as the shelter itself. But they are arranged with care, each occupying its own special spot. On the side where the man sleeps are his weapons. He has his bow and arrows, his spear, a curved throwing stick for killing birds, and perhaps a net for snaring small game. Next to these is his leather pouch—his carryall—containing things like string woven of grass for setting snares, a few arrowheads, the hollow tip of an antelope horn in which he keeps a sticky glob of arrow poison. Also there is a skinning knife, perhaps a steel one bartered from some Bantu tribesman. More likely it is made of chipped stone or sharpened bone.

His wife's possessions are just as sparse. Her chief item is a leather cape known as a *kaross*. It has many purposes in addition to keeping her warm. Belted around the waist, it provides a convenient carrying place. In it she puts her baby, roots and melons collected on the desert and choice pieces of kindling—all at the same time.

In addition to her kaross and its contents, each woman has two other indispensable[c9] items—a digging stick and a "stamping block," her only kitchen utensils.

# Check the Skills

### Understanding the Selection

1.  Do you agree that the exchange of greetings is a ritual? Why do you think as you do?

### Literary Appreciation Skills Figurative Language

2.  Give one or two examples of exaggeration as used in the greeting ritual. What do you think these exaggerations really mean?

### Vocabulary Development Skills Dictionary

3.  Did you use the glossary to look up unfamiliar words? If not, how did context clues help you figure out the meaning of *breechcloth* at the top of page 455 and *ushered* toward the bottom of that page?

# Apply What You Learned in Unit 16

## The Theme

### Rituals

1.    In this unit you read about several different kinds of rituals. You found out that rituals are practiced at many places and times, not only at group meetings. Why do you think people establish certain rituals for themselves to follow?

•     Some people practice daily activities in a ritualistic manner such as brushing their teeth at the same time in the same manner every day. Can you think of any other such rituals? What do you think is the difference between a ritual and a habit such as biting your fingernails?

•     During certain holidays, whether religious or not, certain rituals are performed in the same way. An example is the evening fireworks display on the Fourth of July year after year. What are some other rituals like these?

# The Skills

## Literary Appreciation Skills Figurative Language

2. You saw many different forms of exaggeration in this unit and saw how it could be used to serve different purposes. You will find that many times you will have to ask yourself whether what you are reading is really true or if it is exaggeration. This is especially important when you read such things as a newspaper editorial or an advertisement. Decide for yourself what the facts are. Then you won't be "hoodwinked" as Young Fu was.

• You'll have little trouble understanding most of the exaggerations you encounter. Remember to look at surrounding sentences and think about the sense of the paragraph to understand what the exaggeration means or to figure out the reason for its use.

## Vocabulary Development Skills Dictionary

3. Many times you can figure out the meaning of an unknown word with the help of context clues. But other times you will have to use the glossary or a dictionary. If you use a dictionary, you will have several meanings to choose from. Remember to use the context of surrounding sentences and your own common sense to decide which meaning is the appropriate one.

# Apply the
# Literary Appreciation Skills
## You Have Learned

### Apply the Skills As You Do Your Schoolwork

The literary appreciation skills you have learned in this section will be very useful when you read materials assigned in school. You will see that this is true when you read the following excerpt. It is the kind of selection you find in some textbooks used in reading, language arts, or English classes. This is part of a novel about two Puerto Rican girls in New York. Spook has come to visit her friend Magdalena in the apartment Magdalena shares with her strict grandmother, Nani.

The literary appreciation skills you have learned will help you get the most enjoyment from this selection. You can see how this works by keeping the following questions in mind as you read. Answer them after you finish.

1.   **Realistic and historical fiction.** How can you tell that this is realistic fiction? Refer back to pages 351 and 352 if you need to check literary types.

2.   **Plot and climax.** The plot of this story centers on the friendship of the two girls, and what happens to them. The climax comes after the end of this excerpt. Can you guess what it will be? Do you think that Nani might arrive unexpectedly and find Spook in the bathtub? Why would this be the high point of interest?

3.   **Description.** What is the description at the end of the selection that you could say is an example of sensory imagery?

4.   **Exaggeration.** There is an example of exaggeration in this excerpt. What is it?

# MAGDALENA

Louisa R. Shotwell

"Where's your mother?" Spook asked.

"Mami's dead. That's why Nani came."

"I shouldn't think your mother was old enough to die, but I suppose it can happen to anybody. My little brother Eustaquio died and he was only three. He had asthma. I still have two brothers left and a sister, all little kids and they're always grabbing things. The one I really liked was Eustaquio. How about your brothers and sisters?"

"I'm the only one."

"You're not! I never heard of such of a thing. You and your grandmother rattling around this great big palace of a place all by yourselves? Must be nice."

Spook wandered some more, touching everything. She lifted up the wooden cover that made a table out of the bathtub.

"Whee! If I had a tub convenient like this, I'd take a bath every day."

"I do."

"You do not."

"I do too." Magdalena stifled a giggle.

"I don't believe it."

"Well, I do."

"You care if I take one now?"

"Take a bath? Do you want to?"

"Yes, I want to, but I'm not wild about having your grandmother catch me in her bathtub. How do these things work? Never mind, I get it." The water gushed forth.

The tub began to fill. Magdalena glanced at the clock. Not quite twenty minutes of five. Nani never came home before five.

Magdalena produced soap and sponge.

"Honest, can I?" Spook asked. "Do you mean it?"

"You said you wanted to. I'm not making you."

Spook plunged in. "Help! I'm scalding!"

"No, you're not. It'll feel all right in a minute."

Spook recovered and began to scrub, gingerly at first and then with more and more energy.

## Apply the Skills As You Deal with the World

You'll find these literary appreciation skills helpful when you read material outside of school. The following excerpt is from a story similar to those you might find in a magazine. It is a true story set during the Civil War, more than a hundred years ago. Martin Emery has gone to Washington, D.C. His father is a prisoner of war. Martin misses him very much. Read the questions first and keep them in mind as you read the story. Answer them after you finish.

1. **Realistic and historical fiction.** Which type of literature is this? How do you know?

2. **Plot and climax.** Even in a short excerpt like this, you can probably decide that the plot of the story involves Martin's worry about his father. What is the climax in this excerpt? Remember that the climax is the highest point of interest or excitement.

3. **Description.** Look for examples of sensory imagery. Which ones appeal to your senses of touch, hearing, and sight?

4. **Exaggeration.** The incident is told in a very straightforward manner. So don't look for any exaggerations. How could the author have used exaggeration in describing the height of the man or the hardness of the stone steps?

# MARTIN

Catherine Cate Coblentz

The sun was hot. Martin went over and sat down on the stone steps of the Capitol. The steps were clean and cool.

He heard someone coming down the steps in back of him. But there was plenty of room so Martin didn't move. He just sat there and watched dreamily as a long shadow moved over the step he was on, and went slither-sliding down the step ahead. And the next. And the next. And the next.

Then the shadow stopped still and stayed in one place. A voice just in back of Martin said, "Well, well! How's my little soldier?"

Soldier! When his father's friends said that, Martin had always done as his father had taught him, jumped to his feet and saluted. So, forgetting how tired and sad he had been, he sprang to his feet.

As his fingers touched the visor of his blue cap, Martin's heart began to thud like a drum. For Abraham Lincoln was standing there looking down at him, his sad face losing its look of worry, and breaking slowly into a smile. Abraham Lincoln, himself!

"What is your name, soldier?" the great man asked, gravely returning the salute.

Martin told him.

"Where were you born, Martin?"

"In Vermont. In a log cabin."

The man nodded. "I was born in a log cabin, too."

"I know, Mother told me. She said some day I might get to be President like you."

"All mothers say that, Martin. What does your father say?"

"I don't know." Martin's voice slowed. "You see, he is away. He used to be a cobbler, but now he is your soldier."

"What regiment? And where is he now?"

The lump in Martin's throat was growing worse. It was difficult to make the words come. "The First Vermont—" he managed. And then the sobs had him. "He's in Andersonville Prison," he jerked.

But the great man was bending over. Strong arms were lifting Martin. In another moment the man had taken Martin's place on the steps. Martin was folded into his lap.

The boy's face was hidden now, in Abraham Lincoln's vest.

# Glossary

**Pronunciation Key**

After each entry word, letters and symbols in parentheses show you how the word is pronounced. Some symbols that may confuse you are shown below. Pronounce a symbol as you pronounce the spelling in bold, or very dark, type in the words next to the symbol. For example, ô should be pronounced the same way you say the *a* in **all** and the *aw* in **saw**. For your convenience, a shorter list of these symbols is at the bottom of each right hand page of the glossary.

Sometimes a word can be pronounced in different ways. When that is the case, the more common pronunciation is given first.

A syllable that gets the most stress when spoken is followed by a primary accent mark, as the first syllable in **accent** (ak′sent). A syllable spoken with less stress is shown with a secondary accent mark, as the last syllable in **accelerate** (ak sel′ə rāt′).

A brief history of a word, called its etymology, is given for some words. It is in brackets at the end of the entry.

| | | | | | | |
|---|---|---|---|---|---|---|
| a | apple, h**a**t | o | **o**dd, t**o**p | u | **u**p, p**u**ff |
| ā | **a**ble, s**ay** | ō | **o**pen, h**o**se | u̇ | p**u**t, b**oo**k |
| ã | **a**ir, c**a**re | ô | **a**ll, s**aw** | ü | b**oo**t, m**o**ve |
| ä | **a**rm, f**a**ther | ôr | **or**der, f**or**ce | ū | **u**se, m**u**sic |
| e | **e**levator, b**e**st | oi | **oi**l, b**oy** | ə | **a**bout, giv**e**n, penc**i**l, |
| ē | **ea**ch, m**e** | ou | **ou**t, h**ow** | | lem**o**n, unt**i**l |
| ėr | **ear**th, t**ur**n | | | | |
| | | | | th | **th**in, boo**th** |
| i | **i**tch, p**i**n | | | ᴛʜ | **th**en, smoo**th** |
| ī | **i**vy, n**i**ce | | | zh | mea**s**ure, sei**z**ure |

464

**a bun dant** (ə bun′dənt), in great supply; plentiful.

**a dap tive** (ə dap′tiv), able to be changed or fitted to suit different needs.

**af fec tion ate** (ə fek′shə nit), showing tender, friendly, caring feeling. *Mother gave me an affectionate hug.*

**a ga ve** (ə gä′vē), a tropical plant that grows in the desert.

**a lert** (ə lért′), to warn.

**al gae** (al′jē), a group of simple plants having no roots, stems, or leaves, found in water or damp spots. [from Latin *algae*, plural of *alga* seaweed]

**al ma nac** (ôl′mə nak), a reference book published yearly that contains charts and facts about the weather, tides, moon, stars, and other useful things.

**al ti tude** (al′tə tüd *or* al′tə tūd), height above the earth's surface.

**an ces tor** (an′ses′tər), a relative older than a grandfather, from whom one is descended.

**an chor** (ang′kər), to fix firmly in place.

**an cho vy** (an′chō′vē), a small fish that looks like a herring and tastes salty.

**an ten na** (an ten′ə), the aerial or set of wires on a radio or TV that receives the sound and pictures.

**an ten nae** (an ten′ē), the pair of long, thin feelers on the heads of certain shellfish and insects.

**ap pa ra tus** (ap′ə rā′təs *or* ap′ə rat′əs), equipment, tools, or machinery for a particular purpose. [from Latin *apparare*, from *ad* to + *parare* to prepare]

**ap pren tice** (ə pren′tis), a person who is learning a skill or trade from an expert.

**ap pro pri ate** (ə prō′prē āt), to set aside for a special use.

**ar a besque** (ār′ə besk′), a ballet position in which the dancer stands on one leg and holds the other leg straight back with straight knee.

**ar chae ol o gist** (är′kē ol′ə jist), a person who studies ancient ruins in order to understand life in past ages.

**ar ti fi cial** (är′tə fish′əl), made to imitate something in nature.

**As sin i boins** (ə sin′ ə boinz′), a tribe of North American Indians from Montana and nearby Canada.

**as sure** (ə shur′), to convince.

**at mo sphere** (at′mə sfir), the air surrounding any planet.

**av a lanche** (av′ə lanch), a sudden slide of a large amount of snow, earth, or rock down a mountainside.

**a venge** (ə venj′), to seek justice for a wrong; to get even.

**awe some** (ô′səm), causing great wonder, respect, and fear.

**ba ca lai to** (bä kä li′tō), 1. a small fried fish. 2. a treat made by freezing a carton of soft drink.

**baf fling** (baf′ ling), puzzling; confusing.

**bal us trade** (bal′ə strād), the railing around a porch, balcony, or stairway.

**bam boo** (bam bü′), a grass with long, hollow stems, which usually grows in warm regions.

**bar rier** (bār′ē ər), something that stands in the way.

**bid** (bid), to invite to attend; to summon.

**bland** (bland), mild; agreeable, dull.

**blurt** (blért), to speak suddenly, often without thinking first.

**boar** (bôr), a wild pig.

**boom** (büm), a period of sudden growth.

**bound ar y** (boun′dər ē), a line, thing, or place that forms a border or limit.

**breech cloth** (brēch′ klôth′), a small piece of clothing worn around the hips.

**bri dle** (brī′dl), the head strap or harness used to control a horse.

**bril liant** (bril′yənt), 1. shining brightly. 2. extremely intelligent or talented. [from Italian *brillare* to sparkle]

**buf fet** (buf′it), to strike, hit, or knock against. [from Old French *buffe* a blow]

**bur row** (bér′ō), to dig and then hide in a hole in the ground.

**but ton hole** (but′ ən hōl′), to make someone stop and listen as if by grabbing the buttonhole of the jacket.

**ca pa bil i ties** (kā′pə bil′ ə tēz), possible features and abilities not yet developed. *Scientists are investigating the capabilities of solar energy.*

**car a van** (kär′ə van), a group of people, animals, or vehicles traveling together, often in single file.

**car bon-date** (kär′bən dāt′), to find out the age of once-living matter by measuring the amount of a certain type of carbon left in it.

**car bon di ox ide** (kär′bən dī ok′sīd), the odorless, colorless gas breathed out by humans and taken in by plants.

**car cass** (kär′kəs), the body of a dead animal.

**Car ib be an** (kär′ə bē′ən *or* kə rib′ ē ən) **Sea**, the body of water between Central and South America and the West Indies.

**cast** (kast), 1. to throw with force. 2. to throw off or drop. 3. the set of actors in a play. 4. to give forth, project.

**cat e go ry** (kat′ə gôr′ē), a division in a system of grouping or classifying.

**cat nap** (kat′nap′), to take a short nap; to doze.

**cav ern** (kav′ərn), a large cave.

**cer tif i cate** (sər tif′ə kit), an official document that states that something is a fact. *I need my birth certificate to get my passport.*

**cham ois** (sham′ē), 1. a small, goatlike antelope. 2. a soft leather made from chamois, sheep, deer, or goat skin.

**charge** (chärj), 1. the amount of bullets needed to load a gun. 2. to ask a price. 3. to give an order. [from Middle English *chargen* to load, from Late Latin *carricāre* to load, from *carrus* wagon]

**charmed** (chärmd), protected as though by magic. *Our cat leads a charmed life, always escaping from the dog next door.*

**chink ing** (chingk′ing), the mud mixture used to fill the cracks between logs in log cabins.

**chis el** (chiz′əl), a tool with a strong blade and sharp edge used for cutting or chipping.

**chow der** (chou′dər), a thick soup or stew.

**churn** (chérn), to move constantly with a shaking motion.

**cir cu lar** (sér′kū lər), round in shape, as in a circle.

**cir cu la to ry** (sér′kyə lə tôr′ē), moving around in a regular, fixed pattern.

**cler gy** (klér′jē), official ministers of a religion. [from Late Latin *clericus* a clerk]

**clum si ly** (klum′zə lē), in an ungraceful, awkward way.

**co-an chor** (kō′ang′kər), a person who shares the duties of arranging and presenting a radio or TV news program.

**com bat** (kom′bat), a battle or fight.

**com mence** (kə mens′), to start or begin.

**com mit ment** (kə mit′mənt), a promise.

**com mut er** (kə mū′tər), a person who travels regularly from home to work either by car or public transportation.

**com plex** (kom′pleks), a group of connected buildings.

**con ceal** (kən sēl′), to put out of sight.

**con cer to** (kən chär′tō), a long piece of music written for one instrument, such as violin or piano, to be accompanied by an orchestra.

**con ces sion** (kən sesh′ən), space where someone has the right to run a business or service. *The concession stand at the ballpark sells terrific hot dogs.*

**con di tion ing** (kən dish′ən ing), the pattern of exercise and behavior used to get in good physical shape for an athletic event.

**con fec tion er** (kən fek′shə nər), a person who makes candy. **confectioners′ sugar**, a type of fine white sugar used in making candies and desserts.

**con sec u tive ly** (kən sek′yə tiv lē), following one after another in order or logical sequence.

**con serve** (kən sérv′), to keep from wasting; to save.

**con stel la tion** (kon′stə lā′shən), a group of stars that appears to form a shape for which the group is named.

**con sum er** (kən süm′ər), a person who buys goods and services.

**con ta gious** (kən tā′jəs), easily spread from one to another; catching. *The doctor said the disease was contagious.*

**con ten der** (kən tend′ər), one who takes part in and tries to win a fight, struggle, or contest.

**co or di nate** (kō ôr′də nāt′), to arrange in working order with someone or something else.

**co or di nat ed** (kō ôr′də nā tid), having groups of muscles that work together to produce a well-balanced action.

**co or di na tion** (kō ôr'də nā'shən), the working together of groups of muscles in good timing and rhythm.

**coup** (kü), 1. a clever move. 2. a test of courage. [from French *coup* a blow]

**cove** (kōv), a sheltered part of a sea or lake that cuts into the shoreline.

**craft y** (kraf'tē), sly; clever at tricking others.

**cri er** (krī' ər), an official who makes public announcements.

**crouch** (krouch), to stoop down low with the legs bent close to the body.

**CTA,** Chicago Transit Authority, the organization in charge of public transportation in the city of Chicago, Illinois.

**cus tom** (kus'təm), a usual habit or way of doing things.

**cy clone** (sī'klōn), a violent windstorm; a tornado.

**de ac ti va tion** (de ak'tə vā'shən), to remove a military person or piece of equipment from active service.

**debt** (det), money owed to someone else.

**de cor** (dā kôr'), scenery; decoration.

**de flate** (di flāt'), to let air out. *He deflated the bicycle tires.*

**deft** (deft), quick and skillful.

**del i ca cy** (del'ə kə sē), gracefulness; precise, fine action.

**de scend** (di send'), to come down from a higher to a lower place.

**de spite** (di spīt'), regardless of. *She walked home despite the pouring rain.*

**des ti na tion** (des'tə nā'shən), the place to which one is traveling.

**de vice** (də vīs'), something invented for a special use.

**di gest** (də jest'), to change food in the stomach into a form the body can use.

**din gy** (din'jē), dull, shabby, dirty.

**dis as ter** (də zas'tər), an event or misfortune that causes great damage or suffering. [from Italian *disastro* ill-starred, from Latin *dis* not + *astro* star]

**dis creet** (dəs krēt'), careful; reserved; cautious.

**dis grace** (dis grās'), to bring shame or a loss of respect.

**dis till** (dis til'), to heat a liquid and collect its vapor in order to purify it.

**dis tinc tive** (dis tingk' tiv), serving to set apart and identify.

**dis tress ing ly** (dis tres'ing lē), in a way that causes discomfort or pain.

**dot ty** (dot'ē), weak-minded; crazy. [variant of Scottish *dottle* silly, from Middle English *doten* dote]

**dou bloon** (du blün'), an old Spanish gold coin.

**drab** (drab), dull; not bright or lively.

**draft** (draft), used for pulling heavy loads. *The draft horses pulled the big wagon.*

**drain age** (drā'nij), a system of pipes for carrying off water or waste.

**dredge** (drej), to scoop out and deepen the bottom of a body of water.

**drowse** (drouz), to sleep lightly; to doze.

**dude** (düd *or* dūd), 1. western slang for a city person. 2. an overdressed person.

**eaves** (ēvz), the bottom edge of a roof that hangs over the side of a building.

**e clipse** (i klips'), the blocking out of the light passing from one heavenly body to another.

**e co nom ic** (ē'kə nom'ik *or* ek'ə nom'ik), referring to the distribution of goods and money. [from Greek *oikonomikos* relating to household management, from *oikos* house + *nomos* managing]

**ed it** (ed'it), 1. to revise written work for publication. 2. to prepare a film or recording for presentation.

**ee rie** (ēr'ē), strange; weird; unsettling.

**e lim i nate** (i lim' ə nāt), to get rid of; to remove.

**em blem** (em'bləm), a sign or token that stands for an idea; a symbol.

**e merge** (i mérj'), to come into view. [from Latin *emergere*, from e out + *mergere* to dip]

**em ploy ee** (em ploi'ē *or* em'ploi ē'), a person who is hired to work for pay.

**en cour age** (en kér'ij), to give support or hope to; to promote, urge.

---

a **a**pple, ā **a**ble, ã **a**ir, ä **a**rm; e **e**levator, ē **ea**ch, ér **ea**rth; i **i**tch, ī **i**vy; o **o**dd, ō **o**pen, ô **a**ll, ôr **or**der; oi **oi**l, ou **ou**t; u **u**p, ủ **p**ut, ü b**oo**t, ū **u**se; ə **a**bout; th **th**in, ℸH **th**en, zh mea**s**ure

**en dur ance** (en dúr′ əns or en dūr′ əns), power to last without giving up. [from Latin *in* in + *durare* to harden]

**en gage** (en gāj′), 1. to take part in. 2. to hire for work. 3. to promise to marry. 4. to reserve for use.

**en grave** (en grāv′), to carve letters or a design into a surface.

**en hance** (en hans′), to add to in order to make more valuable or attractive.

**e nor mous ness** (i nôr′məs nəs), greatness of size, amount, or degree beyond normal.

**en zyme** (en′zīm), a substance produced by a living body to start chemical changes such as digestion.

**e qua tor** (i kwā tər), an imaginary line that circles the middle of the earth and forms the halfway mark between the North Pole and the South Pole.

**ev i dent ly** (ev′ə dənt′lē), clearly; plainly.

**ex cel** (ek sel′), to do or be better than others.

**ex panse** (ek spans′), wide, open space or area of land, sky, or water.

**ex pe di tion** (ek′spə dish′ ən), a journey taken for a special purpose such as exploration.

**ex ten sion** (ek sten′shən), a part connected to and stretched out from the main part.

**ex traor di nar y** (ek strôr′də nār′ē), very unusual and remarkable.

**ex trav a gance** (ek strav′ə gəns), something that goes beyond proper limits of reason or expense.

**feat** (fēt), a great deed, showing courage, strength, or skill.

**fer ry** (fãr′ē), a boat for carrying people back and forth across a body of water. **ferry slip**, place at the edge of the water where a ferry is tied between trips.

**fes toon** (fes tün′), to decorate with hanging chains made of leaves, flowers, or ribbon.

**flint** (flint), a hard stone that makes sparks when struck with steel.

**foil¹** (foil), 1. a very thin, bendable sheet of metal. 2. a person or thing who makes another seem better by contrast. [from Latin *folium* a leaf]

**foil²** (foil), to outwit. [from Old French *fouler* to trample on]

**fo rage** (fôr′ij), to search for food. [from Old French *feurre* fodder, food]

**fore bear** (fôr′bãr), a relative who lived in the past. [from Middle English (Scottish dialect) *forebear*, from *fore* fore + *bear* be -er or one who is, from *be* to be]

**for ma tion** (fôr mā′shən), 1. the way something is made or arranged. 2. large body of rocks all made of the same substance.

**foy er** (foi′ ər), front hall. [from French *foyer*, from Latin *focus* fireplace]

**frac ture** (frak′chər), to break or crack a bone.

**free style** (frē′stīl′), a sports event in which the contestants choose their own style or method of performing.

**freight er** (frā′tər), a ship used for carrying a load of goods; a cargo ship.

**fren zy** (fren′zē), great excitement; near madness; out of control.

**frus trat ing** (frus′trāt ing), preventing someone from reaching a goal; making useless.

**ful fill** (fù fil′), 1. to carry out; to satisfy. 2. to bring to an end; to complete.

**fur row** (fér′ō), a long, narrow groove in the ground.

**Gage, Thomas**, 1721–1787, the commander of the British army and the governor of Massachusetts at the beginning of the American Revolution.

**gang plank** (gang′plangk′), a temporary bridge used to get on and off a ship.

**gear** (gēr), 1. to equip. 2. to adjust in order to bring about a certain result.

**ge o log i cal** (jē′ ə loj′ ə kəl), having to do with the scientific study of the earth's crust and of types of rocks.

**ges ture** (jes′chər), to move a part of the body to express an idea or feeling; an act done as a sign of one's feelings. *A handshake is a gesture of friendship.*

**glib ly** (glib′lē), in a smooth, convincing, but less-than-truthful way.

**gloat** (glōt), to look at or think about with great or excessive pleasure. [from old Norse *glotta* to smile scornfully]

**glo ry** (glôr′ē), to rejoice greatly.

**gnarled** (närld), covered with hard, rough knots.

**gourd** (gôrd), the fruit of a squash plant that has a hard rind that can be hollowed out and used as a bowl.

**gour met** (gür'mā), an expert in judging fine foods and wines. [from Old French *gromet* wine merchant's servant]

**grav i ty** (grav' ə tē), a force in nature that pulls objects toward the center of the earth. **center of gravity**, point in an object around which its weight is evenly balanced.

**greed i ly** (grēd' ə lē), 1. in a selfish way, wanting more than one's share. 2. in an intensely eager manner.

**groom** (grüm), 1. a person who takes care of horses. 2. to make neat and tidy. *Her speech was as carefully groomed as her hair.*

**grope** (grōp), to feel the way with one's hands because of being unable to see.

**Gros Ventre** (grō'vänt'), a North American Indian tribe from Wyoming.

**grot to** (grot'ō), a small cave or cavelike room.

**grum bles** (grum'bəls), poetic term for discontent, complaining.

**gus sak** (gus'ak), Eskimo term for people of the Caucasian (white) race.

**hand** (hand), a unit of measurement roughly equal to the width of a hand (about four inches), used especially to express the height of horses.

**han ker** (haṅg'kər), to wish or long for; to crave.

**haunch** (hônch), the hind of an animal including the hip and thigh.

**hec tic** (hek'tik), confused and rushed.

**hen e quen** (hen' ə ken), a type of desert plant whose strong fibers are used in making rope.

**hes i tate** (hez' ə tāt), 1. to stop and wait before acting. 2. to be unwilling.

**hes i ta tion** (hez'ə tā'shən), delay due to uncertainty. [from Latin *haesitare* to stick fast]

**hi lar i ous** (hə lār'ē əs), extremely funny and merry.

**hoist** (hoist), 1. to raise up. 2. to help lift or boost a person up over something.

**hold**[1] (hōld), to have in the hand. [from Old English *haldan* to hold]

**hold**[2] (hōld), the inside of a ship below the deck. [from Dutch *hol* hole]

**ho ri zon** (hə rī'zən), the distant line where earth and sky seem to meet.

**how dy** (hou'dē), western term of greeting; hello. [shortened form of *how-de-do*, how do you do?]

**hun dred fold** (hun'drəd fōld'), one hundred times as much or as many.

**hy e na** (hī ē'nə), a wolflike animal of Africa and Asia.

**hyp not ic** (hip not'ik), causing one to go to sleep or be in a sleeplike state.

**i dle** (ī'dəl), 1. doing nothing. 2. useless; worthless; time-wasting.

**im i tate** (im' ə tāt), to copy; to act like.

**im mi grant** (im'ə grənt), a person who moves to a new country to live.

**im part** (im pärt'), to tell; to reveal.

**im pend ing** (im pen'ding), about to happen; threatening. [from Latin *impendere* from *im* in + *pendere* to hang]

**im plore** (im plôr'), to beg or plead for.

**in cred i ble** (in kred'ə bəl), 1. hard to believe. 2. too unusual to be possible.

**In di an sum mer**, a period of warm, dry weather in the fall after the first frost.

**in dis pen sa ble** (in'dis pen'sə bal), absolutely necessary; cannot be done without. *Food is indispensable to health.*

**in dulge** (in dulj'), to give in to one's own wishes or feelings.

**in ert** (in ért'), lifeless; having no power to move or act.

**i ni ti ate** (i nish'ē āt), to hold a special ceremony to admit someone into a group or organization.

**inn keep er** (in'kē'pər), one who owns or runs a small hotel or restaurant.

**in no cence** (in'ə səns), state of being free from any wrong-doing.

**in spire** (in spīr'), to cause to have a thought or feeling.

**in stall** (in stôl'), to put into place for a special use.

**in stinct** (in'stingkt), an inborn, unlearned knowledge, power, or feeling.

**in stinc tive ly** (in stinkt'iv lē), in a natural, automatic way, rather than in a way that is learned.

---

a **a**pple, ā **a**ble, ä **a**ir, ä **a**rm; e **e**levator, ē **ea**ch, ér **ea**rth; i **i**tch, ī **i**vy; o **o**dd, ō **o**pen, ô **a**ll, ôr **or**der; oi **oi**l, ou **ou**t; u **u**p, ú **p**ut, ü b**oo**t, ū **u**se; ə **a**bout; th **th**in, ₮н **th**en, zh mea**s**ure

**in sult** (in sult′), to treat with disrespect, scorn, or rudeness.

**in te gral** (in′tə grəl), necessary for completeness. *The table of contents is an integral part of a book.*

**in tent** (in tent′), aim; purpose.

**in ter vene** (in′tər vēn′), to come between in order to settle something.

**in tol er ance** (in tol′ ər əns), unwillingness to put up with differences in opinions, beliefs, or backgrounds.

**In u it** (in′ū it), the name Eskimo people call themselves, meaning ''people.''

**in vent** (in vent′), to make or create something new.

**jerk y** (jėr′kē), a strip of dried meat.

**jour nal** (jėr′nəl), a daily written record of events and feelings; a diary.

**ju bi la tion** (jü′bə lā′shən), happy, joyful celebration.

**jut** (jut), to stick out. *The finger-shaped piece of land juts out into the water.*

**ke long** (kē′long), a fish trap and hut built on tall poles over the water.

**kil ter** (kil′tər), good working order. *Our TV set is out of kilter.*

**kins man** (kinz′mən), a male relative.

**la bor er** (lā′bər ər), a person whose job requires hard, physical work but not much skill.

**lank y** (lang′kē), very tall and thin.

**lath er** (laᴛʜ′ ər), 1. foam formed by soap and water. 2. foam from sweating.

**launch** (lônch), to set forth in the water; to set afloat.

**lit er ate** (lit′ər it), able to read and write.

**lob by ist** (lob′ē ist), a person who tries to influence the way lawmakers vote.

**loft y** (lôf′tē), very high; towering.

**lum ber** (lum′bər), to move along in a heavy, clumsy way.

**lure** (lür), 1. to lead on or tempt. 2. anything that attracts. 3. artificial bait used in fishing.

**lurk** (lėrk), to hide and be ready to attack.

**lus ter** (lus′tər), soft shine or gloss; brightness caused by reflected light.

**ma chet e** (mə shet′ē or mə chet′ē), a large, sharp knife used as a cutting tool and weapon.

**make shift** (māk′shift′), used for a while as a substitute. *The sofa became a makeshift bed.*

**Ma lay an** (mə lā′ ən), referring to the race of people living in the island country of Malaysia in southeast Asia.

**mal let** (mal′it), a type of hammer with a short handle and a wooden head.

**mar i o nette** (mār′ē ə net′), a puppet moved by strings from above.

**me an der** (mē an′dər), to follow a winding, unplanned course. [from Latin *Maeander*, from Greek *Meiandros* the name of a winding river in Asia Minor]

**men ace** (men′əs), to threaten danger.

**mer it** (mār′it), to deserve. *Her good work merited a reward.*

**me ter** (mē′tər), a unit for measuring length in the metric system. *A meter is equal to 39.37 inches.*

**me thod i cal ly** (mə thod′ ə klē), in an orderly, systematic way.

**mi gra tion** (mī grā′shən), the movement of a large group of people or animals from one place to another.

**min i a ture** (min′ē ə chùr or min′ə chər), made much smaller than the original.

**moc ca sin** (mok′ə sən), a soft leather shoe of the type first made and worn by Native Americans.

**mock** (mok), not real; imitation.

**moor** (mùr), to fasten a ship to a place at the shore.

**mosque** (mosk), a temple or place of worship for members of the Moslem religion. [from Arabic *masjid* a place of worship, from *sajada* to worship]

**mo ti vate** (mō tə vāt), 1. to provide someone with a reason for doing something. 2. to inspire.

**mus ket** (mus′kət), a long-barreled gun used before the rifle was invented.

**mus sel** (mus′ əl), a shellfish having two hinged parts to its shell.

**mut ed** (mūt′əd), softened or toned down in color or sound.

**Nav a jo** (nav′ə hō or näv′ə hō), a member of a tribe of North American Indians living in the Southwest. [from one of the American Indian languages *Navahu* great planted fields]

**nav i ga tor** (nav′ə gā′tər), the person who plots the course of a ship or airplane. [from Latin *navigare* to manage a ship, from *navis* ship + *agere* to drive]

**Nez Per cés** (nez′pér′siz), American Indian tribe from the Pacific Northwest. [from French *Nezpercé* pierced nose]

**nick er** (nik′ər), to make a low whinnying sound like a horse; to neigh.

**no bil i ty** (nō bil′ə tē), people of important rank by birth or title.

**nos tril** (nos′trəl), one of the two outer openings of the nose.

**nudge** (nuj), to push gently.

**ob struc tion** (əb struk′shən), something in the way; obstacle.

**op po si tion** (op′ə zish′ən), a group that fights against those in power.

**or bit** (ôr′bit), the curved path of one body in space around another.

**or deal** (ôr dēl′), a difficult and trying experience or test.

**or der ly** (ôr′dər lē), a hospital worker who cleans and waits on patients.

**out ra geous** (out rā′jəs), so uncontrolled as to be shocking.

**par al lel** (pār′ə lel), always the same distance apart, like railroad tracks. **parallel bars**, two bars set on upright posts, used in gymnastics and as a support for exercising.

**parch** (pärch), to dry out by the sun's heat or by roasting.

**pare** (pār), to peel [from Latin *parare* to prepare]

**par ka** (pár′kə), a hooded, fur jacket of a design originated by Eskimos.

**pas sage  way** (pas′ij wā), a hall or opening wide enough to go through.

**pa tient** (pā′shənt), 1. calm and understanding. 2. someone under medical care.

**pe di a tri cian** (pē′dē ə trish′ən), a medical doctor who specializes in treating children.

**per ish** (pār′ish), to die. [from Latin *perire* to perish, from *per* through + *ire* to go]

**per sist ent** (pər sis′tənt), continuing; not giving up in the face of difficulty.

**pew ter** (pū′tər), a dull metallic substance made from a combination of tin and other metals.

**pick et** (pik′ət), to tie a horse to a peg in the ground.

**pie** (pī), to mix up or jumble a pile of printing type.

**pieces of eight**, very old Spanish silver dollars.

**pier** (pēr), a platform reaching from the shore into the water, used as a landing place for boats.

**plague** (plāg), to torment or bother. *Insects plague our garden every year.*

**plan ta tion** (plan tā′shən), a large farm. [from Latin *plantare* to plant]

**plu mer i a** (plü mār′ē ə), a flowering plant.

**plum met** (plum′it), to drop suddenly.

**plunge** (plunj), 1. to throw suddenly, with force. 2. to dive.

**pre car i ous** (pri kār′ē əs), risky; not secure. [from Latin *precārius* dependent on prayer or favor]

**pre cip i ta tion** (pri sip′ə tā′shən), rain, snow, or sleet.

**pre dic a ment** (prē dik′ə mənt), an unpleasant, difficult, or troublesome situation.

**pre dict** (pri dikt′), 1. to tell what will happen in the future. 2. to make a guess based on special knowledge. [from Latin *praedicere* to foretell, from *prae* before + *dicere* to tell]

**prey** (prā), an animal hunted and killed for food by another animal.

**prim i tive** (prim′ə tiv), from the earliest times in history.

**prin ci pal** (prin′sə pəl), most important.

**proc ess** (pros′es), to develop film.

**pro claim** (prə klām′), to announce publicly and officially. [from Latin *pro* before + *clamere* to cry out]

**prong** (prông), one of the pointed ends of a fork.

**prop o si tion** (prop′ə zish′ən), the statement of a suggested plan. *The Senate studied the gas tax proposition.*

**pros pect** (pros′pekt), something expected or hoped for; a possibility.

---

a **a**pple, ā **a**ble, ã **a**ir, ä **a**rm; e **e**levator, ē **ea**ch, ér **ear**th; i **i**tch, ī **i**vy; o **o**dd, ō **o**pen, ô **a**ll, ôr **or**der; oi **oi**l, ou **ou**t; u **u**p, ů **pu**t, ü b**oo**t, ū **u**se; ə **a**bout; th **th**in, ғн **th**en, zh mea**s**ure

**pros pec tor** (pros′pek tər), a person who explores an area for valuable natural resources such as gold, silver, or oil.

**pros per ous** (pros′pər əs), doing well; successful; earning money.

**pro test** (prə test′), to object to.

**pro vide** (prə vīd′), 1. to supply what is needed. 2. to state as a prior condition. *I will go provided that he goes too.*

**prune** (prün), to cut branches from bushes or trees to improve the shape.

**pu ri fy** (pūr′ə fī), to make clean.

**ram shack le** (ram′shak′əl), made loosely; ready to fall apart.

**rang y** (rān′jē), having long, thin legs.

**reb el** (reb′əl), person who fights against those in power. [from Latin *re* again + *bellare* to war]

**reck less** (rek′ləs), careless; not responsible; taking chances.

**re con di tion ing** (rē′kən dish′ ən ing) the restoring of good physical fitness to a person or animal.

**re gain** (ri gān′), to get again; to recover.

**reg u lar** (reg′yə lər), member of the permanent army of a country.

**reg u late** (reg′yə lāt), to control or direct according to a set of rules.

**re luc tant** (ri luk′tənt), unwilling; slow to act because of wanting to wait.

**re mote  con trol** (ri mōt′kən trōl′), control of a machine or an activity from a distance, often by radio signals.

**re pul sive** (rē pul′siv), causing a great dislike; disgusting.

**re search er** (ri sér′chər *or* rē′sér′chər), a person who makes a careful, scientific study for facts about a subject.

**res ig na tion** (rez′ig nā′shən), 1. the act of giving up a position, job, or office. A written notice that one is leaving a job, office, or position. 2. an attitude of acceptance or submission to some condition. *He listened to the bad news with resignation.*

**rev er ie** (rev′ər ē), a daydream. [from French *rêverie*, from *rêver* to wander]

**rev o lu tion ar y** (rev′ə lü′shə när′ē), causing an extreme change or overthrow of fixed ideas or government.

**ridge top** (rij′top), the top of the long, narrow strips of ground that have been formed by a plow.

**rouse** (rouz), to wake up; to stir out of a state of inactivity.

**ruse** (rüz *or* rüs), clever trick.

**sat el lite** (sat′ əl īt), an object sent into space to revolve around the earth or another planet.

**scan** (skan), to measure the rhythm of a line of poetry by counting the syllables and accents.

**scarce** (skârs), hard to get; rare. **make oneself scarce**, to go away; to hide.

**scores** (skôrz), a large number. *Scores of fans appeared at the rock concert.*

**scowl** (skoul), to look angry and sullen; to frown.

**scud** (skud), to move quickly; to be driven by the wind.

**scur ry** (skér′ē), to move quickly; to scamper.

**se cu ri ty** (si kūr′ə tē), condition of being safe and free from cares and worry. **social security**, a system in which the government provides money to retired and other dependent persons.

**shun** (shun), to avoid; to keep away from.

**Sioux** (sü), American Indian tribe from the Midwest.

**sis al** (sis′ əl *or* sī′səl), a type of desert plant whose strong fibers are used in making rope.

**site** (sīt), a place or location chosen for a special purpose.

**skiff** (skif), a small, light rowboat.

**skill ful** (skil′fəl), showing great ability in an art or craft.

**skip per** (skip′ ər), the captain of a ship.

**slab-sid ed** (slab′sīd′ əd), having broad, flat, thick sides.

**slack** (slak), 1. loose, not tight. 2. not busy. **slack off**, to lessen one's efforts.

**slate** (slāt), a type of hard, gray rock that is easily split into layers.

**slith er** (sliᴛʜ′ ər), to move by sliding along over a surface.

**smokejumper**, a person who parachutes from an airplane into a forest fire area to help put out the fire.

**smug** (smug), overly self-satisfied.

**smug gle** (smug′ əl), to bring in or out of a country secretly and illegally.

**snick er** (snik′ ər), to laugh in a controlled way that shows disrespect.

**sol emn** (sol′ əm), serious; somber.

**spec i men** (spes′ə mən), one chosen from a group to show what the others are like; sample. [from Latin *specere* to see]

**spec tac u lar** (spek tak′yə lər), making a grand or unusual display.

**spec ta tor** (spek′tā tər), a person who watches but does not take part.

**spe lunk ing** (spi lungk′ing), the hobby of exploring caves.

**spin dly** (spind′lē), having very long and thin legs.

**splay** (splā), to spread out far apart in a clumsy way.

**spon sor** (spon′sər), to support, pay for.

**square** (skwār), to make even; to settle accounts. *He squared his debt by paying for my lunch.*

**sta bi liz er** (stā′bə līz′ ər), 1. a device to keep a person or thing steady or balanced. 2. a device in an airplane or ship to keep it steady.

**stalk** (stôk), 1. a thin stem. 2. the thin structure supporting the eyes of certain shellfish.

**stam i na** (stam′ə nə), strength; endurance.

**sta tus** (stā′təs *or* stat′əs), position; state; condition. [from Latin *status* manner of standing, posture]

**stee ple chase** (stē′pəl chās), a horse race run on a course with obstacles that must be jumped over, so named because riders originally used a distant, visible church steeple as the goal.

**stern**[1] (stėrn), 1. strict. 2. grim. [from Old English *styrne* stern]

**stern**[2] (stėrn), the rear part of a ship. [from Old Norse *stjorn* steering]

**stilt ed** (stil′tid), stiff and overly formal.

**Stone Age**, the earliest period of human society in which people used weapons and tools made of stone.

**Stu ka** (stü′kə), a German World War II, two-seated, dive bomber airplane.

**sub ter fuge** (sub′tər fūj), a plan or trick used to hide or avoid something. [from Latin *subterfugere* to flee secretly, from *subter* below + *fugere* to flee]

**suf frage** (suf′rij), the right to vote in an election.

**su mac** (sü′mak), a small bush or tree with leaves that turn red in the fall.

**sun dry** (sun′drē), 1. various, assorted. 2. each and every.

**su per in tend ent** (sü′pər n ten′dənt), one who oversees a place.

**sur vey** (sər vā′), to look over; to view.

**sus tain er** (səs tān′ər), 1. something that keeps something else in existance. 2. something that provides necessary nourishment.

**sweet gum**, a large North American tree with reddish-brown wood and sweet-smelling sap.

**swirl** (swėrl), to spin around.

**tack le** (tak′ əl), equipment; gear.

**ta ran tu la** (tə ran′chə lə), a large, hairy spider with a painful bite. [from Italian *Taranto*, a city in Italy where such spiders were found]

**tar nish** (tär′nish), to dull the brightness of; to lose color.

**tech ni cal** (tek′nə kəl), having to do with the special facts used in a science or craft.

**tech nique** (tek nēk′), a special method or system.

**tech nol o gy** (tek nol′ə jē), the science that puts scientific ideas into practice.

**tem po rar y** (tem′pə rär′ē), lasting for a short time; not permanent.

**terse ly** (tėrs′lē), in a brief manner; not wasting words. [from Latin *tergere* to wipe or polish]

**thatch** (thach), 1. to cover a roof with straw or leaves. 2. roof covering made of leaves or straw.

**ther a pist** (thâr′ə pəst), a person trained to treat diseases or physical disorders. **physical** (fiz′ ə kəl) **therapist**, a person trained in the treatment of bodily disorders by exercise, heat, and massage.

**thor ough bred** (thėr′ō bred′), a special breed of race horse developed to have qualities of a champion.

**tide** (tīd), the rising and falling movement of the oceans caused by the pull of the moon and sun.

---

a **a**pple, ā **a**ble, â **a**ir, ä **a**rm; e **e**levator, ē **ea**ch, ėr **ear**th; i **i**tch, ī **i**vy; o **o**dd, ō **o**pen, ô **a**ll, ôr **or**der; oi **oi**l, ou **ou**t; u **u**p, u̇ **p**ut, ü b**oo**t, ū **u**se; ə **a**bout; th **th**in, ᵺ **th**en, zh mea**s**ure

**tim id** (tim'id) shy; easily scared. [from Latin *timere* to fear]

**tine** (tīn), one of the sharp points of a fork.

**tra di tion al ly** (trə dish' ə nəl ē), according to a habit or practice that has been in use for a long time.

**tran quil** (trang'kwəl), peaceful; calm.

**tri um phant ly** (trī um'fənt lē), expressing joy over a victory or success.

**troll** (trōl), 1. to fish by trailing a baited line behind a boat. 2. to sing in rounds.

**tuck ered** (tuk' ərd), tired; worn out.

**tun dra** (tun'drə), the huge, flat, treeless plains in the Arctic regions.

**tur ban** (tér'bən), 1. a scarf wound around the head, worn by men in some Oriental countries. 2. a small hat, with little or no brim.

**un in hab it ed** (un'in hab' ə tid), not lived in or on.

**u nique** (ū nēk'), 1. having no equal; one of a kind. 2. unusual; remarkable.

**ur ban re new al** (ér'ban ri nü' əl), the improvement of run-down city neighborhoods by rebuilding or restoring.

**u ro pod** (ūr'ə pod'), one of a pair of lower back limbs of certain shellfish.

**ush er** (ush' ər), to lead one to a place.

**u ten sil** (ū ten'səl), 1. a tool or container used for a practical purpose. 2. an eating tool such as a knife, fork, or spoon.

**vast** (vast), very great in size, amount or area; overwhelming.

**ven i son** (ven'ə sən), deer meat.

**vest** (vest), an old-fashioned word for an undershirt.

**vet er an** (vet' ər ən), 1. a person who has experience in some kind of work. 2. a person who has fought in a war.

**v i brant** (vī'brənt), full of life.

**vi bra tion** (vī brā'shən), a fast, back-and-forth, shaking motion.

**vid e o** (vid'ē ō), television. [from Latin *video* I see]

**vid e o tape** (vid'ē ō tāp'), to record sounds and images on a special tape for showing on television.

**vie** (vī), to compete; to be a rival.

**vig i lant** (vij'ə lənt), ever watchful.

**vis i bil i ty** (viz'ə bil' ə tē), the ability to see under given conditions of light.

**vis u al ize** (vizh'ū ə līz), to form a mental picture; to imagine.

**vi tal ly** (vī'təl ē), in a way that is necessary to life; in an important way.

**vo ca tion al** (vō kā'shə nəl), having to do with an occupation or profession.

**vul gar** (vul'gər), showing a lack of good taste. [from Latin *vulgaris*, from *vulgus* the common people]

**wear i ness** (wir'ē nəs), tiredness.

**weave** (wēv), to go forward by moving from side to side or around objects.

**wedge** (wej), to force or pack in tightly.

**whin ny** (hwin'ē), the gentle sound made by a horse; a neigh.

**white-collar**, describing any job done continually in an office. [from the white shirt that was worn by such workers]

**wind lass** (wind'ləs), a machine for pulling or lifting things.

**with ers** (wiтн' ərz), the highest point of a horse's, or similar animal's, back between the shoulder blades.

**wrench** (rench), to injure by twisting. *I wrenched my back when I fell down the steps.* [from Old English *wrenc* a trick]

**writh ing** (rīтн'ing), squirming in pain.

# Word List

The first time it appears in a selection, a word included in the **glossary** is followed by a<sup>g</sup>. Words in the selections for which there are **context clues** to meaning are followed by a<sup>c</sup>. These words are listed below in alphabetical order by selection.

| Glossary Words | Context Clue Words |
|---|---|

## Vocabulary Development Skills

## Unit 1

*Selection 1*

| | |
|---|---|
| cyclone | (none) |
| dude | |
| invent | |
| tarantula | |
| withers | |

*Selection 2*

| | |
|---|---|
| Assiniboins | bid |
| avenge | coups |
| bid | crier |
| charmed | mounts |
| coup | picketed |
| crier | reckless |
| feat | |
| Gros Ventres | |
| Nez Percés | |
| picket | |
| reckless | |
| Sioux | |

*Selection 3*

| | |
|---|---|
| anchovy | anchovies |
| festoon | festoon |
| kelong | kelong |
| Malayan | squared |
| pier | windlasses |
| plumeria | |
| purify | |
| square | |
| thatch | |
| windlass | |
| writhing | |

*Selection 4*

| | |
|---|---|
| commence | commenced |
| grumbles | grumbles |
| hanker | howdies |
| howdy | tuckered |
| musket | |
| Navajo | |
| ramshackle | |
| slab-sided | |
| tuckered | |

| Glossary Words | Context Clue Words |
|---|---|

*Selection 5*

| | |
|---|---|
| distressingly | shun |
| impart | |
| insult | |
| shun | |

## Unit 2

*Selection 1*

| | |
|---|---|
| baffling | prongs |
| gravity | |
| precarious | |
| prong | |

*Selection 2*

| | |
|---|---|
| anchor | Asturias |
| bridle | haunches |
| catnap | impending |
| draft | |
| drowse | |
| eerie | |
| haunch | |
| hesitation | |
| impending | |
| merit | |
| obstruction | |
| scores | |

*Selection 3*

| | |
|---|---|
| concerto | (none) |
| gourmet | |
| pare | |

*Selection 4*

| | |
|---|---|
| chowder | enzymes |
| circular | furrow |
| enzyme | sustainers |
| furrow | |
| greedily | |
| plague | |
| sustainer | |

*Selection 5*

| | |
|---|---|
| adaptive | devices |
| coordination | parallel bars |
| device | physical therapist |
| parallel | |
| parallel bars | |
| therapist | |

| Glossary Words | Context Clue Words | Glossary Words | Context Clue Words |
|---|---|---|---|

**Unit 3**

*Selection 1*

| | | | |
|---|---|---|---|
| lumber | livestock | | |
| security | shaded up | | |
| superintendent | traitor | | |

*Selection 2* (none)

*Selection 3*

| | |
|---|---|
| co-anchor | grasp |
| consumer | license |
| coordinate | |
| edit | |
| gear | |
| hectic | |
| process | |
| stamina | |

*Selection 4*

| | |
|---|---|
| alert | combat |
| combat | predator |
| digest | ruminants |
| hyena | |
| lurk | |
| menace | |
| mock | |
| vast | |

*Selection 5*

| | |
|---|---|
| decor | discreet |
| discreet | frenzies |
| frenzy | nostrils |
| implore | |
| nostril | |

**Unit 4**

*Selection 1*

| | |
|---|---|
| gangplank | makeshift |
| hold | turban |
| inert | |
| lather | |
| makeshift | |
| stern | |
| tersely | |
| turban | |

*Selection 2*

| | |
|---|---|
| barrier | despite |
| coordination | |
| descend | |
| despite | |
| kilter | |
| stabilizer | |

*Selection 3*

| | |
|---|---|
| groom | (none) |

*Selection 4*

| | |
|---|---|
| meter | burls |
| | meters |

*Selection 5*

| | |
|---|---|
| cast | cast |
| cove | lures |
| lure | skiff |
| skiff | tackle |
| slack | |
| tackle | |
| troll | |

## Comprehension Skills

**Unit 5**

*Selection 1*

| | |
|---|---|
| boundary | boundary |
| certificate | equator |
| circulatory | seamarks |
| equator | |
| freighter | |
| hilarious | |
| initiate | |
| navigator | |

*Selection 2*

| | |
|---|---|
| consecutively | (none) |

*Selection 3* (none)

*Selection 4*

| | |
|---|---|
| Caribbean Sea | immigrants |
| economic | migration |
| immigrant | |
| integral | |
| migration | |
| status | |
| unique | |

*Selection 5*

| | |
|---|---|
| algae | buffet |
| buffet | destination |
| carbon-date | ordeal |
| chamois | |
| destination | |
| ordeal | |
| precipitation | |

**Unit 6**

*Selection 1*

| | |
|---|---|
| avalanche | capsized |
| doubloon | engraved |
| engrave | |
| pieces of eight | |
| triumphantly | |

**476**

| Glossary Words | Context Clue Words | Glossary Words | Context Clue Words |
|---|---|---|---|
| | *Selection 2* | | *Selection 5* |
| enormousness | (none) | altitude | altitude |
| lofty | | apparatus | balustrade |
| resignation | | balustrade | carcass |
| | | carcass | comrade |
| | *Selection 3* (none) | deflate | deflated |
| | | distill | descending |
| | *Selection 4* | plummet | desperate |
| contagious | contagious | plunge | devour |
| | | prey | plummeted |
| | *Selection 5* | | plunged |
| buffet | capabilities | | prey |
| capabilities | conditioning | | |
| conditioning | foraging | **Unit 8** | |
| coordinated | freighter | | *Selection 1* |
| forage | Grand National | chisel | cavern |
| freighter | reconditioning | Inuit | chisel |
| hand | regained | mussel | parkas |
| instinctively | steeplechaser | tundra | wedges |
| luster | uninhabited | wedge | |
| methodically | whinny | | |
| rangy | | | *Selection 2* |
| reconditioning | | constellation | ecliptic |
| regain | | orbit | orbit |
| steeplechase | | | zodiac |
| thoroughbred | | | |
| uninhabited | | | *Selection 3* |
| whinny | | smokejumpers | conservation |
| | | vocational | vocational |
| **Unit 7** | | | |
| | *Selection 1* | | *Selection 4* (none) |
| endurance | assembled | | *Selection 5* |
| gloat | opponent | (none) | sloop |
| intolerance | proposition | | |
| proclaim | status | **Study and Research Skills** | |
| proposition | | | |
| revolutionary | | **Unit 9** | |
| status | | | *Selection 1* |
| stilted | | almanac | humid |
| suffrage | | caravan | humidity |
| | | instinct | indicators |
| | *Selection 2* | scurry | meteorologists |
| brilliant | (none) | | |
| prospector | | | *Selection 2* |
| | | arabesque | airborne |
| | *Selection 3* | blurt | blurts |
| contender | contender | commitment | commitment |
| hoist | heft | concession | concessions |
| meander | hoist | delicacy | delicacy |
| reverie | reverie | fracture | gesturing |
| | | freestyle | rehearsing |
| | *Selection 4* | gesture | tai |
| perish | roused | hypnotic | weaving |
| rouse | scowled | tranquil | |
| scowl | visualized | video | |
| solemn | | videotape | |
| Stuka | | weave | |
| visualize | | | |

| Glossary Words | Context Clue Words | Glossary Words | Context Clue Words |
|---|---|---|---|

*Selection 3*

(none)
- computer program
- electronic
- input
- operator's console
- output
- process
- processing
- programmers
- sequence
- storage

*Selection 4*

| | |
|---|---|
| drainage | flocked |
| forebear | intent |
| intent | lured |
| lure | prospect |
| prospect | |
| vast | |
| vitally | |

*Selection 5*

| | |
|---|---|
| antennae | bait |
| burrow | burrows |
| churn | feeding antennae |
| scurry | plankton |
| stalk | scurries |
| swirl | survival |
| tide | swirl |
| uropod | uropods |

## Unit 10

*Selection 1*

| | |
|---|---|
| antenna | chlorophyll |
| carbon dioxide | decompose |
| distinctive | dissolve |
| Indian summer | moisture |
| muted | pigments |
| researcher | spectacular |
| spectacular | tissue |
| sumac | |
| sweetgum | |
| tarnish | |

*Selection 2 (none)*

*Selection 3*

| | |
|---|---|
| complex | *bonkei* |
| excel | *bonsai* |
| gnarled | gnarled |
| miniature | *kare-san-sui* |
| prune | landscape |
| thatch | miniature |

*Selection 4*

| | |
|---|---|
| abundant | hesitate |
| artificial | imitate |

*Selection 4 (continued)*

| | |
|---|---|
| hesitate | lures |
| imitate | nymphs |
| lure | plugs |
| marionette | reel |
| slither | sinkers |
| vibration | slither |
| visibility | wary |

*Selection 5*

| | |
|---|---|
| agave | agave |
| henequen | fibers |
| machete | machetes |
| sisal | pores |
| | survive |

## Unit 11

*Selection 1*

| | |
|---|---|
| commuter | disaster |
| disaster | employees |
| employee | frustrating |
| frustrating | ICC |
| install | install |
| persistent | slot |
| vigilant | stationary |

*Selection 2*

| | |
|---|---|
| appropriate | appropriate |
| buttonhole | channel |
| deactivation | deactivation |
| dredge | intervene |
| enhance | site |
| intervene | |
| launch | |
| lobbyist | |
| moor | |
| motivate | |
| site | |
| skipper | |
| vie | |

*Selection 3*

| | |
|---|---|
| CTA | CTA |
| spectator | sponsor |
| sponsor | |

*Selection 4*

| | |
|---|---|
| (none) | agencies |

*Selection 5*

| | |
|---|---|
| boom | orderlies |
| eliminate | white-collar |
| literate | |
| orderly | |
| resignation | |
| technology | |
| white-collar | |

| Glossary Words | Context Clue Words | Glossary Words | Context Clue Words |
|---|---|---|---|

## Unit 12

*Selection 1*

| | |
|---|---|
| conserve | conserve |
| predict | sampling |
| technique | snow courses |
| temporary | snowmelt |

*Selection 2*

| | |
|---|---|
| category | advertisers |
| encourage | broadcasters |
| imitate | category |
| incredible | encourages |
| inspire | hassle |
| pediatrician | incredibly |
| regulate | inspired |
| technical | violence |

*Selection 3*

| | |
|---|---|
| atmosphere | atmosphere |
| expanse | |
| satellite | |

*Selection 4* (none)

*Selection 5*

| | |
|---|---|
| ancestor | chop |
| archaeologist | repulsive |
| bamboo | tableware |
| clergy | tines |
| custom | trencher |
| extravagance | utensil |
| flint | |
| gourd | |
| nobility | |
| pewter | |
| primitive | |
| repulsive | |
| slate | |
| Stone Age | |
| tine | |
| traditionally | |
| utensil | |
| vulgar | |

## Literary Appreciation Skills

## Unit 13

*Selection 1*

| | |
|---|---|
| dingy | drab |
| drab | |
| eaves | |
| urban renewal | |

*Selection 2*

| | |
|---|---|
| cavern | backtrack |
| conceal | cavern |

*Selection 2 (continued)*

| | |
|---|---|
| crouch | concealed |
| encourage | crouching |
| formation | encouraged |
| grope | groping |
| grotto | grotto |
| jerky | intersection |
| jut | jutting |
| lanky | marveling |
| passageway | passageway |
| slither | rippling |
| spelunking | spelunking |

*Selection 3*

| | |
|---|---|
| awesome | (none) |
| eclipse | |
| gussak | |
| horizon | |
| parka | |
| snicker | |
| vibrant | |

*Selection 4*

| | |
|---|---|
| bland | deft |
| deft | evidently |
| evidently | opposition |
| ferry | pied |
| Gage, Thomas | principal |
| glibly | rebel |
| jubilation | regulars |
| opposition | timid |
| pie | |
| principal | |
| rebel | |
| regular | |
| scarce, | |
| make oneself scarce | |
| smuggle | |
| sundry | |
| timid | |

*Selection 5*

| | |
|---|---|
| *bacalaito* | innocence |
| innocence | *olé* |
| proclaim | |

## Unit 14

*Selection 1*

| | |
|---|---|
| crafty | chamber |
| debt | concluded |
| gesture | debts |
| hundredfold | generous |
| innkeeper | greedy |
| predicament | gypsy traveler |
| | misfortune |

| Glossary Words | Context Clue Words | Glossary Words | Context Clue Words |
|---|---|---|---|

*Selection 2*

| | | | |
|---|---|---|---|
| disgrace | disgraced | *Selection 3* | |
| expedition | geologist | dotty | dotty |
| geological | knapsacks | scud | |
| laborer | laborer | vest | |
| mallet | perish | | |
| perish | thrashing | *Selection 4* (none) | |
| specimen | | | |
| | | *Selection 5* | |
| *Selection 3* | | assure | assured |
| confectioners' | concentrating | chinking | gloried |
| sugar | decent | despite | journal |
| foil | grammar | glory | protest |
| foyer | mystic motions | idle | warrior's bread |
| remote control | revenge | journal | |
| scan | spell | kinsman | |
| | syllable | moccasin | |
| | vacuum | parch | |
| | via | plantation | |
| | | protest | |
| *Selection 4* | | venison | |
| engage | amazing | weariness | |
| indulge | constantly | | |
| provide | engaged | | |
| ruse | foreseeing | | |
| subterfuge | illustrate | **Unit 16** | |
| | indicated | *Selection 1* | |
| | situation | apprentice | daze |
| | tormented | extraordinary | |
| | trickery | prosperous | |
| | unbearable | | |
| | | *Selection 2* | |
| *Selection 5* | | wrench | (none) |
| emerge | emerged | | |
| fulfill | fulfilled | *Selection 3* | |
| skillful | skillful | hesitate | hesitated |
| | | patient | patient |
| | | veteran | veteran |
| **Unit 15** | | | |
| *Selection 1* | | *Selection 4* | |
| boar | foal | affectionate | affectionate |
| clumsily | nudge | charge | charge |
| emblem | padding | hoist | hoisting |
| groom | splayed | outrageous | outrageous |
| mosque | | ridgetop | scythe |
| nicker | | smug | smug |
| nudge | | survey | surveyed |
| spindly | | | |
| splay | | *Selection 5* | |
| | | breechcloth | descend |
| *Selection 2* (none) | | extension | indispensable |
| | | indispensable | Tshjamm |
| | | usher | ushered |

Acknowledgments (continued)

"Bad-Hop Grounders" from *The Giant Book of Strange But True Sports Stories* by Howard Liss; copyright © 1976 by Howard Liss; originally adapted by *Cricket* Magazine, August 1977; reprinted by permission of Random House, Inc., New York. "Benjamin Franklin" by Nancy Garber from *Highlights for Children*, January 1976; copyright © 1975 by Highlights for Children, Inc., Columbus, Ohio; reprinted with permission. "The Big Fuss," adapted from *I Am Not a Short Adult—Getting Good at Being a Kid* by Marilyn Burns; copyright © 1977 by The Yolla Bolly Press; adapted by permission of Little, Brown and Company, Boston. An adaptation of *Biography of a Giraffe* by Alice L. Hopf; text copyright © 1978 by Alice L. Hopf; originally adapted by *Cricket* Magazine, June 1979; adapted by permission of G. P. Putnam's Sons, New York, and Larry Sternig Literary Agency, Milwaukee. An adaptation of pp. 6 and 8–10 from *The Black Stallion* by Walter Farley; copyright 1941 by Walter Farley; copyright renewed © 1968 by Walter Farley; adapted by permission of Random House, Inc., New York. "Buried Treasure," adapted from *Two-Minute Mysteries* by Donald J. Sobol; copyright © 1967 by Donald J. Sobol; adapted by permission of McIntosh and Otis, Inc., New York. "The Bushmen," adapted from pp. 66–69 of *Yesterday's People* by Robert Martin; copyright © 1970 by Don Meier Productions, Inc.; adapted by permission of Doubleday & Company, Inc., New York.

"Chinese Forebears," adapted from pp. 7 and 9 of *An Album of Chinese Americans* by Betty Lee Sung; copyright © 1977 by Betty Lee Sung; adapted by permission of Franklin Watts, Inc., New York. Excerpts from *Conservation Careers*, a publication of the National Wildlife Federation, Washington, D.C., have been reproduced, as edited, with the Federation's permission. "Coyote and the Money Tree" by Tina Naiche, adapted from *And It Is Still That Way, Legends told by Arizona Indian Children*, with notes by Byrd Baylor; copyright © 1976 by Byrd Baylor; originally adapted by *Cricket* Magazine, January 1978; reprinted by permission of Charles Scribner's Sons, New York, and Toni Strassman, literary agent, New York.

An adaptation of "Dangers Underground" by Mary Zettelmier; copyright © 1978 by Mary Zettelmier; originally adapted by *Cricket* Magazine, August 1978; adapted by permission of the author. An adaptation of "The Day of the Golden Eagle" by Jonathan T. Stratman; copyright © 1979 by Jonathan T. Stratman; originally adapted by *Cricket* Magazine, September 1979; reprinted by permission of the author. "Daydreaming? Good for You!" by Ronald Kotulak; adapted from the *Chicago Tribune*, March 30, 1980; copyright © 1980 by Chicago Tribune; all rights reserved; adapted with permission. An excerpt from *The Desert Is Theirs* by Byrd Baylor; copyright © 1975 by Byrd Baylor; reprinted by permission of Charles Scribner's Sons, New York, and Toni Strassman, literary agent, New York. "Don't Ever Strike a Rhinoceros" by Martin Steinberg; reprinted by permission of the author. An adaptation of *Dragons Hate to be Discreet* by Winifred Rosen; text copyright © 1978 by Winifred Rosen; adapted by permission of Alfred A. Knopf, Inc., New York, and International Creative Management, New York.

"Easy Gourmet Dessert," adapted from *Easy Gourmet Cooking for Young People and Beginners* by Bernice Kohn; copyright © 1973 by Bernice Kohn; adapted by permission of the author and The Bobbs-Merrill Company, Inc., New York. "Esther Morris—Mother of Equal Rights," adapted from pp. 173–175 of *Westering Women* by Helen Markley Miller; copyright © 1961 by Helen Markley Miller; adapted by permission of Doubleday and Company, Inc., New York, and Barthold Fles Literary Agency, Inc., New York.

An adaptation of "Fingers Were Made Before Forks" by Althea Jackson; copyright © 1975 by Althea H. Jackson; originally adapted by *Cricket* Magazine, May 1975; reprinted by permission of the author. "A Foal is Born," adapted from *King of the Wind* by Marguerite Henry; copyright 1948 by Rand McNally & Company; renewed copyright © 1976; adapted with permission. "For Sale" from *Where the Sidewalk Ends* by Shel Silverstein; copyright © 1974 by Shel Silverstein; reprinted by permission of Harper & Row, Publishers, Inc., New York. An adaptation of "Freshwater Fishing," text and illustrations by Jim Arnosky; text copyright © 1979 by Jim Arnosky; illustrations copyright © 1979 by Open Court Publishing Company; originally published by *Cricket* Magazine, September 1979; text adapted by permission of the author; illustrations reprinted by permission of *Cricket* Magazine, La Salle, Illinois.

"The Garden" from *Where the Sidewalk Ends* by Shel Silverstein; copyright © 1974 by Shel Silverstein; reprinted by permission of Harper & Row, Publishers, Inc., New York. "Getting Ready to Study," adapted from page 25 of *Building English Skills, Silver Level* by Kathleen L. Bell, Frances Freeman Paden, and Susan Duffy Schaffrath; copyright © 1980 by McDougal, Littell & Company; adapted with permission. "The Greatest Cowboy" by Tom Macpherson from *Boys' Life* Magazine, August 1976; copyright © 1976 by The Boy Scouts of America, Irving, Texas; reprinted by permission of Marie E. Macpherson.

An adaptation of "Hard Bargain" by Nick Engler; copyright © 1979 by Nick Engler; originally adapted by *Cricket* Magazine, November 1979; reprinted by permission of the author. "Hard-Boiled Eggs" by Tom R. Kovach; copyright © 1977 by Tom R. Kovach; originally adapted by *Cricket* Magazine, May 1977; reprinted by permission of the author. "Hasty Digger" by James H. Carmichael, Jr., from *Ranger Rick's Nature Magazine*, June 1979; copyright © 1979 by National Wildlife Federation; reprinted with permission. An excerpt from "The Honey Guide" by William Riziki Riwa; copyright © 1977 by William Riziki Riwa and Daniel Manus Pinkwater; originally adapted by *Cricket* Magazine, September 1977; reprinted by permission of McIntosh & Otis, Inc., New York. An adaptation of "How Much Is a Million?" by Ellen H. Goins; copyright © 1975 by Ellen H. Goins; originally adapted by *Cricket* Magazine, May 1975; reprinted by permission of Otto Goins, Executor of the Estate of Ellen H. Goins.

"Japanese Gardens," adapted from *Awake* Magazine, February 8, 1979; copyright © 1979 by Watchtower Bible and Tract Society of New York, Inc.; adapted with permission. An adaptation of pp. 7, 9–12, 14, 17, 19–24, 26–28 from *Jim Bridger's Alarm Clock and Other Tall Tales* by Sid Fleischman; text copyright © 1978 by Sid Fleischman; adapted by permission of E. P. Dutton & Co., Inc., New York, and A. P. Watt Ltd., London. An adaptation of pp. 225–228 from *Johnny Tremain, A Novel for Old & Young* by Esther Forbes; copyright © 1943 by Esther Forbes Hoskins; renewed copyright © 1971 by Linwood M. Erskine, Jr.; adapted by permission of Houghton Mifflin Company, Boston, and Penguin Books, Ltd., London. An excerpt from pp. 100 and 101 of *Julie of the Wolves* by Jean Craighead George; text copyright © 1972 by Jean Craighead George; reprinted by permission of Harper & Row, Publishers, Inc., New York, and Curtis Brown, Ltd., New York.

"Keeping In Touch with Reality," adapted from pp. 129–132 of *Without Hats, Who Can Tell the Good Guys* by Mildred Ames; copyright © 1976 by Mildred Ames; adapted by permission of E. P. Dutton & Co., Inc., New York. "Looking Toward the Equator," adapted from *Elementary Science, Learning by Investigating*; adapted by the courtesy of Rand McNally & Company, Skokie, Illinois.

An adaptation of pp. 77 and 78 of *Magdalena* by Louisa R. Shotwell; copyright © 1971 by Louisa R. Shotwell; adapted by permission of Viking Penguin, Inc., New York; and John Farquharson, Ltd., London. "Martin," adapted from *Martin and Abraham Lincoln* by Catherine Cate Coblentz; copyright 1947 by Children's Press, Chicago; renewed copyright © 1975; adapted with permission. An adaptation of certain specified pages from *Meet the Computer* by Bruce Lewis; copyright © 1977 by Bruce Lewis; originally adapted by *Cricket* Magazine, January 1979; reprinted by permission of Dodd, Mead & Company, Inc., New York. "Moisfaa" from *Sam Savitt's True Horse Stories* by Sam Savitt; copyright © 1970 by Sam Savitt; originally adapted by *Cricket* Magazine, July 1979; reprinted by permission of Dodd, Mead & Company, Inc., New York. An adaptation of pp. 3 and 4 from *Mountain Born* by Elizabeth Yates; copyright 1943 by Coward-McCann, Inc.; renewed copyright © 1971 by Elizabeth Yates; adapted by permission of Coward, McCann & Geoghegan, Inc., New York. "Nature Cannot Be Changed," excerpted from pp. 53–55 of *African Folk Tales* edited by Charlotte and Wolf Leslau; copyright © 1963 by The Peter Pauper Press; reprinted with permission.

"Pablita," adapted from *Sam Savitt's True Horse Stories* by Sam Savitt; copyright © 1970 by Sam Savitt; originally adapted by *Cricket* Magazine, August 1979; adapted by permission of Dodd, Mead & Company, New York. Pronunciation Key from *Thorndike-Barnhart Intermediate Dictionary* by E. L. Thorndike and Clarence L. Barnhart; copyright © 1974 by Scott, Foresman & Company, Glenview, Illinois; reprinted by permission of the publisher. "Puerto Rican Americans," an adaptation of the introduction to *An Album of Puerto Ricans in the United States* by Stuart J. Brahs; copyright © 1973 by Franklin Watts, Inc.; adapted with permission. "The Purple Plug" from *Stories of the Inner City* by Benjamin M. Ashcom, Morton A. Maimon, and William W. Reynolds; copyright © 1970 by Globe Book Company, Inc.; reprinted by permission of the publisher. An adaptation of "The Quarter" from *Stories from El Barrio* by Piri Thomas; copyright © 1978 by Piri Thomas; adapted by permission of Alfred A. Knopf, Inc., New York.

An adaptation of "The Real Thing" by A. R. Swinnerton from *Boys' Life* Magazine, February 1977; copyright © 1977 by The Boy Scouts of America, Irving, Texas; reprinted by permission of the author. "Redwoods Are the Tallest Trees," adapted from *Redwoods*

## Illustrations

## Editorial Credits

Managing Editor: Kathleen Laya
Assistant Editor: Elizabeth M. Garber
Director of Design: Allen Carr
Design Assistants: Ken Izzi, Marcia Vecchione

Editors: John Hancock, Manya Pleva, R. Lucinda Smith, Carol Steben